The Feature Writer's Handbook

*With a Treasury of 2,000 Tested Ideas
for Newspapers, Magazines, Radio, and Television*

The Feature Writer's Handbook

With a Treasury of
2,000 Tested Ideas for Newspapers,
Magazines, Radio, and Television

by Stewart Harral

NORMAN : UNIVERSITY OF OKLAHOMA PRESS

Books by Stewart Harral

The Feature Writer's Handbook (Norman, 1958)
Profitable Public Relations for Newspapers (Ann Arbor, 1957)
Profitable Public Relations for Cosmetologists (National Association of Cosmetology Schools, New York, 1956)
Keys to Successful Interviewing (Norman, 1954)
Tested Public Relations for Schools (Norman, 1952)
Patterns of Publicity Copy (Norman, 1950)
Successful Letters for Churches (New York and Nashville, 1946)
Public Relations for Churches (New York and Nashville, 1945)
Public Relations for Higher Education (Norman, 1942)
Publicity Problems (editor) (American College Public Relations Association, Washington, 1940)

Library of Congress Catalog Card Number: 58–11601

To my students
Who have taught me so much

Acknowledgments

In writing this book the author has incurred a heavy debt of gratitude to many people. I am especially indebted to my colleague, Dwight V. Swain, for his counsel and encouragement, and to Clyde Davis, my assistant, who joined me in the search for story ideas. To Ruth Owens I am indebted for typing assistance.

Grateful acknowledgment is made to the following individuals and organizations who co-operated so generously in providing suggestions and ideas:

Ed Lipscomb, National Cotton Council of America; Gene Potes, Southwestern Bell Telephone Company; Mary Howard Ellison of the Girl Scouts of America; Leslie G. Stratton of the Boy Scouts of America; Edwin H. Powers of the American National Red Cross; Len Arnold of the American Library Association; Jean R. Packard of the National Parks Association; William L. Browne of the National Institute of Dry Cleaning; J. H. Cunningham of the Bituminous Coal Institute; Hal Allen of the National Committee of Boys and Girls Club Work, Inc.; The Institute of Life Insurance; and the National Arborist Association.

Special thanks are due to the many top-flight writers who took time from extremely busy schedules to share their ideas on feature writing. Grateful acknowledgment is made to the University of Oklahoma Press, which gave permission to use a number of ideas and suggestions from my book, *Keys to Successful*

Interviewing, in writing chapter four. To all I feel a deep sense of indebtedness.

STEWART HARRAL

Norman, Oklahoma
May 6, 1958

Why You Need This Book

WHAT ARE the three main things you need as a writer?

Here they are:

1. Hundreds of fresh and salable ideas for feature stories.

2. Professional writing "know-how"—secrets of successful writers.

3. Devices and patterns to give your stories that priceless ingredient—living action.

Armed with these keys, you'll crash markets you've dreamed about. Your words will rise up and shine. You'll see drama in the commonplace. And the words you type will carry power—power to influence editors and readers and power to step up your placement and profits.

Good writing is two things: (1) Wise use of techniques and devices, plus (2) a writer's reserve power—his creative ability. Mix these two ingredients in the right proportions and the result is a high-octane feature.

I want to share with you a collection of tested ideas, devices, and techniques used by noted feature writers, columnists, publicists, reporters, free-lance writers, Sunday magazine editors, public relations copy writers, television and radio newsmen, magazine writers, and correspondents.

Things like: how big name writers keep their idea tanks filled; some specific devices which make any story click; some idea stimulators which will give you enough feature tips to last for years.

You'll find all three in this book—in tested patterns fundamental enough to work in a wide variety of situations. You can use them just as well in a feature showing future possibilities of the Univac as in a personality sketch of Jed Perkins upon his retirement as court house custodian.

Above all, the "Treasury of Feature Ideas" contains more than two thousand salable ideas. And they're listed alphabetically for instant reference—from "accidents" to "zoos." Each one suggests possible angles and approaches, as well as the best source to contact for the material.

Best of all, the ideas are adaptable to a wide variety of markets—general magazines, newspapers, feature syndicates, trade magazines, news-gathering associations, Sunday magazine sections, radio and television stations, and others.

Using this book, you'll soon find your creative talent beginning to expand. Your thinking will yield more and more creative dividends. You'll develop into a better writer, make more money. Just try it and see.

Contents

Illustrations

The Feature Writer's Handbook

*With a Treasury of 2,000 Tested Ideas
for Newspapers, Magazines, Radio, and Television*

1. What Every Writer Should Know

IF YOU want to succeed as a writer—stick to tested strategies.

Sounds simple, doesn't it?

Yet certain basic principles are likely to be overlooked by many writers. And you ask, "What are they?" "Who devised them?" "Are they all sure-fire?" "Will they work for me?"

Yes, they work. They came from a variety of sources—interviews, books, articles, experience, observation. And even from trial-and-error. But the list isn't complete. It isn't meant to be a formula. But by following these guideposts of successful writing, you can move ahead faster along the road to readership.

1. *To write a story you must first think a story.*

Give an idea time to develop. When an idea flutters by, resist the temptation to rush to the typewriter and start pounding. Think out the angles, the outline, the specific devices. Visualize the completed article.

2. *Meditation precedes inspiration.*

"Live with your material and absorb it," Harry Shaw, formerly of *Look*, declares. How can you do this? Mr. Shaw explains, "Pre-write your material before you sit down to put it on paper. Don't sit down to think what you shall write. Do sit down to write what you have thought. The best articles come that way."

3. *Ask yourself, "What am I trying to say? To whom?"*

This will keep you on the track. It should give you a sense of direction. And certainly you should know if the completed feature will interest debutantes or detectives—or both. When you know your audience, you can talk in their language—in terms of their interest.

4. *Dig deep for your facts.*

Gather three times more material than you can use. Roger Dakin, former editor of *Collier's*, once said, "It's too easy for the rare talent to depend upon skill with words rather than perseverance with research, too tempting for him to write around the facts instead of making the facts carry the story." Research alone gives you the "feel" of your subject.

5. *Give your best to the lead.*

You must make the first few words—to be read in a few fleeting seconds—really count. The more you can woo the reader with words—words that intrigue, words that pull, words that say "Wake up!" to his mind—the more effective your lead. Your beginning can make or break your story, no matter what comes afterward.

6. *Remember: it takes a simple style to hit the masses.*

As Lewis Mumford reminds us, "A book has one leg on immortality's trophy when the words are for children and the meanings are for men." Simple writing has the power of acting invisibly. That is its magic. The writer uses words—but the words themselves are never seen. Only the ideas emerge.

7. *Streamline your article but keep it chock full of interest.*

Let's not forget that the human mind has a terrific capacity for resisting information. So you must dramatize events, use anecdotes which strengthen the story, employ a change of pace, keep the reader involved, and employ other devices to keep interest at a high level. Here's the main thing: Keep showing instead of merely telling.

8. *Make some of your moods visual.*

If your central figure is disgusted and breaks his putter and tosses it into the lake, don't just tell what happened; describe the action so that the reader can visualize it. This is a fictional technique which can be extremely effective in a feature story.

9. *Put your best into every story.*

Let's remember the advice given to a young writer by Willa Cather. She said, "Be a spendthrift with your effort, your ideas, with the best you have in you every single time you sit down at the typewriter." Extra effort pays extra dividends.

10. *Know the rules of writing before you try to break them.*

Get the basic patterns right and then try:

variations	conversation
angles	reiteration
new approaches	transitions
emotion	off-trail reactions
illustrations	

11. *Give the reader the feeling that things are happening to him.*

Every reader wants to feel that he is taking part (at least emotionally) in the scene or incident. So get him involved from the beginning. And keep him sitting on the edge of his chair until the last word.

12. *Rewriting is the route to success.*

"Good rewriting is the difference between the artist and the amateur," someone declared. And that's right. Oh sure, you can write—that's easy. But it's the manipulation of material—adding a paragraph here, rephrasing a sentence there, substituting a better incident in the middle, revising diction and sentence structure —that makes the big difference.

13. *Read—read—read!*

Old advice? yes. But it's still needed. Unless you rub elbows with the writers of all ages, you will never learn the magic of words. Study the clarity and drama of the Bible. Watch how O. Henry makes a fascinating story from a trivial incident. Read Charles Dickens and see how he describes his characters. Analyze today's best seller. To sum up: Respond to good writing wherever you find it.

14. *Anticipate the reader's point of view.*

Mr. Reader wants HIS point of view played up. That means that you keep YOU alive throughout your article. Answer all of the reader's questions. "It takes two to speak the truth," Thoreau said, "one to speak, another to hear."

15. *The usual may make a better piece than the unusual.*

Let's let Marc Rose, senior editor of *Reader's Digest*, explain: "It is the phenomenon of the spectacular, the hard to find, the extraordinary, being far less often magazine material than the commonplace, yet personal incident." Right here is an obstacle which makes the transition so difficult for the reporter turning writer. A "Believe-it-or-not" approach is good only if it hits the reader's self-interest.

One last word: these aren't laws. A competent writer can break some of them and get away with it. Nor can these hints become a formula. Rather, they are signposts. But you must find your own way. How you use them and move along will depend on your reserve—your imagination—your development of story sense. Keep your mind and your eyes open. Experiment with writing devices. Keep asking yourself questions—all sorts of questions —about the things you see. Work to polish and improve each idea. Do it often enough and you'll soon begin to produce more pieces with "check appeal."

2. 25 Ways of Sparking Story Ideas

NEED story ideas?

You do? Then begin to stretch your creative muscles.

"Talent is our affair," said Gustave Flaubert. You can let this creative gift shrivel through disuse, or you can build it up by cultivating activities which are most likely to strengthen the imagination.

Practically everything that happens to you can spark story ideas. Your creative ability can keep growing year after year in pace with the effort you put into it. "Imagination grows by exercise," said W. Somerset Maugham, "and contrary to common belief, is more powerful in the mature than in the young."

Irvin S. Cobb said that he could look at a sack of popcorn and write a novel. By using his creative imagination he could see suspense, romance, conflict, and drama in an ordinary sack of corn. The story, you see, wasn't in the popcorn. It started in Cobb's creative faculties.

Idea-finding for writers is packed with questions like "How about?" "What if?" "What else?" "How about this angle?" "What if I used this approach?" "What will happen if I mix this incident with that quotation?" "Why is this person interesting?" "What will happen if I reverse this point of view?" "What have I overlooked?" "How was this caused?" "What happens after?"

Self-priming is a must for you. Actually, you can intensify your enthusiasm by making a start. One of my friends boosts his

7

interest in a prospective interview by setting down various head-lines or titles which might be used over the published story. This does two things. First, his goal becomes more graphic. Secondly, such a practice steps up his interest. Whether self-generated or not, an intense interest is needed to fully command the services of our imaginations.

"The world is so full of a number of things" that feature ideas can jump from a great variety of sources. And the best part of it is that no one has a monopoly on the treasure chest of ideas. As a writer, you can use creative imagination to see stories all around you. Here are 25 idea sources used by top-flight writers:

1. *Read behind the headlines.*

Your newspaper mirrors life—life with its hopes, its dreams, its disappointments. Here is the story of mankind. Ideas for fea-tures often pop from unexpected places. Hal Curtis, who has sold feature stories to many metropolitan newspapers, admits that he reads every column for ideas. Why? Largely because he once found a tip for a feature in an obituary column! Hidden near the end of an obituary was this line: "Mr. Blank was a boyhood friend of O. O. McIntyre, the New York columnist." Curtis found three other boyhood friends of McIntyre living in the city and inter-viewed them. Naturally, the whole thing made a delightful story, filled with anecdotes, boyhood pranks, and the heartaches and thrills experienced by a country printer's devil on the road to fame. Day after day, you'll find more feature ideas per column inch in newspapers than in any other source.

2. *Mine magazines for hidden ore.*

This is easy. You pick up a copy of a magazine and notice an article entitled, "Our Schools—Afraid to Teach?" Do schools play down basic studies in favor of snap courses? What do par-ents think? Kids? Teachers? Administrators? Any angle is worth a follow-up story.

3. *Keep an active file of ideas.*

Let's listen to Dwight Swain, magazine and newspaper writ-er, tell us how his system works:

The most important thing to remember, for my money, is that you want to end up as a writer and not a librarian. So keep your system simple and geared to your own personal needs!

For myself, I try to jot down ideas and angles wherever and whenever they develop, with no effort to decide at the time whether they're strong or weak.

Then, sometime within the next twenty-four hours, in one of those ten-minute breaks that crop up every day, I check over these notes, typing up the items that still seem worth-while and throwing out the others.

As for the mechanics of file maintenance, these three tricks have helped me:

1. Use a full sheet of paper for each idea. That way, you've got plenty of space to elaborate, yet your data's easily handled in standard file folders.

2. Limit yourself to one idea per sheet, so that you can classify data easily for filing.

3. Keep your headings flexible. Mostly, this means splitting up folders that grow too thick, combining those that stay too thin, and abandoning "dead" headings that you come to realize are too far afield from your own interests and/or specialties for practical development.

Personally, I have a strong prejudice against piling up factual data (as distinct from ideas) before they're needed for a specific writing job. Maybe it's because I've known too many writers who spent endless hours clipping and copying, only to find in the end that most of their information was obsolete when the time came to use it.

4. *Uncover ideas from scrapbooks.*

Look up on that shelf. Yes, there are your bulging scrapbooks of clippings. Old stories? Yes, but some of them were used so long ago that they can be revised, brought up to date, given a new angle or twist. There's the story you did on the plans of physicians to improve their public relations. They planned to answer more night calls, they asked that their patients feel free to inquire about fees—you remember? That was four years ago. Did everything work out as planned? Are doctors still conscious of their public relations? Use these questions for a follow-up story. Take an occasional glance at your scrapbooks. A yellow clipping may give you the germ of an idea for a bright feature.

5. *Stay off the tourist trail.*

Travel yields ideas, but not when you follow hordes of tourists on a "conducted tour." Watch for off-the-trail pieces—about people, buildings, events, ceremonies, traditions, or customs. Free-lancer William Folprecht found a restaurant in California where a series of rooms in the basement represent the Holy Land, with a life-size figure of the praying Christ kneeling in Gethsemane. His feature describing the scene sold to *Sunday Digest.* Leslie Kennon, whose travel stories appear in many magazines, suggests that we look for "some unusual aspect to give it a beginning punch-line." Talk to people, for here is a rich source of colorful anecdotes.

6. *Experience the situation.*

There's nothing new about a writer "living" his story to experience the condition or at least the environment. And it's still resultful. In fact, it always carries more flavor and authenticity than an article created from a half dozen reference books and a couple of stilted interviews. Living another life does not always yield facts. "More often than not," Morton Sontheimer, a magazine writer who has "lived" many of his pieces, reminds us, "your personal experience will have no place in the story but it takes a very large and helpful place alongside you when you sit down to the typewriter." You may have to force yourself to spend a day or two as a beggar, taxi driver, or elevator operator. Sontheimer admits, "I have to fight inertia about going after personal experiences, and I imagine most writers do. In the first place, you can usually get away with not doing this type of research. That's a big temptation. Most articles don't have it, therefore it isn't generally expected of a writer, unless he builds a reputation for it. . . . Finally, it often takes a lot of nerve to pull them off." But there's a pay-off: Readers will see your piece and say, "This guy really knows what he is talking about."

7. *Discover drama behind figures.*

Dull research reports? Usually. But often a significant story lies hidden beneath staggering figures. Remember what Leo Cherne did? He took a Department of Commerce booklet listing statistically the consumer increases necessary to maintain the economic health of the United States. Then he gave the idea personal reader application. The result? A best seller, *The Rest of Your Life.*

8. *Anniversaries produce news angles.*

Nationwide observances, such as the Jubilee of Light (to honor Thomas Alva Edison's discovery of the incandescent lamp) can give you anniversary angles. But so can the birthday of practically any institution—whether it's a museum or a match factory —on its twenty-fifth, seventy-fifth, or one hundredth anniversary.

9. *Watch for hidden angles at conventions and conferences.*

Obviously, you must "bone up" on the event you are to cover. But over and above this, you must be alert to report what Lester Markel has defined as "the deeper sense of the news." Here's an example: With many people wondering, "Why so many trips to the Antarctic? Can Admiral Byrd and others add to the world's knowledge of weather?" Robert C. Cowen, natural science correspondent of *The Christian Science Monitor,* found the answers by covering the meeting of the American Association for the Advancement of Science and digging for them. The result: A series of five dispatches showing that twelve nations would set up a network of more than thirty bases to cover the unknown "seventh continent." At the next convention, watch for news possibilities in speeches, exhibits, demonstrations, elections, reports, prominent persons in attendance, and future plans.

10. *Write stories that parallel the news.*

Watch today's headlines for clues to tie-in stories. Several months after President Eisenhower's heart attack, *U. S. News and World Report* queried a group of heart specialists on the advisability of his seeking office again. The result: a feature story flashed around the world.

11. *Dig new angles for stories.*

You've read the criticisms of several male columnists and feature writers about women "meddling" in politics. Let's turn the idea around. Ask a number of women who are prominent in political life about the shortcomings of the male sex in public positions, and about unique traits or qualifications possessed by women.

12. *Take a second look at your hunches.*

You know how this works. You "see" a story in a situation, and yet there's no evidence. You know it's there. You stick with your hunch, and finally the story pops. Herbert Bayard Swope of the *New York World* (called by Lord Northcliffe "The greatest reporter in the world") felt that Herman Rosenthal, the gambler, had police protection. Finally, his hunch proved true. He tilted lances with the "System"—New York City's alliance of police and underworld—and won. In cracking the celebrated Rosenthal-Backer case, he wrote one of the great crime stories of all time. So stick with your hunch—it will probably hit the headlines.

13. *Make publicity releases work for you.*

Here's an example: In a publicity release from General Motors you read that the corporation paid its employees for 352,316 suggestions for improving safety and working conditions in a 13-year period. Find a large organization which uses the employee suggestion system. Does it work? Are winners given cash awards? What are some of the best ideas which have been submitted?

14. *Take a long look at advertisements.*

A nationally-syndicated columnist admits that he got the idea for a "cars of the future" story from an ad illustration which showed a "car of tomorrow." "Big advertisements?" you ask. Yes, read them for ideas, but don't overlook smaller ads. A writer for *Collier's* revealed that he found the peg for a feature article in a classified ad in a weekly newspaper!

15. *Some orators still say something.*

You locate ideas from speeches in several ways. Here are some: (1) watch programs and announcements of speakers and topics which might make a feature; (2) scan printed copies of speeches in newspapers, magazines, reports, newsletters, and other media; (3) listen to speeches—on radio and TV, at your club, and at church; and (4) interview a speaker following his address for additional comments on some idea which you can develop into a feature.

16. *Watch the world through television.*

Again—television programs of many types will result in ideas in proportion to your alertness and imagination. And just as in the other media, you won't find a story peg which calls attention to itself. The important thing is that you watch for clues in all types of shows—dramatic, quiz, comedy, news, music, variety—everything that viewers see.

17. *Don't discount your own experience.*

Pearl Buck visited several orphanages, and her reactions made a shocking story. For some strange reason, you are likely to pooh-pooh your own ideas. But wait! How did you react to some experience? With pleasure? Fright? Contentment? Then perhaps other persons would experience the same excitement in reading about it.

18. *Uncork your imagination.*

As a writer, you look for material. But at times you change what you have found. You switch, mix, enlarge, reduce, or interpret. "Creative effort," Joseph Jastrow reminds us, is "the imagination that looks forward, foresees, supplies, completes, plans, invents, solves, advances, and originates." Exercise your creative muscles and watch the output of ideas increase.

19. *Take a peep behind the stacks.*

"Forget your idea of the library as that old tomb on the hill," Warren Kuhn, librarian and writer, advises us in *The Writer*. And he's right! Today's library is more than books hidden away. It still has books, to be sure, but the modern library also has special collections which are teeming with ideas and facts. Varied sources of knowledge—letters, bulletins, photographs, ledgers, journals, courthouse records, historical documents, speeches, surveys, government reports, proceedings of meetings, old newspapers—these and many other source materials await you. Maybe you're lucky enough to live near a library which also houses museum objects which will stimulate your jaded imagination. The door to the library is the door to a world of features. Go in and see!

20. *Put the postman to work.*

Haven't you often wanted comments, advice, suggestions, facts, or opinions from persons who live far away? Travel expenses usually prohibit personal interviews. Why not try letters and questionnaires? For best results, you should follow these steps: (1) Decide upon your specific objectives. (2) Select the persons from whom you want replies. (3) Beam your request—letter, letter and questionnaire, or whatever method is used—so that the respondent will be motivated to reply. (4) Adapt the terminology and questions to the specific person (you can't send the same questionnaire to a brain surgeon and a band director). (5) Design your presentation (letter, envelope, questionnaire, or reply form) as attractively as possible. (6) Use extreme care in wording the questions. (7) Write your copy long enough to tell your story—and quit. (8) Give your reader something to do, make it easy for him to do it, and tell him he should do it now. Response speeder: Offer results to each person.

21. *Observe closely and then ask questions.*

Ruth Boyer Scott and members of her family used the automatic telephone weather reports. She wondered how they worked. Then she did live research—found out how actual weather forecasts are written, talked to top brass in the telephone company, visited the supervisor who trains girls to serve as the cheerful weather voice, and wrote officials of telephone companies in other cities with automatic weather reports. From these and other sources, she found enough information to write five thousand words. And in aiming for an article of seven hundred words, she came out in her first draft with about seven hundred words. Live research paid off. Her article, "Forecasts at Your Finger Tip," was published in the *Saturday Evening Post*.

22. *Dead men and dinosaurs do tell tales.*

Been to your museum lately? If not, you'll probably be surprised how they have brightened the place. Chances are that the museum is displaying something new—a recent gift or something on loan. Whether it's an old sword or a spur, it may be worth a feature.

23. *Stroll along the book beat.*

You can quicken your creative spirit when you read books not just for contents but as springboards for story possibilities. Newer books have no monopoly on ideas. Think of all of the literature which has been written from Bible-inspired ideas. Try this in reading books: When you come to a stirring passage, mark it or make a note in the margin. In "How to Read a Book," Mortimer Adler says that the art of reading "includes all the same skills that are involved in the art of discovery; keenness of observation, readily available memory, range of imagination, and, of course, a reason trained in analysis and reflection." You will gain new ideas as you read with imaginative effort.

24. *Tune in on conversation.*

You hear a shopper in a supermarket tell her friend, "I'd let John shop more but he pays no attention to costs." So you begin wondering, "Do men turned loose in a supermarket buy more than women?" "Do they buy more expensive foods?" "Small talk" can be the start of a big feature.

25. *A glimpse into tomorrow.*

Every alert writer takes the keenest pleasure in witnessing history in the making, and wants to share that pleasure with his readers. But he must watch for stories which answer the eternal question of all readers, "What's next?" He must tell what happens and what it means—in terms of both the present and the future. It is the job of the interpretive writer to fit what happened this afternoon into the patterns of history. How can you develop this skill? Only by making a never-ending study of the matrix of society, with its changing patterns, old forces, new personalities, and unfolding events. The interpretive reporter finds in his facts the patterns which give them meaning. What's more, he selects those which may illuminate the past, explain the present, and, to a greater or lesser degree, indicate the future. So watch for features that can be built around predictions, forecasts, "things-to-come," and the possible outcomes and results of present-day happenings.

3. Devices Do It!

Do you know the difference between a bore and a charming person?

That's easy. The bore tells you all of the dull details of a dull existence. But the happy person shares the interesting things that happen to him. When a famous artist was asked how it was that all of his portraits turned out so beautifully, he replied: "The secret is . . . I never show the bad ones."

So it is with your writing. You must tell your reader interesting things—things which intrigue and captivate him. And you say, "But every topic isn't interesting." True. But we can remind ourselves of the advice an old city editor gave Westbrook Pegler: "Always look at every situation long enough so that you will see something which no one has ever seen in it before. Then you'll have a yarn worth telling."

Keep your reader on the hills of interest. Focus on the dramatic.

How?

Easily! You must woo the reader with words and devices—words that intrigue, words that say "Wake up!" to his mind.

You'll stumble on some big stories—but not many. Seldom is a feature labeled "This is terrific stuff." No sir. Most of the time you'll have to dig for sparkling features. It will take a lot of hard work, aggressiveness, and ingenuity.

Here's the big idea: You must keep your reader emotionally

involved from the first word until the last. You must keep the story moving all the time!

But let's be more specific. As you write your story follow these four steps:

1. Pick your subject. Decide specifically what you want to write about.

   Do you want to—

   Show how to be a fast reader?
   Reveal human nature as seen by a taxi driver?
   Describe what atomic war will be like?
   Tell the dramatic history of the American flag?
   Explain what makes a successful person click?

2. Spotlight the main things you want to do in the feature.

   portray a personality   focus on an interesting object
   share an experience   bring a smile or tear
   show how to do something   tell an exciting story
   change the reader's mind   give the facts behind the
   describe a sensory percep-   headlines
        tion   point a moral
   interpret the news   warn the reader
   predict the future   strengthen the reader's ego

3. Pinpoint the highlights with specific devices.

4. Keep "hooking" your reader by use of devices and situations which keep him interested.

   Every feature that clicks conforms to this four-step pattern.

   Now comes the most important job: How can you choose devices and hooks which will hold the reader? What makes a story march? How can you make the reader hit the sawdust trail? What will give your feature a combination of pull and interest?

   Dominant traits in writers may differ, but all top-flight word-smiths possess specific and clearly defined techniques and characteristics. Many of these patterns—these keys to successful writing —will be revealed to you in the pages that follow. One thing is certain: by adding these devices to your present stock of "know-how," your stories will contain that rare ingredient which makes all great writing click: LIVING ACTION.

Stick to the specific:

Be specific! That's the most important rule to follow in your writing. What do we mean by this? It's concreteness—it's getting down to facts, cases, people, things, colors, sensations, sounds, scenes, movement, dialogue, and events.

Old stuff, you say. Just a platitude. Every writer knows it. Every writer does it without thinking. Are you sure?

Great writers concentrate on details. But the great mass of writers seem to ignore this great principle. As a result, their words are weak. Being a successful writer without being specific is impossible.

How do you do it? You must focus on the visible, the audible, and the measurable. You must give names, places, facts, dates, and figures. You repeat exactly what was said. If you find something abstract, you translate it to the concrete.

As you see, this principle involves more than commas and periods, what words to use, and how to make an outline. Rather, it is a deep feeling for reality—a feeling for people and things— for Bach, boogie woogie, can openers, model planes, ice cubes, Mickey Mouse, TV comedians, bulldogs, paper flowers, mortgages, gadgets, and women's hats.

Now let's be frank: concreteness isn't something you sprinkle on your words like salt and pepper. It's deep inside you. Its power lies in the depth of your perception. See what I'm driving at? You will be specific in your writing only if you live deeply. So keep your mental antennae up. Stick close to the stream of life. Watch the drives which propel your friends. Be alive to the meanings which make people act as they do—at the theater, at the county fair, or at the beach. Output depends on intake. For how can you make your readers see what you have never seen yourself?

Put action in your verbs:

Paste this in your hat: put action in your verbs. Strong verbs are dynamic and on the move. They give your writing a bounce and they hold the reader's attention. *Time* writers often take a much-discussed situation and give it a freshness. Note how one of them makes good use of verbs to write something fresh about New York:

> Once it was just an island between two rivers, with a bedrock which *defied* digging. But it had a magnificent, deepwater harbor and a river which led to the hinterland. Slowly its farms *turned* into city blocks, its mud streets *grew* cobblestones, its docks *stuck* fingers into the sea. First its sewers, then its wires, and finally its trains *went* underground. The higher its buildings *rose*, the deeper *went* their foundations. Its bowels *became* a vast catacomb *laced* with the ganglia of communication. It was an aggressive organism; it *touched* everything within reach, *attached* itself to everything it *touched*.

What does this prove? First of all, you see that active verbs bring sentences to life. And secondly, they shorten them as well. The reader gets the idea that something is going on—that something exciting or important is happening.

Each verb conveys its own meaning. So never use the conventional ones (usually those which first pop into your mind) when others might convey the meaning better. Compare these commonplace verbs with some possible substitutes:

pull	tug, lug, yank, haul
run	dash, speed, hasten, whisk
shout	bawl, bellow, roar, cry

One thing is sure: There's as much difference between an active verb and a passive one as between a moving picture and a still photograph. So keep your word pictures moving!

Use the "YOU" gimmick:

Every good piece has a "you" angle—direct or implied. As

one successful feature writer reminds us, "You may be a brilliant reporter but unless your cocoon of facts is spun around the reader, the resulting article will seem remote."

By using "you" as early as possible in the article (and repeating it from time to time), you involve the reader. Result? You get reader identification and participation. At times you can combine the "Hey!" technique (catching the reader's attention) with the "you" device. Paul W. Kearney, writing an article about the Empire State Building for *This Week*, merged the two at the start: "Would you like to visit a place where rain is sometimes red—where snow falls up—where kissing can be really shocking?"

Howard Whitman combined the same two devices in an article, "Why Some Doctors Should Be in Jail," in *Collier's*. Here's his opening: "The nation's ethical doctors want to clean the chiselers out of their profession, but they need your help."

See how easily another writer uses "you" in his opening paragraph: "Are you one of the 25 million Americans who are forced to loosen the belt a notch or two . . . or who are having trouble making the hooks and eyes meet?"

In some types of features, you may wish to inject the "you" element from time to time in the story. Here are a few of the many ways to do it:

You can tell at once . . .
As you might suspect . . .
But suppose you don't know.
Will you make them your own?
And you are right.
"That's disgusting," you say.
Ask your electrician to explain . . .
You're asking, "What do I do first?"

You shouldn't be too concerned.
Fatigue can play such tricks on you.
For example, you have noticed . . .
Your sense of humor hits on all eight when . . .
So always make sure that you . . .
Maybe you think it sounds silly but . . .

Enliven with quotations:
Your reader likes to hear people talk. Not just any kind of

talk, but conversation which hangs together, which moves the story along. Remember: it must be going somewhere. Here's a way to test the use of a quotation: can you leave it out and still have the same story? Yes? Then cut it. Short, to-the-point talk is preferred. Good quotations have hooks between each speech.

And let's not forget this fact: people talk differently. A Tennessee hillbilly doesn't talk like a native New Yorker. Furthermore, people talk differently than they write. Bear down on the feeling so that you have enough emotion to carry the facts. Your quotations will really pull the reader if you have one person trying to achieve something and another person resisting.

Warning: in writing features based to a great extent on interviews, you cannot create dialogue as the fiction writer does. But in many instances, you can select material from the interview and use it in such a way that it advances the story.

Avoid quotations which are pleasantries or small talk. Instead, use bits of speech which establish character, mood, and, in the final analysis, interest.

Example? Got one right here. This is an excerpt from an article written by Quentin Reynolds for *Reader's Digest*. "Babe" Didrikson Zaharias and her husband, George, had just left the specialist's office. He urged immediate surgery for cancer.

"We'll fight it together," George said. "I'll be with you every minute."

"I know," Babe said in a small voice. She was dry-eyed, but George knew that she was crying inside, and there was nothing he could say to comfort her. "I'll never play golf again, George," she said, brokenly.

"You'll play all right, honey." George tried to make his voice convincing. "Remember, you're the champion, at everything you've set your mind to. You're the best there is."

Make use of analogies:

Sometimes you must bridge the gap between what the reader knows and something new. A *Time* writer took a technical subject and gave it a "looks like" twist, as follows:

"When a blood clot in a coronary artery causes a heart attack, one result may be an aneurysm—something like a big blister—bulging from the heart muscle."

Vivid figures of speech:

Any time you use an eye-catching phrase or a vivid figure of speech—simile, metaphor, or others—you paint a word picture for the reader. It gives your reader an emotional buzz. But remember to use them wisely and be sure they're good. Like these:

As cool as the other side of the pillow.

She was wearing her voice an inch above the humline of the conversation.

Definition: Local bus—a device that makes mountains out of molehills.

Old saw resharpened: Opportunity knocks only once, but temptation bangs on the door for years.

Observation: People with time to spare usually spend it with someone who hasn't.

Philosophy: "The whole secret of life is to be interested in one thing profoundly and in a thousand things well."

Headline boner: "Egg-laying Contest Won By Local Man."

No matter how flat your conversation, a woman likes to have it flatter.

Epitaph for a dog: His tail still wags in my heart.

Description: A face full of autobiography.

Simile: Easy to bite as a dentist.

Types: There are two kinds of women—one who wants to correct a man's mistakes and the other who wants to be one.

The longest word in the English language is the one following the phrase, "And now a word from our sponsor."

Advertisement for diamond rings: "Try these for sighs."

Early winter—Novembbrrrrrrr.

It was quieter than a turkey farm on Thanksgiving afternoon.

Bridging emotion:

If you have enough connectives and hooks, your story will keep moving. So in many instances you can write the last sentence of a paragraph so that the feeling—the emotional note—carries over into the next paragraph. For instance:

Resentment in his heart, he stalked out of the laboratory.

And somehow, he was still resentful four years later when he saw her again. (You see that this is a bridge of emotion. Here your reader feels that the story has continued and nothing of interest has happened in the elapsed time.)

Suspense:

Suspense is a good word, but don't let it throw you. You've experienced it all your life (particularly if you've stood in front of telephone booths and wondered what people were saying). It's nothing in the world but curiosity. You create suspense by keeping the reader excited—restless and wondering—until the problem is solved. In the following brief passage, see how much of the atmosphere, character, situation, suspense, and drama are given:

The minute Selma's bare feet hit the kitchen doorsill, Mrs. Dean stopped getting supper to say: "Time you made home tracks. What's all this about you quittin' school?"

Make a problem:

Unless you plan and think an article through, you may end up with an incident—often lifeless and dull—instead of a live story. Ordinarily, an incident has only one problem or none. So you must often show two forces of equal strength, each fighting for supremacy. And you can step up readership by emphasizing that the losing force is stronger until the end.

Suppose you are doing a personality sketch on Dr. J. K. Blotz, a research wizard. In gathering material, you find the clash of two forces. So you go back into Dr. Blotz's high school days and show how he was torn by two forces inside: whether to follow his father's profession and become an attorney or whether to enter medical research—a course strongly urged by his chemistry teacher.

Break up a big idea into small units:

Your reader is frightened by material which looks long, statistical, slow, dull, or complicated. So break up the main idea into little ideas. Try these:

Here is the situation at a glance.

It's a long process. Briefly here's what happens ...

He had to solve three problems: (1) What caused the rise in temperature? (2) Did the sediment always form? (3) Would the use of oxides boost manufacturing costs?

Result—a dozen federal grand jury indictments and another vein of corruption dug up by the Porteous nose.

Quickly, let me tell you what subjects in newspapers interested these young officers most.

Briefly, the policy laid down by President Eisenhower, at the urging of economic advisers, is this: Make it easier for business to raise money.

You'll find some stories which lend themselves to the "question and answer" format. Here is an example:

Q. Russia is a big food-producing country. Why the food shortage?

A. Because the regime takes everything to prepare for the coming of the "world revolution"—the next war.

Q. Are men in the army spied upon, too?

A. Every man in the Red Army knows that he is being watched, possibly by his buddy or his wife.

Notice this simple device used by *U. S. News and World Report* to break up what could have been a long, ponderous paragraph:

Expanding industries. The government estimates are in line with such expansion plans as these, laid out by business leaders—

Power companies are to increase the amount of electricity they can produce at a rate of 6.5 per cent per year for the foreseeable future.

Cement companies are to add 17 per cent to their plant capacity this year.

25

Steel companies are to increase capacity by 15 million tons, or 12 per cent, within three years.

Oil companies are to step up production of crude oil from about 6.8 million barrels a day to barely 7.9 million, or 16 per cent, within four years.

Now, let's suppose that you want to give advice or suggestions in small doses. Here's the problem: how can you list a number of pointers and still keep the material from looking long and dull? Try this: alternate do's and don't's. Then your suggestions will look like this:

DO: Find the right people to contact. Depending on the problem, there are many sources for a sampling frame: customer records, previous survey records, advertising inquiries, trade directories, and your own sales force.

DON'T: Try to be too cute or humorous. State your purpose in an explicit covering letter that presents a good physical appearance. A few paragraphs should suffice. The job of reproduction should be double-checked for spacing, errors, and other seemingly minor details that mean so much.

Good personification:

You'll remember this device from your college composition course. You don't remember? It's this: you give life or living characteristics to an inanimate object. But, like other devices, it must have polish and sparkle to really click. Here's a good one created by Marian Sims: "Leaves gossiping among themselves." And here's another example from *Time:* "Like most self-educated men, Disney pulled himself up from nowhere by grabbing the tail of a runaway idea and hanging on for dear life."

Philosophical contrast:

A man learns more from one bad hangover than from ten good temperance lectures, or so it is said by those who have suffered both.

Admonition plus figures:

We don't bring them up to run them down, but the National

Devices Do It!

Safety Council tells us that 4,100 youngsters under fifteen years of age were killed in traffic last year.

Live quotation:

"He was the best damned soldier in this division," said Major Nathan M. Quinn, Spencer, Massachusetts. Shorty would rather have that sentence over his grave than his own name plate.

Specific incident:

Then came August 27, and the fight in Lenaires. It was extremely important that he be good that afternoon. First, because he was near his home town; second, because the rising young matador, Louis Miguel Dominguin, was on the same program. (Note how this incident also builds suspense.)

Prediction or forecast:

"What's ahead?" your reader asks. So you can often use a prediction like this:

Within a year or two, the average housewife may reach into the pantry, not the freezer, when she needs orange juice. She'll use a revolutionary new product: dehydrated orange juice that costs about one-half less than frozen, tastes better and has the vitamin C content of the fresh juice.

Characterization:

Your reader wants to know what the person looks like. So you can give a glimpse like this:

Or take Slim Horne. He is a heavy-shouldered man in his thirties, standing a good six feet in his bush socks and weighing about 225 pounds. His title is site superintendent.

Description of a scene:

Use a scene to hold interest. Notice how H. L. Mencken did this in a story he wrote for the *Baltimore Sun:*

The preacher stopped at last and there arose out of the darkness a woman with her hair pulled back into a tight little knot.

She began so quietly that we couldn't hear what she said, but soon her voice rose resonantly and we could follow her. She was denouncing the reading of books. Some wandering book agent, it appeared, had come to her cabin and tried to sell her a specimen of his wares. She refused to touch it. Why indeed read a book? If what was in it was true, then everything in it was already in the Bible.

Flashback:

All stories do not begin with the words, "Once upon a time—." Your material may sometimes be put across most effectively by following the chronological pattern—but not often. Instead, you will keep reader interest on a higher plane by using flashbacks which provide cues to later behavior, events, beliefs, or situations.

Watch this: never drag in a past incident unless it adds to the major theme. And, just as important, space the flashbacks so that the article keeps both continuity and unity.

See the way Joseph E. Doran of the *Cincinnati Post* uses a combined flashback and contrast approach in this lead:

Pat Doran, that's my boy, marched away with the Marines today. . . . But watching him walk away into that new life sort of started the calendar flipping backward to more important days . . .

That day when I first heard him holler about 2 A.M.

That day, one of his first at school, when he got lost on the way home

That day up at the lake when he caught his first fish

That day when he was editor of the high school paper

Here are some other ways of jumping backward:

It started this way:

As a sophomore in high school, he noticed . . .

One day he was watching his father plowing . . .

He got the idea on a train.

But the story actually started in 1941.

Backtrack to January, 1895.

At one time, TVA had 42,000 men at work.

Even before he quit school, however, he was in politics.

There, on the day when an old man down the road gave him a dollar for drawing a picture of a horse, Walt decided that he wanted to be "an artist."

Henry must have been about twelve when, along the road that ran from the Ford farm to the Plymouth carding mill, he saw a belching locomotive.

But he hasn't always captivated crowds. He can remember the snickers and guffaws which drowned him out the first time he competed in the Greer County oratorical contest.

Use carry-over connectives:

You lose the reader when the thought ends with the paragraph. So you must keep him moving along with some kind of hook. One way is to link the first sentence of a paragraph with the last sentence of the preceding paragraph. Notice these examples:

> But this will never happen.
> Now you will ask, "What are . . ."
> Let's take another example.
> But that's only half the answer.
> That is true. But our modern authors . . .
> And now let's see how Stevenson would do it.
> You may wonder how all of this is possible.
> Just don't be too sure.
> Here is another angle:
> That raises the question, "Shouldn't you wait for prices to go lower?"
> Not really; a high proportion of all houses are made . . .
> I will give you an example.
> Mr. Jones has noticed this himself. One day last summer . . .
> Nor could she tolerate success.
> All right, here's a gift shop in an Eastern suburb. It could just as easily be one in Ohio or California or Texas. All say the same thing.
> Now get back to your town. If it has a Better Business Bureau . . .

The drive succeeded. A man with ten years experience, John K. Milnot, was named full-time manager.

The pioneering isn't over yet—not by a long shot.

Impossible? It might have been during World War II, but . . .

Human interest plus suspense:

Always remember that personalities interest people more than ideas. So somehow or other you must keep talking about people. For instance, you cannot talk about Salk vaccine without considering the people who made it, the people who control it, and the people who feel its effects.

Show something happening to somebody—a druggist, a teen-ager, a junk dealer, or an expert on etiquette. Then build up the incident with suspense and drama. Like this:

Saturday, July 11, was just another morning to Dr. J. P. Boudreau; that is, until 9:40. (How much better than writing, "It was on Saturday morning, July 11, at 9:40, that Dr. J. P. . . .")

Mix Fact and Emotion:

Your reader will feel your story—he will identify himself quicker and stay with you longer—when you get a fact and a feeling, an idea and an emotion, into as many sentences as possible. You can use this device even in describing a scientific experiment. Like this:

His curiosity piqued, Griffith took ten grams of melamine, added formaldehyde, and heated the product on a watch crystal. Then he stared in wonderment.

Overlapping paragraphs:

This is another form of "hook." You can use the same words or ideas at the end of one paragraph and at the beginning of the next. Here's an example:

There was nothing to do but hang up and wait.

And he had waited. He had waited all through the afternoon and now it was five o'clock. Quinton Hardy, he knew, had done this deliberately.

Dialogue at cross purposes:

The technique of using dialogue at cross purposes is usually effective. Two people do not understand each other—each attaches a different meaning to what is said. A child, for instance, may say something innocently which rocks adults with laughter, because for them it has another meaning. Two persons meet, and each imagines the other to be someone else. The resulting dialogue could be very funny. Here's one way of using dialogue at cross purposes:

A man opens the door to the doctor's office and, in a hoarse voice, whispers to the pretty receptionist, "Is the doctor in?"

She glances around the room. She peers this way and that way. Then she whispers, "No. Come on in."

Contrast:

Think of the many contrasts around you—night and day, black and white, successful and unsuccessful, rich and poor, educated and illiterate. You can use this device to keep the reader interested because it shows a sudden shift—something has happened. Here's an example:

Twenty-three years ago Bert Ramsey was awarded first place for his collection of rocks at the Bryan County Fair. Yesterday he was elected president of the Geological Society of America at its national meeting held in Chicago.

Sometimes you may wish to show the difference between truth and rumor, or between fact and fiction. Look how Sylvia Porter punctured myths of the stock market in a very specific way:

Folklore: There's nothing like a first-rate war scare to send the stock market soaring because war means big armament orders, feverish buying, and vast profits. This, incidentally is a favorite accusation of the Kremlin and people all over the world who believe it.

Fact: In almost every case in modern history, the market's initial reaction to war news has been a slump. In the 21-year period, there were 58 days during which the stock average moved

2 per cent or more on war or war fears. On 51 of those days, the market plunged.

"Show and tell":

You want to use a fairly long quote. But you have used so many that you hesitate to run in more. What can you do? For one thing, show what the news source did while he answered. Bill Stapleton made use of this device in an article in *Collier's*. Here's the way he wrote it:

> "Look here," he said, walking over to a hurricane map of 1954 on a nearby wall. "As you see it on this chart, each hurricane path appears to be a straight or gradually curving line. Actually it's not. A hurricane zigs and zags. We don't know the reason for its erratic behavior, but we do know that if Edna had zigged when it obviously zagged, Connecticut would have been hit again instead of Massachusetts and Maine."

Flavor with anecdotes:

"The life blood of every good article," Stuart Rose of the *Saturday Evening Post* reminds us, "is the anecdote." Suppose you are doing a sketch on a racing driver. Do this: emphasize his daring and courage not through superlatives but with a string of anecdotes. A penetrating anecdote can make a personality come to life, "whether he's a hero or a heel, a wit or a lummox, a Good Samaritan or a Scrooge," Mort Weisinger says.

What's a sure way to get good anecdotes? Interviewing the subject? Talking to friends? Scanning the subject's scrapbooks? Those methods may yield a few good ones. But Maurice Zolotow swears by this technique: accompany the subject as he goes about his daily routine.

Once, assigned to do a profile on the late Mike Todd, Zolotow attached himself to the producer and wouldn't let go even when Todd went into a shoe store. Zolotow's leech-like tenacity paid off. He observed that when Todd bought shoes, he purchased fourteen pairs at a time, and this fact provided a fine anecdote.

For variety's sake, avoid overselling one trait with too many anecdotes. If you have four or five anecdotes to show how a baseball manager has the courage to tear into umpires, then, with a swift transition, serve the reader a contrasting anecdote which shows how shy and reticent he is when asked to speak in public.

How many anecdotes do you need? At least twice as many as you can use in your piece. And from this supply you can pick only those which (1) reveal the "real person" whom you are writing about, (2) keep your piece marching, and (3) carry the reader to your desired goal.

The humorous touch:

Every reader welcomes an opportunity to laugh or smile— not just in reading humorous stories and jokes, but even more so in serious matters. So serve a dash of humor when you can—an anecdote, a wisecrack, something to "break the ice." For instance:

Rossini, the Italian composer, discovered that some wealthy admirers in France were planning to erect a statue in his honor.

"How much will it cost?" the composer asked.

"About ten million francs," was the answer.

"Ten million francs!" gasped Rossini. "For five million francs I will stand on the pedestal myself."

Avoid dragging in a story. Rather, be sure that the anecdote or humorous quotation has a point which strengthens your story. At times a humorous quotation is more convincing than the most telling argument. You couldn't find a better description of Arthur Godfrey's voice than that written by George Reim when he said, "He sings like a frog with a man in his throat." You couldn't emphasize the necessity for slow driving better than the King Features writer who said, "A motorist is a person who after seeing a wreck drives carefully for several blocks." And if you write about ignorance, you might do worse than quote the remark of the little girl who explained that "Ignorance is when you don't know something and somebody finds out."

Summing up: add a dash of humor when you can. It can lighten material and keep your piece moving. Best of all, your reader welcomes it.

Narrative:

This device is effective because it is swift. But it doesn't make pictures very well. Use it? Yes, indeed. But vary it with other devices. Be sure you are telling an interesting story. In a sketch in *Reader's Digest*, Farnsworth Crowder supplies an example:

> One morning in 1884, with sleeping bag, gun and fishing tackle, he started to walk. He kept on walking for 3,500 miles, until on the 143rd day he reached the Pacific. If what he wanted was to try himself, the West did not let him down. He had to fight winter over the Rockies. Near Colorado State Prison he had to slug it out with an escaped convict who jumped him for his rifle. Awakened in an abandoned cabin, he had to face a prowling wildcat. Crossing the deserts he met storms, heat and thirst. In an Arizona canyon he broke his arm in a fall, set the bone himself, bound it up and went on.

Repetition:

Since, as Samuel Taylor Coleridge pointed out, a reader much prefers recognition to surprise, repetition is a standard and frequently used device in all forms of literature. Actually, a reader has to slow down when you present him with a surprise, a puzzle, something novel or new. But when you repeat something—whether a phrase, an idea, an action, a word, or a bit of conversation—you make it easy for the reader.

But here's something to watch: repetition does not mean repeating the same line over and over again. Edgar Allen Poe, in his poem, "The Raven," took extreme care that "Nevermore," the word repeated by the bird, was the answer to a different question each time it was uttered. So each utterance carried a different meaning. Repetition can be varied in meaning, length, or sound. Notice this simple way of using it:

That day, that most unusual day, started like any other.

Sharing sensation:

Can you make the reader see, hear, smell, or feel something? Does he really experience the sensation? You'll probably get hun-

This is the feature writer's audience—people—180 million of them,
living mostly in cities, but in important numbers
in towns and around the countryside.

Courtesy *Oklahoma City Times*

*Ideas are the stock in trade of the newspaper city editor,
whose job is to keep reporters occupied on dull days
as well as busy ones:* Ralph Sewell, Oklahoma City Times
city editor, *and* Mary Goddard, reporter.

Photograph by Dick Peterson; courtesy *Oklahoma City Times*

gry when you read these words Alberta Wilson Constant wrote for the *Southwest Review:*

> You could smell a peach cobbler all through the dinner, and when Mattie opened the oven door to take it out you had to swallow quick because that aroma would make the taste buds of a mummy burst into bloom. Cobblers came to the table in long black pans and were put in front of Mama on two asbestos mats, while the juice bubbled and oozed through the fancy gashes cut like fern fronds in the brown crust.

Ask questions:

As you write, remember the reader and the questions he might ask. Sometimes you can point out what lies ahead by asking several questions. Robert Ginna and H. B. Darrach, Jr. did it this way in an article in *Life:*

> Why do these things make no sound? What power urges them at such terrible speeds through the sky? Who, or what, is aboard? Where do they come from? Why are they here?

Specific incident plus suspense:

Note how Karl Detzer builds suspense with an incident:

> At 4 A. M. on December 5, 1929, an Indiana industrialist named Frank H. Sparks climbed out of bed, went to his desk and wrote a long memorandum to himself. He had just decided what to do with the rest of his life.

Hey! How about going back and reading these devices again? This time notice the uniqueness of each. See how each one does its part in flashing green lights ahead of the reader. And notice that each one is not just a string of words. Rather, each device has an emotional overtone because it is a shared experience.

Now—right now—start building your device file. Grab that stack of old magazines and newspapers and start clipping. If you wait, they may get lost. How about it? Read for devices. You'll find the types shown here—and a lot more! Keep adding to your files. Then put these devices to work in your features.

And you'll be surprised
    how much "check appeal" you can add to your features;
    how quickly your acceptances begin to climb;
    how you'll hit those markets you've dreamed about;
because—devices do it!

4. The Art of Asking Questions

Ever asked yourself

"How can I become an expert interviewer?"
"What strategies will make people respond?"
"How can I get material for a personality sketch?"
"Can reticent interviewees be softened up?"
"Where can I learn the secrets of top-flight writers?"

Yes, you can improve your skills as an interviewer. You can learn to ask the right kind of questions. And your questions will bring the desired answers. How?

Not by using a neat little formula. Nor by following a set of strict rules. Interviewing is more than questions and answers. As a writer you must have a knowledge of environmental forces, news values, human behavior, and interviewing skills and techniques—all of which are valuable in getting information, color, and opinions from individuals.

Now here's Fred. Armed with all kinds of questions, he jumps into an interview. But he doesn't get the material he wants. Somehow or other his informant does not respond as he should. Finally, Fred gives up. What was wrong?

First of all, Fred should remember that the whole process depends upon countless factors—tangible and intangible. Did he anticipate the mood of the interviewee? Perhaps Fred thrust some of his big questions too early in the interview. Was the whole affair rushed? Was the interviewee worried, nervous, incoherent, afraid? But here's the most important thing: Did Fred tie in his approach and questions with basic interests of the interviewee?

As a writer you watch people. You study their actions. You know that Mr. Bigdome is different from Mr. Highpower. "No two people are alike," you say. And that's right. But do you remember that basic fact in getting ready for an interview?

Now, let's go a step further. Without a complete picture of the interviewee you will probably be astonished. Mrs. Sourpuss at home may be Mrs. Charm when she serves on the greeting committee at Dornick Hills Country Club. Don't forget that you may have to talk to her when she is down psychologically. And you must be ready to raise her spirits—to give her a feeling of satisfaction and enjoyment—through your interviewing techniques. Then she will respond.

Let's remember as writers that most human behavior is the result of mixed drives. We do not always attend meetings of the Scribes and Scribblers, for instance, purely to listen in on the discussions. Nor do we usually play tennis merely for the exercise. Every person, whether a debutante or a ditchdigger, has scores of drives operating simultaneously. What is more, these drives all flow into one another, generating widespread chemical and muscular changes. But only some of them reach proportions sufficient to give activity a specific character.

Here's the all-important must: Only as you understand WITH a person can you polish your interviewing techniques. This means that you must see the expressed idea and attitude from the other person's point of view, in order to sense how it feels to him and to see how it has personal meaning for him. But that is not all. You must see how his attitude is combined with emotional factors. Psychologically, you must achieve his frame of reference in regard to the subject he is talking about. You must see the world through his eyes.

Let's dissect the anatomy of your interviewee's attitudes for a moment. Here is Mr. Emory Q. Spellbinder. Whatever happens to him—in business, at his civic club meetings, or on a fishing trip—will be interpreted in accordance with his predispositions.

Here's something else: His likelihood of reacting a certain way depends upon his habits of evaluation, which are conditioned by his environment. Remember that his attitudes include the way he looks at things, the way he feels about them, and the way he is prepared to act. These three factors are interrelated. Each one influences the other two. Psychologists call this sort of arrangement a dynamic interrelationship.

You plan to interview Mr. Spellbinder. So by looking at his attitudes from three sides, you have three possible levers with which to control them. First, find out the way he looks at things. Secondly, try to discover how he feels toward them. And then, if you know these attitudes, you are likely to know how he will react under given circumstances.

Suppose Mr. Spellbinder refuses to co-operate. What caused his reticence? All the forces working on him from his existence as an embryo to the time he did not respond to your questions provide the reasons. In other words, his failure to respond was not due to a single cause. Rather, his behavior was the result of many forces, most of which are unknowable.

Here's what expert interviewers say: There's usually more than one cause behind a respondent's failure to talk. How often have you said, "If I could just find the reason why he doesn't talk I could get the material I need?" And I used to believe that, too. But today most psychologists say that we should not isolate any single factor as the sole reason for a person's behavior. Rather, Mr. Spellbinder's behavior, like our own, is the result of the interaction of millions of forces inside and outside of him.

You must get more than facts and opinions to write a sparkling personality sketch. Why? Largely because a well-written personality piece gives the readers a vicarious visit with the subject of the sketch. And information alone can't accomplish this. Roger Dakin reminds us, "People do not sit down to read information per se. If this were true, *Encyclopaedia Britannica* would be the best-selling book in the nation."

So we must entertain the reader. Mr. Average Reader is bombarded today from all sides by communications stimuli—radio, TV, magazines, newspapers, direct mail, speeches, exhibits, demonstrations—and he simply doesn't have enough time to see or react to them all. Now: to hold the reader's attention we must amass a tremendous amount—more than we can use—of anecdotes, character traits, sidelights, opinions, and facts.

In interviewing and in weighing and analyzing your material, keep asking yourself the question, "What makes this person tick?" As former *Life* writer Jeanne Perkins Harman reminds us, "When you have found that, you're half way home."

And let's not forget that people generally do not talk about very personal matters—matters which you usually must have. Take the Boy Scout motto: Be prepared. Read everything—articles, clips, books. Talk to the interviewee's friends and associates. His relatives. And know as much about his field as you can.

Sometimes this isn't easy. Lincoln Barnett, who did the excellent *Life* science series, decided he wanted to do a piece on Einstein. But before even asking to see the scientist, Barnett took an intensive course in physics at Columbia University. The result was first a magazine piece and later his book, *The World of Dr. Einstein.*

What are the differences between the expert interviewer and the amateur? After all is said and done, it is the know-how—the specific and minute techniques—that you find in the polished performer. By some peculiar magic—which you can acquire—the expert gets more than facts and comments from an interviewee. Coupled with that ability, he has a news sense, a sense of seeing something exciting even in drab human experiences.

Remember this: you have known all along that you must understand people before you can gain any facility in handling them. And because you want to step up your interviewing skills, you will keep adding to your stock of workable strategies.

You can shorten the road to success in interviewing in two ways: first, through experience, and secondly, by studying the methods used by the experts.

If you are eager to increase your ability, you must constantly add to your stock of knowledge. To learn, one must do. After each interview ask yourself: "Did I plan it well enough?" "Did I sense the interviewee's attitudes?" "Were my questions planned with care?" "Was I able to see the situation from the interviewee's point of view?" "Did I get the full meaning of each statement?" "Were my questions geared to the interests of the interviewee?" "Was I careful to avoid stock questions?" "Did I get the story which I sought?" Use a follow-up evaluation of your actions and you will soon climb higher on the ladder of proficiency.

Follow these guideposts in stepping up your interviewing skills:

1. Plan each interview with care.
2. Make the right approach.
3. Do everything possible to build an atmosphere of co-operation.
4. Make the other person like you.
5. Avoid thrusting big questions early in the interview.
6. Accept things from the interviewee's angle.
7. Learn to sidestep arguments.
8. Size up the interviewee—his drives, beliefs, prejudices, and habits.
9. Don't give up too soon—tactful persistence pays.
10. Get the beliefs behind the quotations. The meaning of the facts are more important than the facts themselves.
11. Resolve to do your best on every assignment, and then people will know you are trustworthy.
12. Be a good listener.
13. Use conversational "hooks" to keep the interview moving.
14. Be on the alert for unusual angles, unexpected slants, and new facts.
15. Obtain all the facts and opinions needed for a well-rounded story.
16. Write your story while the information is fresh.

Somehow or other, you've got to get the "feel" of the situation. You won't get it by telephone. Nor by rewriting old material. Meyer Berger of the *New York Times* writes his own stories without the aid of the rewrite desk. Why? He says, "A good story doesn't take on dimension until you see it. I always try to get sound and motion . . . and the only way you can do it is by being there."

In the final analysis, remember that the best interviewing is the result of a battery of skills and abilities which the interviewer uses. His knowledge, his understanding, his sensitivity, his expertness in knowing human behavior—these are keys which open up the other person. And always, the expert interviewer knows that motivation is the moving force in the interaction of person with person.

Jules Archer, a successful free lance writer, gives the most succinct and probably the best advice on writing the personality piece. He says, "Get under that halo and look for the dandruff!"

Briefly now, let's look at some basic ways of acquiring successful interviewing strategies: (1) Keep your curiosity about people alive—watch them, talk to them—keep asking "What makes them click?" (2) Steep yourself in current books and magazine articles on psychology—strengthen your knowledge of association, interest, suggestion, identification, and other phenomena of human behavior. (3) Practice looking at life from the other fellow's point of view. (4) Overcome your natural tendency to hear and write only those facts and opinions which harmonize with your own. (5) Do not fall into the practice of regarding all interviewees as types, but rather try to discover the uniqueness of each person to whom you talk. (6) Understand WITH a person and then gear your questions so that they will tap his basic interests. (7) Remember that preparedness pays. If you've studied the facts, the person, and the situation, made allowances for unforeseen behavior, and tried to prepare all of the other ingredients which make a successful interview, you may be surprised how smoothly it will go and how productive the experience can be for you.

Here's the most important thing: use a planned approach, not a canned approach.

5. Let's Listen to the Experts

THAT SHIFT in paragraphs, your decision to add two more incidents near the end of the article, the lifeless figures you chopped from the middle of the piece—will these changes step up the readership of your story? Are you sure?

Today there is more competition for the reader's attention than ever before. Even if your story appears in print, it is in direct competition with others for the reader's time, attention, and dollars. Did you ever count the number of stories, advertisements, and pictures in one issue of a metropolitan newspaper? Or a national magazine? If your story is to stand out and be read amid that sort of competition, it must be prepared with unusual ingenuity and skill.

And you say, "But first of all, I must write a story which hits the editor." And you are right. How? For one thing, your story must be tuned an octave higher than run-of-the-mill pieces.

How can we learn to write articles that click? It's simple! Let's get some helpful suggestions from some top-flight word artists. We'll just listen to them and learn some of the secrets of their success.

"Human appeal . . . is secret of feature"
Robert Richards, Staff Writer
Memphis Press-Scimitar
The secret of any successful feature story lies in its human appeal.

Once I did a daily feature (1945-48) out of New York City for United Press. When I started doing it, I had the problem of writing a piece that would go over in Boston, or Memphis, or Oklahoma City, or San Francisco. I decided, after a short while, that the features which were printed the most—on the basis, I may add, of factual checking of clips from the newspapers—were interviews with different people who let themselves go and told their feelings about life, or, at least, about a given situation in their lives.

If the reader is able to identify himself with the person in the feature, he is bound to read the story. It's the same principle that makes people read a novel, or go to the movies. They put themselves in the position of the hero—and laugh or cry with him.

Recently United Press's Hugh Baillie wrote that it isn't enough for a wire service to present just the big news. The people, he says, want the so-called "little" news too. I agree with this. I also think it is essential that a good feature have a "point of view." I don't mean that the writer should editorialize, in any sense. But he should tell enough about the main character in his feature so that the reader senses what the character is trying to accomplish, or what he hopes will happen tomorrow. If this isn't done, the feature remains flat and one-sided, and the feeling doesn't get across to the reader.

Ernie Pyle learned that the ordinary man is the key to the reader's heart if he is treated with the respect and interest that he deserves.

To me, the fewer gimmicks a feature has—and the more honest interest and integrity—the better.

"It's how you write it"
Leif H. Olson, Financial Writer
The *New York Times*

I have only one principal pointer in writing feature stories. It's not what you write, it's how you write it. Learn to handle words, then look for your story.

One of the *Wall Street Journal's* finest feature writers once told me: "If a story is worth writing once, it's worth writing twice." What he meant was that a good writer should be able to write a story in at least two interesting ways.

When a writer lacks the knowledge of working with words, then he's in danger of missing a good story. The poor writer is apt to overlook good features because he's looking for an unusual, exciting story

44

that will look good in print no matter how it is written. The good writer, on the other hand, is confident that no matter how simple the story, it will be interesting because of the way he writes it.

"Feature writer gets excited"
F. K. Arthur, Assistant Editor
AP Newsfeatures, New York City

Most good feature writers are good newspapermen first. Conversely, there are many excellent reporters who never seem to get the feel of a feature. The primary difference seems to lie in an ability not only to get the story but to write it in personal human terms—not simply as a collection of facts.

To do this, the good feature writer works up a real feeling for his particular job of the moment. It may be anything from sympathy for the subject to a deep and abiding interest in a project. A good feature writer gets excited about what he's doing and, corny as it may sound, submerges himself in it.

The average newspaperman probably would abhor having anything he does called artistic. Not the good feature writer. He has immense pride in his creation and will fight for every word.

As for what makes a good feature, you have to be wary about generalizing. But here again it comes down largely to the personal and human—it's a story with which a reader can identify himself because the writer stirs a response that gives the reader a feel of the person or problem.

Here too, however, the writer must first be a good reporter—he must get all the facts and get them accurately, his story must be as thoroughly buttoned up as an account of a murder; if he's dealing with a controversial subject, he must take special pains to interpret it with complete objectivity. So a good feature story comes down to the writer and his ability to draw a picture understandably, entertainingly, and accurately.

You could get a lot of answers to the most important things a feature writer needs to know. But here are three:

How to dig, and a willingness to do it. There's no substitute for thorough research. This may involve endless hours of reading, of talking to people, of hunting for facts on both sides of an issue, of interminable questioning to get at essentials. It often involves outwitting an unwilling interview subject; it sometimes lays the reporter open to embarrassment and even personal danger, but it has to be done.

How to be selective. How to throw away four facts for every one used, yet still wrap up all the angles, putting together a story without holes.

How to organize. How to put together the facts he's dug out and selected. How to paint a picture which a reader can grasp easily, without having to stop and puzzle out a single phrase; how to point up dramatic highlights to capture and hold a reader's interest; how to emphasize the human elements; how to use direct quotes effectively.

All this requires one other important thing: time. Good features take a lot of it. The reporter who can sit down and bang out a readable feature like deadline was ten minutes away is rare indeed.

There may still be another question that needs answering: are good feature writers born or made? Probably some of both. A writer either has a flair for the color, enterprise, and creativeness inherent in any good feature, or he hasn't. On the other hand, it takes a lot of application and experience to turn a good reporter into a polished feature writer. The good ones go right on learning.

"Keep track of ideas"
Cary Robertson, Sunday Editor
Louisville Courier-Journal

My best contribution to anyone who wants to be a feature writer or a feature editor is a suggestion to help in keeping track of ideas. Any basic theme or little sidelight should be typed up on a file card and classified under headings that will soon suggest themselves. Cards are easily spread out on the desk or filed under different headings, whereas lists seems to be unwieldy.

I find the daily papers the best source of ideas for feature stories. Sometimes an individual who is mentioned in the news will write one himself. Sometimes an event or place will be in the news and will form a source for a complete story. The news is constantly changing and bringing new things to the surface.

"An eye for details"
Sterling Bemis, Sunday Editor
Independent Press-Telegram
Long Beach, California

After observing feature writers, good and bad, for more than twenty-five years, I have found that they fall into two classes:

1. Those who can spell.

2. Those who write "sargent," meaning a military man with stripes, and "vetaren," meaning a man who has lost his stripes.

Generally speaking, there is some hope for a man who has learned to spell. He obviously has some powers of observation, and these powers are the Number One essential in my book for the prospective feature writer. A person with an eye for details will strike gold even in an overworked lode and will know how to have it assayed and be aware of the general location of Fort Knox.

So that's Number One. Pay attention to details. I remember the case of a brigadier general recruiting Flying Tigers for Claire Chennault who became lively copy when an alert reporter noticed one of his cuffs was wrinkled. "In a hurry, son," said the general. "Don't have time to send out my laundry. Wash my shirts every night in the hotel lavatory." Claire Chennault's men hurried—and washed those Japanese right out of their hair.

Number Two. A good feature writer learns to think up a working title before he starts to write. The working title helps to give the writer a sense of direction and it eliminates a lot of chaff. It is also very handy in querying an editor. An editor may be interested in seeing a yarn about an amputee who is making a name for himself on a college diamond. He is more likely to be interested if the writer teases him with a question like this: "How would you like to see 'Mr. Peg Leg Learns to Pitch'?"

Number Three. The good feature writers of my acquaintance have all been hard to cut. That's because they've packed the facts away tightly, cramming them into short sentences and padlocking with periods instead of semicolons and commas. I think a feature should be so crisp and compact that it will give the editor a mildly frustrated feeling. "Dammit!" he muses, "this is really a little more than we asked for, but it has so many interesting facts it wouldn't be fair to the readers to whack it down."

When you have an editor worrying because he can't reasonably whack you down, you've got something.

"An utter inability to take anything at face value"
Lance Zavitz, Staff Writer
Buffalo Evening News

If I have any "secrets" they are a characteristic and a belief. The trait is an insatiable curiosity, an utter inability (perhaps because of a mind afflicted by wanderlust) to take any situation at face value. The belief is that a feature story can be written about any object, person, or event in the world (the would-be writer must decide, of course, whether the story will be worth the effort required).

Let me illustrate: You have a waste basket somewhere near your desk. Probably it is decorative as well as utilitarian. If you have an insatiable curiosity, the mere presence of the waste basket starts your mind going like this: "When was the first waste basket (in an office, school, etc.) used? Who invented it? What did people do with waste paper in such places before it was invented? The open-mesh wire basket has almost disappeared; why? What are the advantages of solid metal baskets? (One is that if it is turned upside down it will smother a fire that may have started in it.) Do women (and men) have preferences with respect to waste baskets? How many persons will pass a scrap of paper on the floor near a basket before someone picks it up and puts it in the basket?"

You can go on like this indefinitely, of course. Research will supply the answers, but sooner or later you must decide whether the information you have acquired (or amassed) is worth putting into a story; in other words, will anyone want to read what you have written. Experience will lead you to make this decision sooner, rather than later, thereby saving a great deal of research which is fascinating but not remunerative.

Apart from the ability to write, which is essential to any form of successful authorship, a feature writer needs to know facts, all kinds and sizes of facts, and people of every variety.

Knowledge of facts will make it possible for him to determine whether any specific feature story is worth writing.

Knowledge of facts will make it easier for him to write the feature stories which come to his attention.

"People make best features"
Hoke Norris, Staff Writer
Chicago Sun-Times

What makes a good feature story? People doing things. Not statistics or depersonalized facts. But people—one or two or three to a story—doing a thing, sometimes a quite commonplace thing.

What are the three most important things a feature writer needs to know? I wouldn't be dogmatic about "three things." How to write. How to approach people and draw them out. Perhaps that's all.

Secrets? Each writer must find his own.

"Good story is a matter of feeling"
Alfred Segal, Staff Writer
The Cincinnati Post

It's harder to tell how to write a feature story than it is to actually write it. I just sit down and start writing it. Maybe my facility at this has to do with a long experience of life and of newspaper work. I have learned that to write a good story is not a matter of literary mechanics but of feeling. That is to say, the feeling that has to do with knowing and caring about people—ordinary people. If you feel the people in your story, it may turn out warm and heartwarming. That way, I have been able to develop a routine situation into a story that clicked some-how. It's all in how a guy looks at his story—looks behind it to know better those who are mixed up in it.

"Choose a subject that interests you"
Inez Robb, Feature Writer
United Feature Syndicate

I wish I had some secrets that I could pass on, but the truth is that I don't.

I have sold a good many features to magazines and the only thing that I can tell you about it is that I first choose a subject that interests me and then hope that it interests the public. I simply couldn't write about anything that bored me because then it would surely bore the public, too. By that, I mean that if it bored me it would be reflected in the way in which I would attack the subject.

I believe that anyone who starts out to write professionally should acquire a good agent. Such an agent knows what the magazines want, and, in turn, he knows where to place an article. In my opinion, a good agent certainly earns the 10 per cent he receives for his services.

"The angle is the important factor"
Eddie Beachler, Staff Writer
The Pittsburgh Press

In my opinion, the most important factor in a feature story is the "angle." It must be written to catch the reader fast, then continue to suck him in with humor, human interest, suspense, or some such tactic, and finish with a good kicker.

I believe that a good feature writer can take almost any subject and make a readable story out of it simply with skillful writing. Frequently, it is the writer who makes the story and not vice versa.

Good, solid news stories write themselves. Most features do not. They are created by the writer.

There is no set formula for "what makes a good feature story." Usually though, a good feature must have a current news "peg" on which to hang, or something else to make it timely, such as the season of the year, a holiday, or an anniversary of some sort.

A feature frequently is the sidelight or light side or, sometimes, the very heart of the current news.

News sense is just as vital to the feature writer as a green thumb is to a gardener. And it may take just as much digging.

Reading books, magazines, and news stories is helpful. Many feature stories are inspired by an idea expressed in another story.

Style is extremely important, but a writer who always uses the same style will rapidly find himself in a rut and lose readership because it sounds like "the same old story."

A feature writer must be able to adapt his style to the story—when it requires humor, he must have a light touch; for tragedy, he needs a sense of feeling and yet enough restraint that it doesn't "slop over."

In a personality-biography type feature, which perhaps is the most common, the little details and incidents of a person's life frequently are the most revealing.

These are hardest to get, especially from a prominent person who has been conditioned to think in terms of high spots. And often the person being interviewed hasn't the faintest idea what is or is not important.

The feature writer must: (1) disarm the person being interviewed; (2) gain his confidence; (3) not only ask questions, but pass along ideas that may set off a chain reaction by causing the subject to recall incidents that will make him come to life for the reader.

Every reader welcomes the humorous touch. (See Chapter 3.)

Photograph by Jean Mattox

*All of man's hopes, fears, and aspirations are present
at a national Presidential convention. (See Politics).*

Courtsey *The Chicago Tribune*

"Cultivate a sensitiveness to current trends"
Frederick H. Guidry, Staff Writer
The Christian Science Monitor

The writer who clicks with his editor or his reader seems more often to be the skillful craftsman rather than the great idea man. A feature story idea rarely is so good that it can survive careless or shallow writing. On the other hand, many an obvious and oft-used angle has been made to seem new by an imaginative writer.

A particular feature story may click with some readers and not with others, for reasons of individual background or current interests. But some writers have the knack of bringing the reader into almost any subject with equal success, no matter how complicated or foreign the subject matter may be. The difference would seem to me to be in the writing—especially of the opening paragraphs, by which the reader is drawn into the story. The far-fetched or strained beginning may annoy the discriminating reader, who will feel he has been cheated by overwriting if the balance of the story does not live up to its first promise.

I have backed into the second question you ask: "What makes a good feature story?"

It is a well-structured, deftly written piece; one that enlists the reader's sympathy or arouses his curiosity. It more nearly fits the child concept of "story" than the information-packed straight news story. A news feature vivifies a current issue or situation as a statement of mere fact can rarely do.

Being a newspaper reporter, rather than a magazine writer, my concept of a good feature story includes a solid peg to current news. I am always on the lookout for news features that will deepen reader interest in, or knowledge of, something worthy of his concern. A story that dramatizes for the reader a current question on which he may soon have to make a decision or express an opinion is fun to work on as well as helpful to read.

As for the "three most important things a feature writer needs to know," I would list them as:

1. *Familiarity with his material.* He should know it inside out, if time permits, before he writes a word. He should make the story elements "his own"—be so familiar with the facts that he can practically write the story out of his head.

2. *Skill in his craft.* He must be able to write clearly and inter-

estingly without sacrificing accuracy in the process. Without bogging down in details, he should give the readers sufficient facts and background to bring about a satisfying sense of comprehension and informational gain.

3. *Awareness of his readers.* If the writer knows what audience he is trying to reach, he may have more success in communicating with them. This will help him set both the tone and the content of the article within limits reasonably likely to find a receptive readership on hand.

As for my "secrets" in seeing a feature story in an otherwise routine situation, I must tell about the time I almost missed a good story for lack of vision.

When the first troops were to be entrenched near an atomic bomb test—which was also to be shown for the first time nationally on television—I decided to poll a special group of local (Boston) viewers for their reaction. The group I had selected for interviewing were parents of local boys who would be in the trenches. I had their names from Army publicity releases.

On the morning of the blast I waited until the minute when the parents would have just seen the explosion on television. Then I called the home of one of the boys.

I talked to the mother of one of the boys in the Nevada trenches. She had seen the blast on TV and thought it was "wonderful." This puzzled me, for she should have shown more anxiety, I thought. I asked if she didn't have a son in the service. She said she had one in a camp out west—in Nevada somewhere, she thought. She obviously didn't know her son was in the test. I didn't tell her.

Like the green reporter who was sent to cover a wedding and told his editor there was no story because the groom had failed to show up, I almost muffed this one. Assured by fellow reporters that there was still a story in my phone call, I wrote up what happened. Later I received many kind comments on my story headlined "Atom Test—A Mother Does Not Know . . ." which ran as a sidebar to the main test story.

If the writer will cultivate a sensitiveness to current trends—an awareness of ever-changing climates of opinion both nationally and in the community where he lives and works—he will be able to spot those minor events that need to be set in proper context through a larger, more definitive article. A small news item can be the key to a major story. What questions are posed by the situation it describes? How many of these questions need airing or exploring at this particular time? Before long the single loose thread may lead to the colorful whole cloth of the first-rate feature story.

"Feature is news in 3-D"
Louis Cook, Staff Writer
The Detroit Free Press

A good feature story is a good news story. It is the news in 3-D, technicolor, and hi-fi. It tells what happens in such a way that the reader feels he is there while it is happening—seeing what the reporter sees, feeling what people are feeling, smelling the same odors, hearing the same sounds.

A feature writer needs what every reporter needs: compassion, ethics, and a working knowledge of grammar. There is no such thing as a routine situation. Wherever there are people, there is infinite variation.

"Reader identification with subject"
Dick Pearce, Editor, Editorial Page
San Francisco Examiner

In newspaper feature writing the common nerve is, as it has always been, human interest.

There are only two kinds, those about people and those about animals.

In the most successful feature there is reader identification with the subject. The story is good because it is about a common experience, a common emotion, or a common hope.

Vague as the above is, I'm afraid I cannot be more definite. I never write by the rules.

"A word-inspired visual image"
Watson Davis, Director
Science Service, Washington, D. C.

It is very difficult to codify or 1, 2, 3, the analysis of a feature story.

The trick is (without being tricky) to relate with a word-inspired visual image, what the story is to tell, to something the reader already knows about. This can be done in scores of ways, and there should be no formula if the writing is to be fresh, vivid, and readable.

53

Writing is at least as much art as science—even with science stories—and probably even more. There are many gimmicks, such as using emotional or psychological appeals like sex, horror, fear, gold, and all the other emotion-arousing effective clichés.

However, as much of science lends itself to features, the product does not need to be overdressed in order to be salable and readable.

After all, the task in writing features is to pick information of interest and importance; that is the new, or at least timely. If one does not have to ballyhoo something, either for publicity purposes or because some editor has a funny preconceived notion, it is quite possible to pick and choose what one writes. That is one of the attractive features of being a writer.

"Evoke men's minds and emotions"
George W. Cornell, Staff Writer
The Associated Press, New York City

First of all, I would say that a good feature story usually must concern itself with intimate details that are ignored in the general run of news. A news story is news because it is big. Or at least tends in that direction. A feature story is a good feature story because it includes little things, the minutiae of life, the close-up views, the tingles of emotion, the gestures, the color, the stumbles, the strain, and the dreams—and not just the blatant, crash-bang sequence of events that go to make up news.

This doesn't mean that a feature story should be cluttered with dull facts and figures. Even more care is required in selecting the details of a feature story than in carving a news story down to the bone of salient facts. It is easy to learn to skim the dead weight off a news story and keep its essentials in more or less descending order. But in a feature story, it seems to me, a great deal more fineness of taste and recognition of the ruling drives in human nature are needed. A good feature story must touch the heart—or the funnybone—or the brain in its more thoughtful moods. News often just satisfies a superficial curiosity. A feature story should do more than this.

Of course, there are all kinds of feature stories, those that explore some abstruse subject or explain some complicated item that arises in the course of news events, those that tell of insignificant occurrences that have a universal ring of truth, and those that seek out the comic and tragic and heroic in the little affairs of people. But I would say that in all of them there must remain that close adherence to the per-

54

plexities, hungers, and urges of individual men and women. In other words, the well-told feature story must deal with those microscopic elements of human conduct that dominate their lives—but which usually don't break into the news except in outward forms and end results.

As to what makes a feature writer tick, or at least tick effectively, I would say that discrimination is the mainspring. He needs an introspective approach, one that sees the hidden spark, the novel twist, and the overlooked facet of a situation that is often the clue to the real truth of the matter. He must look behind what has been said before. Usually, news coverage works just the opposite. The old news hand gets so he sees a news story just because it has been news before. The news columns are full of repetition. Choice of news gets so it comes by imitation. If it was news when Mr. Smith shot his wife, then it's news when Mr. Jones shoots his wife. Undoubtedly there are weaknesses to this formula, even though there are good reasons for it. My own impression is that it often is carried out the window. Some editors seem to have a kind of compulsion that they've got to give space to the news that is established by precedent as news before they get around to looking for something that is more truly new. There's always this inclination—and perhaps there is a sound basis for it—to play up what past headlines have built up as the expected news diet or what the prevailing mood of society has latched onto as the subject of the hour. And so you keep on playing the same old tunes, with some of them at times a bit more popular than at other times. They're sort of like hit songs—a few variations but always about the same.

This same deadening element doesn't apply to feature stories, or feature writers. They often fall in stereotypes, too. But in the case of feature stories, unlike news, there is no justification for it. A feature writer can approach a subject from almost any angle, with almost any technique or style, and the selection of subject matter also is just as free. While the news writer is limited to telling quickly and specifically the broader, and consequently coarser facts of events, the feature writer is bound to no such flat, routine pattern. It is his to do a little pioneering. If he doesn't, he is missing the trick. He should try to branch out into the unusual avenues of men, deeds, and institutions. He should try to find in the commonplace, in the little things, the story that has not been told in the crass jangle of news. He should search out the delicate undertone and hidden shadings that ordinarily don't show through the outer glare. It is in these overlooked, though often plain places that he will find the gems that bring the smile, the memory, the tear, or the wonder. Because the ground rules of feature writing are so unfixed and so free, the course has to be charted anew each time the writer tackles a subject. He must be able to find in himself the possibilities of a response the subject contains. There are really no rules to guide him, except his own sense of what will evoke men's minds or emotions.

He himself, I believe, must be not only sensitive to, but objectively aware of the things that attract, repel, and stir the feelings of people, and of the things that appeal to their imagination, their hopes, and their quests for understanding. It is only on the basis of such perception that the feature writer can know what to discard that is dull and lifeless, and what he must retain that will excite and prick. Certainly in putting together a feature story which has been well backgrounded, the writer is going to have to throw away more than he keeps. And in the feature field, it is harder to know what part to keep, because the path has not been laid down for you, as it has in the handling of news.

As for advice to the feature writer, I would say this:

Keep away from easy approaches, such as questionmark leads and overall quotation leads. These are lazy and usually inane.

Shun the brash "unprecedented, biggest-in-history" type of lead.

It's better to start off with a low-key sentence, and build into the world-shaking significance in the second or third paragraph, sort of like a piece of music. That is, in a feature story. For spot news, it's different.

Keep the paragraphs short, particularly the opening ones. Break up longer sentences with very short ones.

If dealing with a complicated subject, find the rudimentary key— the simple basic kernel of the subject—that will bring home the meaning to an ordinary person.

Start out with that fundamental core, and then move later into the details that gave rise to the case or situation. If a story is worthwhile, there's always some elementary issue or point that gives it universal application to people. That should set the opening scene.

In a personality profile, some interesting or revealing incident involving the person is always a good starter.

Or sometimes it works best to open with some aspect of the field or profession with which the person is connected, and then ring the person himself in later, with his role or views on the field. Then go on with the personality sketch.

Don't load the lead paragraphs down with titles, physical descriptions, or big-shot pomposity. Start with the intimate side and go into the big generalities later. Readers are more interested in the familiar side.

Also, on features in general, it's always better to handle one microscopic facet of a situation neatly than to try to cover the whole world in one jump.

Always remember that the thing that sounds the most imposing is often not what strikes the human fancy. The part of your material you'd relate in a bull session with friends is usually the best stuff. What strikes your own interest is a good guide.

You ask what I consider the three most important things a feature writer needs to know. I'd say:

1. An awareness of the response zones of people—humor, knowledge, security, comfort, love, power, and all the little morsels that feed these appetites.

2. The perspective to reduce complicated issues, old entrenched problems, places, situations, and people down to fresh, simple, revealing terms.

3. The discipline to write simply, clearly, and modestly, without showiness.

"Writer has built-in feel for story"
Cynthia Lowry, Staff Writer
AP Newsfeatures, New York

I frankly don't know how to pin down a good feature writer. It is as unanswerable as "How long is a piece of string?" I might say that good feature writers are good newspapermen first. That doesn't answer anything either. Some of the best newspapermen I know are magnificent leg men and go all to pieces when confronted with a typewriter.

Some of our best rewrite men are lost, unhappy souls when they are out on the street. I suspect that most feature writers operate on a sense of smell for a feature, and have a sort of built-in feel for it. Certainly no two of them are alike in anything I can discover, except that they like to assemble or research their own material, sweat out the stories in their own particular ways, and—when in mid-feature—are completely concentrated on it.

What is a feature? That alone can be many things, ranging from informal writing which deliberately breaks the inverted pyramid rules of hard news writing with a leisurely lead, an anecdote, or a premise, to material which would fit into the hard-news style but which is "featurized" somewhat by the insertion of interesting but non-essential intelligence, or even humor. Features can be broken up into an infinite number of categories—special interest pieces (chess, stamps), personality pieces (and let's not forget obituaries), "color" stories, and interpretives which are presumed to take a rounded look at any question. There are some writers who are good at one thing, others who are good at another.

The digging equipment a reporter-turned-writer brings into his job can be varied. I know some excellent feature writers who are lousy interviewers. I know some dandy interviewers who can turn out slick profiles but who do miserable jobs on situation stories. Some write emotionally, dramatically; others specialize in humor, satire, the small detail.

Feature writing requires all the qualities of hard news writing. Then there's something else which an editor can spot, the writer can feel, and neither one of them can do more than hint at. Anyway, they all like to write—or at least they all like to have written. And all of them are editor-fighters who go down bleeding when the blue-pencil, tasteless slobs cut, substitute, or otherwise mutilate one single word of their copy.

6. What Makes a Title Click?

YOUR STORY title is like a traffic light.

It stops the reader or waves him on.

You must capture the reader's interest or he walks out on you. This means that you must take advantage of a few fleeting seconds. You must make every letter of every word count. Actually, the title of your story can often be the "sink or swim" part.

How can you make the first contact count? You must strike hard. You must break through the apathy barrier. Somehow you must say something interesting—dramatic—compelling—something significant.

Let's suppose you are doing a piece showing the new interest of business firms in emphasizing spiritual values. You find that several corporations have added chaplains to their staffs. Many boards of directors open their meetings with prayer. Small chapels are provided by several corporations.

Now you start to work on your title. You experiment with several. You put down: "Now It's Prayers by Executives." That's a little too flat, a little too obvious. You try other ideas. You type out one phrase which gives the reader a little mental jolt. And another which arouses his curiosity. After about twenty attempts, you come up with this one: "Businessmen On Their Knees."

Revise Your Punch

Good titles rarely come from sheer inspiration. Most of the

time you write an impressive one—an arresting one—after you write and rewrite, polish and revise. Your title should have an idea in it which makes people want to read the article.

Now let's look at some examples. But first, let's remember that it is our job to construct a title so that it will reach out from the page and arrest the attention of the reader. You must change the reader's indifference into interest. Note the following:

Weak: Comic Books and Crime
Better: Comic Books—Blueprints for Delinquency

Weak: Arsonists On the Increase
Better: Why Is a Firebug?

Weak: How Middletown Fights Rising Divorce Rates
Better: Ganging Up On Divorce

Weak: Now It's One Million New Homes a Year
Better: Going Up! One Million Homes a Year

Weak: Alarmists in the Business World
Better: The Paul Reveres of Business

Weak: How Your Health Depends on Food
Better: Your Body's Wizardry With Food

You see, the better title always carries a little extra punch—an extra quality which carries it an octave higher than a matter of fact statement.

"The best title," a veteran magazine writer once told me, "is so unique that it can be used only on one specific story."

Since titles cover such a wide variety of stories, it is difficult to classify them into exact types. So the categories which follow by no means exhaust the list. Rather, they are given to illustrate some of the principal kinds of titles used by newspaper and magazine writers today.

What Makes a Title Click?

Significance

Your reader wants more facts. He wants more than a situation. When he reads about guided missiles, for instance, he may ask a lot of questions like, "Have they been perfected? What are their uses? Do they help our standing in the global armament race? How rapidly are they being manufactured in communist nations?" For these reasons, the title which shows the meaning—the significance of a situation—may catch your reader's attention. Obviously, this type of title should be used only on a story which interprets the "why" of a situation.

High Taxes Cause Inflation
What the Mess in Moscow Means
How to Make Peace at the Pentagon
The U. S. Mail Goes Through
The Bloody Price of Coal
Eleven Coming Issues in American Politics
Guatemala: What the Reds Left Behind
Here Come the Commercial Jets!
Why There Can't Be Another War
The New Religion in Our Schools

Personality

What do you and your friends usually talk about? That's easy. Other people. Your reader is a gregarious creature and likes to be with others. But he also enjoys reading about persons—both notables and unknowns—who have done something, experienced something, or created something different. Crackpots and capitalists, musicians and movie stars, convicts and clergymen are catapulted into the headlines.

Dot Hall—Radio's Most Widely Known "Ham"
John Foster Dulles: A Very Complicated Man
Lawrence of Pittsburgh: Boss of the Mellon Patch
Alvarez: Everybody's Family Doctor
Sinclair Lewis at His Best
Mencken: Comedian Playing Hamlet

> Dr. Rosenbach: The Tycoon of Rare Rocks
> Gilbert Stuart: America's Portrait Master
> What Makes Lausche Run?
> The One and Only Benchley
> He Carried Hope in His Saddlebags!

Direct Quotation

Your reader likes to hear what others say, how they feel, how they react. So make use of quotations in titles and headlines. Not just any kind of quotations—not just talk. Rather, select picturesque statements which make a difference. Pick an unusual statement, place it between quotes, and readership will always zoom.

> "Do It Themselves? Impossible!"
> "I'm Bringing Up My Daughter to Live Alone"
> "And Proud of It!"
> "Frau McCloy Lights the Fires"
> "Why Didn't Somebody Tell Me?"
> "What We Don't Know Will Hurt Us"
> "The Americans Betrayed Us"
> "I Bought a Man for $50"
> "Pardon Me, I Like Money"
> "What's in a Name?"—Millions!

"How to"

"How to" are words which carry arresting power. You will find them particularly effective when you show the reader how he can improve himself or his situation. Keep yourself in the frame of mind of talking to one person at a time. Try to make your reader feel that you are appealing to his own needs and sense of values.

> How to Repair a Damaged Reputation
> Learn at the Grand Canyon
> Make Money With Your Hobby
> How to Make Your Own Breaks
> The Way to Sidestep An Argument

What Makes a Title Click?

Make Your Money Go Further This Year
Borrowing on Your Life Insurance
The Art of Packing a Suitcase
Where to Get the Facts Before You Invest
How to Talk to the Boss

Puns

Should you use a pun in your title? Before using one: (1) be sure it's good, and (2) be sure that the original one is familiar to your reader. Never strain too hard—because it shows.

A Wolf in Sheik's Clothing
Oh Say, Can You Ski?
The Neighs Have It
The Best Years of Your Wife

Direct Address

"Hey you!", direct or implied, usually stops the reader. Often you omit the word "you" in your headline or title, but it can seem to be there nevertheless. You can use this device as a warning. Or as a test. Most important of all, you can use it to call the reader's attention to some situation which he should know about.

Uncork Your Imagination!
Test Your Table Etiquette
Beware Bicarb!
Look Brother—Your House is on Fire
Watch Out for the Raw Silk Bonanza
Avoid a Mediocre Marriage
Live in the Country—and Live!
Don't Get Gypped on Auto Repairs
Beware of Dental Bootleggers
Now You Tell One!

"Believe-it-or-Not"

Robert L. Ripley's "Believe-it-or-Not" cartoons strike at the very heart of a universal interest—a curiosity about the unusual.

For one thing, there is surprise in the unusual. It arouses curiosity at once, simply because it is out of the ordinary. So if your facts show a departure from the ordinary, use the unusual slant to catch your reader's attention.

Nine Lives for Labor
Death on Parade
God Hates a Coward!
The Sub That Wouldn't Stay Down
He Talked 1600 Hours With the Russians
The Whole Town Goes to School
A Secretary With Eighty Bosses
The Toothpaste Tournament
The Man Who Reads Corpses
This Town Has Just Become a Father!
They Tattle—For Pay
The Lost Art of Doing Nothing
Love Is Not a Statistic
Queens Are His Business

Revelatory

It's human nature to react to anything which proclaims, "This is the inside story. These are the facts. Here is the lowdown." Sometimes you may wish to deflate an idea which most persons believe. On other occasions, you seek to expose something which should be brought into the bright light of publicity. One thing sure: this type of title gives your reader a mental tug.

Why Fad Diets Fail
Why You Can't Adopt a Baby
We Can't Cure a Cold
The Myth of the "Terrible Tonsils"
Why I Can't Write About America
Big-Dam Foolishness
The Great Moon Hoax
I'm Glad I Married Late
The Truth About Safety Belts

What Makes a Title Click?

> The Vicious Scandal of Funeral Fees
> Phony Correspondence Courses

Declarative Statement

Often a simple declarative statement—which shows some-thing—carries a stronger punch than something catchy. Not just any kind of declarative sentence is enough, however. It must say something. How can you do that? That's easy. Make your phrase so sharp that the reader will see it and say, "What's this? Sounds interesting. I'd better read it."

> Museums Don't Have to be Stuffy
> A Veteran Speaks Up to Congress
> What Baseball Owes to Babe Ruth
> The FTC Makes Business Police Itself
> The Secret of Japan's Super-Battleships
> The Best Defense of Freedom
> His Court Is a Classroom

Varied Quotation

Many of the greatest titles result when a familiar saying is given a new twist. Sometimes the change of only a word or two gives greatly increased effect—resulting in a title which is catchy and which lingers in the mind.

Psychologically, you quickly establish a common meeting ground with the reader with a clever adaptation. Like any good title, this type can be written only after experimenting, digging, and revising. They come the hard way. But the result is worth the labor.

> The Man Who Came to Dinner—and Stayed Five Years
> Lo, the Poor Octopus!
> They Whittle While They Work
> If at First You Don't Succeed—Change Hobbies
> Dead Men Tell Him Tales
> For Whom the Bell Clanks
> What To Do Until the Psychologist Comes

Rats Bite the Dust
East Meets West—at Chicago Airport
Little Dobe Homes in the West

Confessions

The next time you stop at your favorite newsstand, look at the many articles with a confession slant in their titles. Why so many titles of this type? Why so many confessional magazines? Just this: many readers get a vicarious thrill out of sharing the experiences of others. Mix an unusual experience with equal parts of first person, and you get a higher reader response.

Why I Remain a Negro
I Learn to Live Again
I Married a Stingy Husband
I Used to be a G-Man
I'm Married to a Working Mother
My Private War with Dr. Barnes
I Sent My Wife to Vassar
Everybody Laughs at Me

Freshness

Your title will carry more attention value if it's fresh. You can give it this quality by using an apt phrase, giving an old idea a new switch, or pepping up the words.

Harvard, Here I Come
No Stars Fell on Georgia
As A Man Thinketh: Psychomatic Medicine
One Foot Out of the Grave
Digging the New Jazz
The Raid on the Indian Reservations
There's No Substitute for Parents
4,000,000 Bankers Can't Be Wrong
Improve Your Sight Without Glasses
Houses Off the Assembly Line
The Light That Has Failed

Questions

Nothing will stop the reader like a personal question—a question which strikes at the heart of something important to him. At times, you ask a question which carries strong personal interest. Here's an example from *Your Life:* "Are You a Sociable Person?"

Then you have a situation in which you use a question which you hope will interest the reader. You pique his curiosity. Here's an example from *Newsweek:* "Can 14 Key States Win for Adlai?" Here are others:

Why Do Men Fight?
Have Fathers Neglected Their Jobs?
Is Big Business Too Big?
What Price Money?
Who Is Guilty of the Katyn Massacre?
How Long Will You Live?
What Makes Billy Run?
How Smart Is a Fish?
What Happens When We Pray?
What Has Billy Graham Got?
How Good Are Aptitude Tests?
Hate to Keep a Family Budget?
How Big is Your Vocabulary?

14 Ways to Test Your Title

As you see, you can't write a catchy title by following a formula. Titles get built one by one. Each has a uniqueness which you must find. We must keep reminding ourselves that the strongest title we can write—for any situation—is the one that catches the interest of the most readers. Test your titles one by one. Here are fourteen questions to ask in your testing:

1. Does my title fit the tone of the publication?
2. Will this title interest the specific reader I am aiming at?
3. Have I made promises or offered benefits to lure the reader?

4. Is my title believable?
5. Would the reader be pulled into the feature story after reading the title?
6. Is my title in harmony with the tone of the article?
7. Does the title ring little bells that say "Wake up!" in the mind of the reader?
8. Have I avoided a label title which might be used over other similar features?
9. Does the title carry the meaning it is meant to convey?
10. Have I used fresh words? Concrete words? Action verbs? Picture-making nouns?
11. Does the title answer a basic question in the reader's mind?
12. Have I compressed the factors of reader interest into a few key words or a phrase?
13. Would this title "jump out" at the reader when he is scanning the table of contents?
14. Does the title really click?

Get over on the reader's side of the fence before you start writing your title. Spend a lot of time learning what he wants, what he seeks, what interests him. Then woo him with words. And he'll read the title and the story—he'll respond because you have beamed your idea at him.

A Treasury of 2,000 Feature Ideas

A Treasury of 2,000 Feature Ideas

Accidents

Two-thirds of all falls (21,000 deaths annually from accidental falls) are in and about the home. What are some typical hazards—basement steps, for instance—which should be watched?

What have been some of the most peculiar highway accidents in your section within recent years? How could some of them have been avoided? Are they likely to occur again? Best source: highway patrolman who has been stationed in your county for several years.

Adults

Grownups are swarming back to school, particularly to night classes. Why? To keep up with new ideas and trends in their work? To learn a hobby or craft? To be with people? Or maybe because their education was interrupted?

Advertising

Should women pictured in magazine and newspaper ads always be hilariously happy? Isn't there such a thing as drudgery? Is each task a delightful event? Ask a number of women if they believe that the gals pictured in ads are real? Would an unhappy or impatient woman, shown occasionally, help the situation?

Some advertising slogans, although old, still sell—"The skin you love to touch," "Even your best friends won't tell you." What makes a good slogan? Who writes them? How are they used? Do people associate the slogan with the product?

Do pictures of pretty women tend to sell goods more to men than to women? One expert believes that each sex identifies itself with the person shown—the woman with the pretty woman, the man with the handsome man. Get the opinions of advertising experts who use several media: direct mail, newspapers, magazines, and outdoor advertising.

Advertising novelties are used by many groups and individuals. What are some of the older types which are still effective? What are some of the newer ones? What makes a good advertising novelty?

Boners occasionally creep into advertising. In St. Louis a laundry advertised that "We don't mangle by hand." Localize this by asking the classified ad manager of a newspaper to recall some of the boners which got into print—and the results!

Trace the origin of some of the better-known advertising slogans, both of products and services and also of stores. Are some of the slogans just as effective as they were when first used? What are some of the best-known slogans of local products and stores?

What have newspapers, radio stations, the Better Business Bureau, and other agencies in your community done to combat bait advertising? How do they wage a constant battle against false advertising of all types?

Modern advertising has been blessed and cursed. Some say it's responsible for our high standard of living. Others say it breeds discontent, presents false claims, and is sometimes unethical and unsavory. What do your neighbors think of advertising? What do *advertisers* think of advertising?

Do Americans take advantage of the products and services offered to them from radio stations in Mexico? Powerful stations with transmitters just south of the Rio Grande blanket the United States with sales pitches for scriptures, song books, cure-alls, and astrological techniques that foretell the future. How successful are these stations with advertising that in many cases would not be allowed in this country?

Who writes radio commercials and newspaper ads? How do writers get "sell" into their copy? Is a different technique used with a different product? What's the difference between writing a radio spot and writing newspaper copy? Writers at your hometown radio station and newspaper office will be glad to tell you their story.

In a recent direct mail campaign, 180 per cent more people answered those advertisements printed on pink paper and 12 per cent more people answered when a postal card was enclosed with the ad! Effective direct mail advertising has become a science. What other devices for getting response have been tested and tried in direct mail advertising? Talk to a successful direct mail ad man.

Agriculture

Tie-in date: The United States Department of Agriculture was created February 11, 1889. Do a summary story, for publication on this day, showing how the services of the department reach into your county.

Experts predict that the world's population is increasing faster than the food supply. What is happening in your county or state? Is net farm income up or down? Are farmers moving to cities? Any new crops being grown?

News items concerning crops and livestock in your area are probably compiled by an agricultural statistician of the U.S. Department of Agriculture. Interview him and see how he compiles figures, who sends them to him, and to whom he sends facts and figures on agricultural conditions.

Air Conditioning

Nowadays, homes, offices, even cars are air conditioned. Air conditioning salesmen say their product increases the work efficiency of employees. Ask the office manager of an air conditioned plant how it's helped in work output. Has the air conditioning paid for itself in added office or plant efficiency?

Alimony

"Alimony is her idea of a guaranteed annual wage," quipped a cartoon character. Upon what basis is alimony decided? And how long must payments be made? What is the largest sum ever required of a former husband in your community?

Ambitions

How many men and women are now doing what they wanted to do when they were in high school? In Hartford, Connecticut, seventeen years after David Cohn's high school class book reported he "aspires to be a mayor," he was appointed acting mayor. How many high school ambitions are realized?

Ambulances

Can anyone drive an ambulance in your city? Or do drivers have to take physical examinations? Pass a course in first aid? Pass a strict drivers test? Are all drivers licensed by the city? What is average age?

American Legion

The American Legion was incorporated by an act of Congress on September 16, 1919. Get a history of the local post. Named in whose honor? What are some of the principal projects through the years? Any charter members still active?

Amusement Parks

The cop at your local amusement park has a story to tell. Why does he think most people come to the park? Does the park try to interest people of all ages? How does he handle "trouble-makers"? Show his duties and responsibilities.

Anesthetics

Dr. Crawford W. Long went down in medical history because he was the first physician to give ether as an anesthetic. What developments have been made since? What are the advantages and disadvantages of ether compared to other anesthetics? Does the amount of ether required by individuals vary? Does more have to be added from time to time during an operation? Describe some of the newer anesthetics.

A medical expert decries the indiscriminate use of the drug sodium pentothal. Do certain anesthetics enjoy a popularity and then get replaced by others? What are some of the factors considered by a surgeon and his anesthetist before an operation?

Animals

Trappers in the far north say that a fox can detect a scent five miles away. What domestic animals have the best developed sense of smell? Does a wild animal have a better one than a domestic animal? Zoo keepers and veterinarians should have the answers.

When a camel takes a drink, it's just satisfying a thirst and not storing up water for a dry day, it is revealed by Duke University scientists. And they say that the camel's hump is not a water storage tank. Check these statements with the director of the zoo.

J. Y. Henderson, in his book *Circus Doctor*, tells of his experiences in taking care of seven hundred animals of the Ringling Brothers and Barnum and Bailey Circus. Interview the veterinarian who is employed full or part time by your city zoo. What animal is hardest to work on? What ailments are common to certain animals? Under what conditions is an anesthetic necessary?

We used to call it the "dog pound"—but in a large city it is now the "animal shelter." And the old dogcatcher is no longer a bogeyman; he is a poundkeeper. Why the change in names? Are many people cruel to animals thoughtlessly or ignorantly? What are some of the plights into which animals get?

Animal stories always pull. Try this angle: List how many different kinds of animals (and other pets) can be purchased in your city. Show how pet dealers handle some rare requests.

Does your community have a monument erected in honor of an animal? If so, who was the animal accorded this honor? What group sponsored the monument and dedication?

Have you done a feature on blessed events at the local zoo? What animals are the most prolific? What baby animals are the most valuable? What special care must be given to certain young animals?

Most dog owners are content with teaching Rover to sit up, fetch, and roll over. But other dogs, or their owners, are more talented. Interview dog lovers to find out how tricks are taught. How many tricks can an intelligent dog learn? Who works harder in learning a new trick: dog or master?

75

Arbor Day

Does your state observe Arbor Day? The first formal observance of Arbor Day as a time for planting trees was on April 10, 1872, in Nebraska. Some schools observe the day with special programs. If your state observes the day, who sponsors the program? What are the objectives of the annual observance? What group or groups participate?

Architecture

Windows in modern churches often have interesting stories behind them. One church, for instance, has a collection of stained glass windows typifying birth, education, agriculture, home, transportation, law, labor, and business. Check the newer churches of your city for interesting windows.

How many different doorways can be seen in your community? What are some of the unusual ones in public buildings, churches, stores, or homes? Is there a special story behind the construction of any of them? What types of architecture are shown?

Armed Forces

A New Jersey man named Goldbrick asked court permission to change his name before he entered the army because he said his name would prove "most embarrassing." What are some of the reasons why persons want their names changed? Are they usually young persons? Are such requests usually granted?

Practically every unit of the armed forces, whether stationed in the United States or abroad, does something special for children at Christmas. Abroad, it is sometimes known as "Operation Cheer." Combine the Christmas activities of the units in your region for a roundup story.

From time to time the USO urges that everyone take part in its USO Mail Call. Here's the basic idea: write regularly to the young people in service. To what extent has the public co-operated? Do many persons feel that correspondence isn't too important when there are no hostilities? Check with your postmaster or USO officials.

A group headed by James Doolittle was set up after the war to make a study of "democratic" processes in the service. They accomplished much as they tried to lessen the gap between officer and enlisted man. What do soldiers themselves think of such efforts? Does it work? Can it work. The contrast of views among officers and men—career personnel and those who plan to serve only one hitch—will make interesting reading.

Armistice

Who are some of the bygone heroes of your state or county? What are some of the medals which have been awarded to them? Interview a hero of yesterday and ask his opinions concerning U.S. defense policies.

Armories

Take a swing around your armory and you'll probably get a good story. What is some of the newest equipment? How is it used in training National Guard members and others? Describe other facilities of the armory and how they are used.

Art

A common expression in an art gallery is: "I don't know much about art, but I know what I like!" What makes an enduring work of art? Is art more appreciated by the average person now than fifty years ago? Have national periodicals increased appreciation of art? The art teacher or art director can give you some facts that will make an interesting feature.

Art belongs in the kitchen as well as the living room, says Lester Laba, Missouri-born columnist and fashion show producer who staged an exhibit of "Paintings for Gourmets." His collection ranges from baseball-size peas to a six-foot single carrot. What are local housewives doing to brighten up their kitchen? What kind of art do they prefer?

Why do some people paint or draw mustaches on posters and printed sheets? Are they amateur artists? Or is it just something they cannot resist? Source for comments: a psychologist.

Do a feature story on the most outstanding art gallery in your state or region. How was it started? What are some of the most valued paintings? Are works of local or state artists featured in the gallery? To what extent is the place visited by student groups? Tourists?

Locate a well-known bird painter. And then find out how he familiarized himself with bird life. Does he visit wildlife refuges? What are the markets for his output? What does he consider the most interesting birds? Did he sketch birds as a kid in school?

Practically all great artists have been men. Why? This fact does not keep hundreds of women from studying art. Does a man possess some unique trait or ability? Seek the views of an experienced teacher of art.

Modern art gets more than its share of lumps from the average American, who admits, "I don't know much about art, but I know what I like and I don't like that!" How do art teachers explain modern art? Or do they say it can be explained? Does public feeling for or against an art form affect the development of that form?

Do you have a local artist who specializes in religious paintings or art? How does he get ideas? Where are some of his paintings found— churches, homes, art galleries? When did he first become interested?

Some seamstresses make pictures with needle and thread. Indians make pictures with sand. Children nowadays use finger paints. What other methods do artists use to picture life? Has there been a change in paints used by modern painters?

Astronomy

Space travel books, movies, and TV shows have increased interest in astronomy. Scores of American families are scanning the heavens through inexpensive telescopes and discovering an exciting hobby. How many persons build their own telescopes? What is the cost of a small telescope? How far can you see with an inexpensive telescope?

Atomic Power

Nuclear power will supplant conventional sources of energy, scientists predict. How soon and to what extent will this new form of energy activate the generators essential to meet the growing need for power? Will atomic power take over the whole load? High officials of an electric power company should be able to give you some provocative comments.

Auctioneers

How did the auctioneer's chant get that way? Does he really say anything? What devices does he use to start the bidding? Why are so many farm auctioneers called "Colonel"? Where did he learn the chant?

Authors

Former President Harry Truman spent more than five hours autographing copies of his book, *Year of Decisions*. Attend the next autographing party in your city. Do most readers want special autographs? How much does the appearance of the author boost sales? What are some of the usual autographs used by authors?

It's been said that many an author would like to have his book banned in Boston, feeling that that would assure success elsewhere. How true is that statement? Are there books that have been frowned on in one part of the country so much that other readers have read the book just to see what caused the frown? Are there review boards for books or movies in your state?

Autographs

When Davy Crockett's popularity was at its height with the small fry, an Illinois automobile agency offered free "autographed" pictures of Davy to children. Other autographs are more authentic, and there's a good feature in how they are bought, sold, and traded. What makes an autograph valuable? How valuable are some collections? Is there one autograph in the world today that is considered more valuable than any other? How do dealers in autographs work?

Are local kids autograph hunters? If so, who has the most impressive list? What heroes and heroines are most sought after? Does some oldster have a collection of famous autographs of yesterday?

Automation

Will automation remove workers from their jobs? Will the increase of automatic devices in business and industry result in overwhelming problems of readjustment? Or will increased production absorb many of the workers? Get views on both sides.

Automobiles

Chances are that someone in your community collects license plates. How have they changed in size and color? Are today's prices higher than those paid by car owners many years ago? What were the makes of some of the early cars on which the tags were used?

Seen on the back of a 1940 model auto in Memphis: "Out of Date—but Out of Debt." Jot down some of the signs on the cars of your community and someday you'll have enough for a feature. How many of the signs have a religious theme? Do some promote civic events?

With new cars coming out in all colors of the rainbow, why don't you find out what are the most popular? With men? With women? How many prefer black? Paint manufacturers issue color identification charts to all paint and body men. Ask these workers how to keep the paint on a car looking new. What causes paint to fade—dew, heat, moisture?

About 12 per cent of the car-owning families in the United States today own more than one automobile. How many own a second car as a necessity? How many families own an extra car just for teenagers or older kids? Does the movement of people toward the suburbs mean that more families will need additional cars?

Attendants at the city's largest parking lot or auto hotel can give you enough comments for a story. Peculiarities of motorists; dealing with feminine drivers; keeping records of the cars; busiest days; most interesting travelers.

Try this approach on your next safety feature: Ask the veteran safety officer on your police force what he considers the main causes of accidents. Is the driver who has never had an accident, for instance, likely to believe he won't have one and thus become careless?

Almost 2 per cent of the passenger automobiles in the United States have been driven nineteen years or more. What do safety experts think about people driving old cars? Do they believe that a car may be unsafe after it has been driven so many miles even though it has been checked by a mechanic regularly?

In 1915 buyers had their choice of 116 established makes of cars, from the brass-nosed Model T at $490 to the Cadillac limousine at $3450, with a new V-8 engine and a three-year-old innovation called a self-starter. How many major models of cars are being sold today? What were the names of some of the cars now forgotten? Do automobile dealers believe that it is better to have fewer and better-known cars on the market?

Highway troopers in Oklahoma were wondering why their high-speed cars couldn't catch some bootleggers when they got in a race. Then they found out: bootleggers had purchased the old highway patrol cars. What happens to the high-speed police cars when they are traded in or sold in your community? Are there always customers waiting to buy a police car?

Car manufacturers now give purchasers a choice of literally dozens of colors and color combinations. Ask car dealers what percentage of cars now sold are more than one color. Which colors are most popular with men? With women? Does the age of the car buyer have anything to do with the color he is likely to choose?

Cars and trucks scrapped today average 14.2 years, according to figures released by the Automobile Manufacturers Association. How does this figure compare with your salvage and junk yards? Can salvage dealers tell if owners are driving cars longer today?

A safety expert urges that each prospective buyer of a used car pay a mechanic to give it a thorough check. What do mechanics think of this suggestion? Used car dealers? Find out from mechanics some of the ways of checking a used car.

What should you look for in buying a used car? To get the answers, talk to several dealers. Should you ever buy a car that's been in a wreck? What repairs are necessary to get it in good running condition? How does the motor sound? How can you tell if the previous owner has taken good care of it?

Aviation

Fliers have a lingo of their own. Interview a veteran and find out some phrases which have been used for a long time. Has the coming of jets added new words to the profession? What is the origin of some of the phrases?

Some airplanes use more than six hundred gallons of fuel every hour. That means refueling in mid-air is necessary many times. How is it done? Is the operation as delicate as it seems? How many gallons of fuel can the big tanker planes carry? Which plane controls the flow of the fuel? What's the rate of flow? Ask aviation men if mid-air re-fueling is ever necessary in smaller aircraft.

Helicopters are being used more and more in a variety of ways. And bigger ones are being made. Does your city have a "heliport"? Are helicopters used by any business man in your community?

The increase expected in private flying after World War II didn't materialize. Ask your airport manager and local flying enthusiasts their opinions on this apparent lack of interest. Is it the expense? Mis-information about the safety of flying?

You hear people talk today about planes flying by instruments. What does it mean? In the old days the pilot had to see ahead to be sure that he didn't hit any obstructions. Talk to the tower observer at your airport and find out exactly how instruments are used. Does the tower operator guide the pilot by radioing to him messages about the cloud ceiling?

Charles A. Lindbergh, the first man to make a solo flight across the Atlantic, was born February 4, 1902. You may use this date as a tie-in with the history of your local airport, its management, its progress, and its services.

Orville and Wilbur Wright made the first successful flight of a man-carrying powered airplane at Kitty Hawk, North Carolina on December 17, 1903. Use this date as a tie-in on your local airport—its history, its growth, its personnel, and its plans for the future.

Do a feature story on the manager of your local airport. At what age did he become interested in aviation? Has he had experience in private and commercial flying? Did he serve in the Air Force? What does he think about the future of air travel?

Do you have a Whirly Girl in your city? If so, she is a member of one of the world's most exclusive women's clubs—she is a helicopter pilot. If you find one, ask her when she learned to fly, what course she took to get the special license, and how she thinks helicopters will be used in the future.

Farmers and ranchers in the United States now operate more than ten thousand planes, about half of which are equipped to do dusting and spraying. What are the advantages of a plane in doing these types of work? Are farmers and ranchers finding new uses for planes?

Babies

Great strides have been made in childbirth safety. Interview an obstetrician and find out about some of the new developments. What were some of the dangers facing mothers of yesterday which have been eliminated or reduced? How is your local hospital equipped to handle special problems which may occur at delivery?

Why are babies born prematurely? Are they more susceptible to such things as cerebral palsy, mental retardation, physical malformations? Why do so many of them die in infancy? Ask several obstetricians about the facts of premature births.

Is it healthy for young children to cry? "They're usually unhealthy if they don't," declares Dr. Katherine Bain of the United States children's bureau. Why do children cry? Do they cry for something they need? Is it important to find out why they cry? Pediatricians can give you comments enough for a feature story.

A baby photographer needs a whole repertoire of games, stunts, noises, and toys to get good pictures, Josef Schneider, specialist in child photography, says. How much patience is required? What are some ways of getting a child to laugh or smile? What type of child is the most difficult to handle? Do parents usually have a certain pose in mind when they bring the child to be photographed?

Babies begin to talk almost at birth, Donna Guyer says in *Bookhouse for Children*. Even at four weeks they actually start "speaking" with gurgling and babbling sounds. These sounds are attempts at communication, and are language to parents and child experts. At eighteen months, children speak at least ten words. Girls learn a bit earlier than boys. These facts should give you a big start on an interesting story.

How do couples in your community find babies to adopt? To what agencies or homes can couples go when they are seeking to adopt babies? What makes up a preliminary examination of home life and relationships before a baby can be adopted?

The stork arrives in odd places at odd times. Do a feature showing how births have occurred in uncustomary places—stores, taxis, or other places. Good sources: ambulance drivers and doctors.

Bachelors

The bachelor clan, as every woman knows, is a group apart. It is also a sizable segment of our population. What makes a man a bachelor? Is it chance or deliberate intent? Are some afraid of the risks of married life? Select some outstanding bachelors and get the answers to these questions.

Balloon Ascension

Sometime before January 9, which is the anniversary of the ascension of the first balloon in the United States, do a local story showing if balloon ascensions pulled crowds at your county fair years ago.

Bands

Your region probably has at least one band—perhaps a school or fraternal group—which is much in demand for parades. If so, why is it so popular? Marching formations? Colorful uniforms? Attractive majorettes?

Banking

Uncle Sam says the life of the average dollar bill is nine months. But some of them are ripped and torn much sooner. What does your bank teller do with mutilated money. How much of it is collected in an average month? How is the new currency shipped in? Is it true that new bills are likely to stick together?

Some people have trouble making correct change for a dollar bill, but bank tellers handle thousands of dollars each day and then balance to the penny each afternoon at closing time. How long does it take for a new teller to learn to handle money quickly as well as accurately? If he's a dollar short at the end of the day, how is it found? If it's not found, who makes it up? If he is a dollar long, where does the "extra" dollar go?

Every time you cash a check today, the bank that does the cashing gets involved in about twenty-eight different operations. Do a story showing what happens when a check is cashed.

Bank officials are using many methods and gimmicks to teach thrift to kids. Your largest bank is probably using an amazing number of approaches in getting the small fry to save. At what age should a child start a savings account? To what extent must parents co-operate in teaching thrift to youngsters? What are some of the unusual ways in which school boys and girls earn money for their savings accounts?

Many persons keep their valuables in safety deposit boxes in banks. Do they ever ask to store anything unusual in the boxes? Does anyone ever move to another city and forget about the contents of his box? What do most people keep in the boxes?

How does a banker judge the trustworthiness of a man or woman applying for a loan? What basis other than the applicant's previous credit rating is used to justify the loan? Are persons in certain occupations or professions particularly good risks? What percentage of small loans have to be written off? Talk to your banker.

Large banks now assign certain officials to make customer contacts. They circulate among firms and individuals and ask questions like, "How can we help you more? Are you satisfied with our services? What are we doing that you dislike?" Interview one or more persons doing this work and show how they use their findings in improving bank services.

Approximately 10 per cent of bank officers are women. What is the percentage in the banks in your city? Has the number increased within the past ten years? What are the backgrounds of the women officers. How did they become interested in banking and finance?

You've heard of the wag whose wife wanted him to give her a joint bank account, and he did. "It had just two names on it," he said, "her married name and her maiden name." How many husbands and wives have joint bank accounts? Is the number increasing? What are the advantages of such an arrangement?

A Texas bank cashier is known for his ability to add a long list of figures on a deposit slip quickly without the aid of an adding machine. Does one of your banks have a wizard at adding figures? How did he or she develop this talent?

What happens to worn out currency? Is a local bank allowed to destroy it? Do banks take bills mended with Scotch tape, for instance, and keep them out of circulation? Will a bank accept a bill which is partly torn away?

Barber Shops

Yesterday's barber shop usually made the *Police Gazette* available to its customers. What types of magazines are popular in barber shops today? Do they have women's magazines for women customers? Comics for the kids?

Idea for humorous feature: Should bald-headed men pay full price for haircuts? Is this an old gag heard by barbers? Are bald-headed men razzed about the lack of hair on their domes?

Does your city have a school for barbers? What is the normal enrollment? How many women barbers finish the course? On whom do the students practice? What are some of the subjects stressed? Is there a shortage of barbers?

Glamorous haircuts for men have been urged by the Associated Master Barbers and Beauticians of America. Do many men want fancy haircuts? Are most satisfied with ordinary styles? Are men particular about a certain type of haircut? Your barber will have the answers.

Baseball

World Series pools flourish every year when the two leading baseball teams clash. How large are some of the pools? Are they illegal? Explain some of the ways in which pools are divided.

Baton Twirlers

How do baton twirlers learn to "strut their stuff"? Short courses are sponsored at some colleges and universities. How much practice is required to do a wrist-twirl, figure-eight, two-hand twirl, pass-around-back, and other movements? What special abilities help in baton twirling? Handy source of information: band director.

Bazaars

One of our major American fall institutions is the church or club bazaar. How do you plan a bazaar? What should be the price range of most articles? What are some of the best sellers? What about location of booths? Sizes? Publicity? Get the comments of several women known for their success in directing bazaars.

Beliefs

How do beliefs influence a person's behavior? William James, the great psychologist, said, "Believe life is worthwhile, and your belief will help create the fact." What beliefs should be instilled into children? Seek the opinions of ministers, teachers, and other youth leaders.

Beverages

Soft drink sales in the United States in a recent year were enough for every man, woman, and child in the country to have 180 bottles! Who drinks most of them: children or adults? How seasonal is the soft drink business? Which flavors sell best? How hard is it to introduce a new flavor? Your local bottler can give you the answers.

Bibles

Thirty-five million Americans read the Bible once a week; twelve million every day, reports a survey in *Catholic Digest*. Is there an increase in Bible reading in your community? Have Bible sales jumped? Check with ministers and book dealers.

The oldest known New Testament in the language spoken by Christ and his disciples is in the Library of Congress, Washington, D. C. Known as the Yonan Codex, it is more than sixteen hundred years old. You probably won't find so rare a book locally, but you probably can locate some person who has a collection of old Bibles.

Bicycles

Does your community have one or more distance bicycle riders?

Men and women? How often do they ride? Who holds the record for distance? Who is the oldest? Youngest?

Birds

Uncle Sam finally succeeded in bird-proofing the United States treasury department. The cost: about $60,000. How was it done? Mainly by stringing charged electric wires. Have your city or county officials had a problem in ridding buildings of birds? Have they succeeded? What methods have they tried?

Every now and then someone watching birds in the sky may ask, "What is the fastest bird?" Ask a local ornithologist. What are birds' methods in flight? What birds fly the highest? The farthest?

There are now an estimated two million "free lunch counters" or feeding stations for birds across the country. How many are located in your community? What types of food are best for birds? Should food be made available all year? What kinds of food should not be given?

All jokes and cartoons to the contrary, birdwatchers are quite normal people. They study the habits of birds, learn their distinctive markings, and also make accurate counts of the various species of birds. Does your city have an Audubon Society? If so, describe its activities. What different professions are represented in its membership? What rare birds have been seen in your region?

The National Audubon Society, 1130 Fifth Avenue, New York City, sponsors bird count week during December each year. Check with local officers of Audubon Society to see if they will take part in observance.

If there's a branch of the National Association of Audubon Societies active in your community, use the anniversary of the birth of John James Audubon—April 26, 1785—as a date on which to release a story. Show the activities of your local bird group—its officers, history, and aims.

Several species of birds can be taught to talk. Parrots were the chief talking birds of some years ago. Parakeets nowadays do lots of the talking in the American home. How many words can a bird be taught? Got any in your own town with extensive vocabularies?

An expert declares that an ostrich cannot fly, but its twelve-foot stride carries it along at forty miles an hour. What else is unique about this bird? What is its life span? What food does it like? If there's an ostrich in your zoo, do a story on it.

Blacksmiths

Has the village smithy been driven out of business by the garages? Chances are that you will find a blacksmith. Find out how many still need his services, the kinds of jobs people ask him to do, and his views of modern machinery and equipment.

Blind

Find out about the careers followed by the blind persons of your community. If possible, tie it in with an anniversary angle: Louise Braille was born January 4.

Many Lions clubs sponsor eight conservation projects and activities. Check with officers of your local club.

Helen Keller's birthday is June 27. Use this date as a peg on which to write a story showing the objectives and projects of the blind in your community or state. Be sure and list the many groups, like Lions International, which emphasize activities for the blind.

Blotters

Have you seen "The World's Handiest Blotter"? It has a fisherman's measure "so you can exaggerate without really lying." Designed by Irvin Levy, it also has a handy compass (point arrow towards North and you'll know which way is East, West, and South) and other clever illustrations. How many of your local business firms use gadgets and gimmicks in their advertising? What have been the most effective? Do merchants feel that the devices boost sales?

Bonuses

Many firms offer bonuses to employees who offer suggestions that are helpful to the company. How many companies in your town have such a plan? Has it paid off for the firm? How do they reward or recognize the individual who submits the suggestion? What percentage of the suggestions offered are accepted?

Books

John Steinbeck once took aim at the constitutional deficiencies of literary critics from an author's viewpoint. What are the functions of a reviewer? To assess the value of a book? To judge the effectiveness with which the story has been presented? Contact a book critic and get his viewpoint.

Encyclopedias are kept up-to-date with new printings and annual supplements. But who compiles them originally? How long does it take to gather and edit material for a twenty-volume encyclopedia? Are there other problems publishers of encyclopedias have that other publishers do not have?

Complete Bibles are published in some 200 languages, New Testaments in 257 others, and parts of the Scriptures in another 605. It's the best seller of all time. How many publishing firms print Bibles? How many are printed and sold each year in the United States? Are sales seasonal? Has the publication of the Revised Standard Version of the Bible affected sales of the King James version?

Are war books obsolete? Ask librarians how readers' tastes change in wartime and peace. Do readers want books dealing with non-war subjects in wartime?

Here's a startling statement: in this country more money is spent on comic books than on textbooks for all elementary and secondary schools! Comic books sell at the rate of a billion per year—at a cost of $100,000,000. How many persons find work in this tremendous output? How many different titles are there? What is the most popular with small fry? Does popularity come and go? How are comic books used to teach? (Many big corporations and associations put their message across with comic books.)

Are the offerings of book clubs as popular as they were a few years ago? Would many readers prefer to choose their own books from a local bookseller? Has the sale of paperbound books reduced the membership of book clubs? Seek the comments of librarians, book dealers, and persons who have held memberships in book clubs.

Amazingly few people read books. Columbia University staff members found that only 52 per cent of adults ever open one after they leave school. What's happening in your community? Who are the most avid readers, as revealed in library figures? Does your librarian believe that TV has affected the reading of books? If so, in what way?

Too many school books, particularly those on science in the fourth, fifth, and sixth grades, are too hard for children, three educators discovered. What do teachers in these grades think about this criticism? Are the science books any harder than those in other subjects?

Some people use very peculiar bookmarkers, it is revealed by a librarian in Pennsylvania. Among items in returned books are: a one-hundred-year-old marriage license, a social security card, an unopened letter, and snapshots. Ask your city librarian what comes back in the books.

Who reads the technical books in your city library? Are they growing in popularity? What percentage of the total volumes are devoted to technical subjects? Are many of the newer volumes being written in a popular style? Talk to the librarian.

Cheap paperback reprints and originals have been published in the United States for more than a century without becoming a stable factor in the book business. But today the paperbacks are becoming respectable. And many of them are serious books. What paperbacks are in demand? Are many of the old classics being read again? Talk to your bookseller.

Does your county or state library use bookmobiles? If so, find one which covers a rather large area and find out how many communities it serves? How often does it make the rounds? What is the total circulation for a year?

Bosses

An official of a big corporation told a national Junior Chamber of

Commerce convention that the old hell-fire-and-brimstone boss is gone, or on the way out. He said the new boss is one who can persuade men under him to do what is needed. What do men in local businesses think about such a statement? Have their policies changed in the past ten or twenty years? If there has been a change, what are the results?

Boy Scouts

Boy Scouts are an international group with members in more than fifty nations. How does Scouting promote world understanding and unity of purpose? Have any Scouts or adult leaders from your community ever attended an international meeting?

Scouting knows no barriers of race or creed. Furthermore, Scouting stresses the twelfth point of the Scout law: "A Scout is reverent. He is reverent toward God. He is faithful in his religious duties and respects the convictions of others in matters of custom and religion." There are distinctive awards for Scouts of Protestant, Catholic, Jewish, and Mormon faiths. More than half of the Scouting units are sponsored by churches or synagogues. What are your local Scouts doing in their religious award activities?

More than 190,000 American women have a vital part in Scouting. They are den mothers who help boys in the eight-to-ten age group —the Cub Scouts. What are their duties? How do they go into Scout work?

About 44 per cent of America's Scouts live in rural communities. How does this program help boys in rural communities? What special skills and crafts can they learn in Scouting? How many rural boys work for the special merit badges (twenty-seven of the one hundred merit badges deal with farm interests).

Boy Scout programs depend to a great degree on the devoted efforts of adult volunteer leaders. What are the many assignments for adult leaders? How are the talents and interests of men used? What are some of the reasons for so many men volunteering to serve? Who is the oldest adult leader in your community?

Boy Scouts help in many community enterprises. The "Get Out the Vote" campaign is an outstanding example. What have been some of the unique contributions which Scouts have made to your community? Is there any activity which they perform for the community year after year?

Scouting is for all boys who want it—including the physically handicapped. Many of them have fulfilled requirements for various ranks. Look around and see if Scouting has brought satisfaction to any crippled, deaf, or blind boys in your community.

Boy Scouts can explore any of the hundred activities covered by the merit badge program and thus "sample" a wide range of activities before making a choice of life work. How many adults feel that their careers were influenced by their merit badge work in Scouting?

The anniversary of the chartering of the Boy Scouts of America, February 8, 1910, makes a timely peg for a feature. Do a round-up story showing the history of scouting in your region—milestones, adult leaders, and growth.

Brains
Brisk exercise of the brain is one of the best methods of staying young, Dr. Wilma Donahue, University of Michigan psychologist, states. "Without using it constantly," she said "brain cells atrophy just as muscle cells when there is lack of exercise." Interview three or four oldsters who are alert, healthy, and happy, and see if they agree.

Brands
What happened to Chalmers cars, Force cereal, Sweet Caporals cigarettes, and Wilbur's Chocolate Buds? Years ago they were well-known, but their producers quit advertising. Why must every seller keep advertising? Why are the biggest concerns the most consistent advertisers in all media? Get your comments from a top-flight executive in an advertising agency.

Bridge
Who is the champion bridge player in your community? When did he or she become interested? Other angles: memories of exciting moments in tournaments, suggestions to amateurs, and the value of the game.

Budgets

If the Gallup poll has things figured out right, you will find that out of ten families, six of them do not keep a household budget, three of them do, and one tries but can't quite make it. Why doesn't the average family follow a budget? Does a budget promote thrift and economy? Does it check wasteful spending? Does a budget mean less worry? Talk to a number of folks, and their answers should add up to a good story.

Buildings

The Jaycees in a Virginia town bought the old jail and converted it into a clubhouse. In Oklahoma City a former drive-in was converted into a church. Does your community have a building whose use today is altogether different from the purpose for which it was erected?

Does your community have a clock tower which is visible at night? How old is it? How far can it be seen on a clear night? Does the clock strike during the night? Has the clock ever needed repairs? Can the mechanism be repaired by local jewelers, or is it necessary to obtain the services of out-of-town experts?

Do highschool kids in your community paint signs or class numerals on watertowers, railroad bridges, and other property? If so, try to find the oldest sign, get the views of the high school principal or superintendent, and ask some of the kids—if you can find the right ones.

Building Codes

Few persons understand building codes. So why not show what they mean, why they are necessary, and how they are subject to change. Who enforces them? How can citizens co-operate in making them effective?

Burglars

Do burglars still use ladders as they are pictured doing in some cartoons? How do modern burglars gain entrance to homes? What can a homeowner do to protect his home against them? Talk to police about unique methods used by burglars to break in.

Burglar Alarms

More and more homes are installing burglar alarms. Does a wave of burglaries usually result in the installation of more alarms? Are they installed after certain homes have been burglarized? Do some of the people who have alarms also keep dogs for protection?

Business

Many workers pride themselves on faithful service. Lots of them work for years without ever missing a day's work. Encourage good work habits by interviewing several local folks with absent-free records. Which plays a greater part in being able to stay on the job, luck or persistence? How important is good health?

Business sponsors of motion pictures and slide films now spend more than fifty million dollars a year among the largest producers. How are the large organizations using film—sales, public relations, institutional efforts? What makes a successful film? What is the cost of a typical business movie?

Callers can get the correct time in most cities by simply dialing a certain number. How does the system work? How many calls for this type of information are received in an average day? What's the most number of calls received in a single day? What does it cost a business to "sponsor" this type of telephone service? What are peak load times during the day?

Ever consider how much paper work is involved in the average business or industry? Invoices in triplicate, interdepartmental memos, route slips, correspondence, and all the rest of it. Chances are even the manager of the plant near you doesn't know how much paper it takes to run his business. Make a survey for him. Use the facts for a feature. How much paper is bought in a month or a year? Is most of it eventually thrown away, or is it filed and used? Or filed and forgotten?

Living and working conditions for plant employees have improved tremendously in the past fifty years. Ask a long-time worker what changes he's most grateful for. Compare today's hours, wages, buying power, vacations, sick leave, bonuses, and stock plans with those of two generations ago. Is the additional leisure time most of us have being put to good use?

Piano tuners are hard to find in many communities. Is piano tuning becoming a lost art? Are there fewer pianos being played in American homes? Where does a piano tuner learn his trade? Is it harder to tune an inexpensive piano than an expensive one?

American homes have more windows and bigger windows now than ever before. Yet with all this additional light indoors, electricity used for residential lighting is expected to hit a record seventy billion kilowatt-hours by 1963. How is additional home lighting being used? How are America's light and power companies going to meet increased demands? How much extra power is needed for the dozens of electrical appliances now being used in most homes?

The number of salesmen in this country has increased only 18 per cent since 1942, while the volume of goods sold has increased 80 per cent. Members of Sales Executive clubs and others are trying to interest more young people in salesmanship as a career. How are they doing this? What are the qualities of a good salesman? What are the advantages and disadvantages of making salesmanship a life career?

An enterprising restaurant proprietor in Omaha hung out a sign: "Come In and Eat Before We Both Starve." Watch for amusing signs when you visit business houses of your community, and also when you are on trips, and the result will be an interesting feature.

Some businessmen have charged that colleges and universities teach too much theory and not enough down-to-earth practical techniques. They say students should be taught the sometimes unpleasant facts of business life. Do businessmen of your acquaintance agree? How practical should teaching be? Should a student be taught that in some jobs he may have, the boss will always be right, or should he learn about unpleasant employers when he gets out on the job?

A worker in an army ordnance plant in South Dakota won $135 for her efficiency suggestion: that the army abolish her job. There must be employee suggestion techniques with happier endings. How widespread is the practice of using suggestions of employees? How are workers paid for their suggestions?

There's no guesswork in industry today. One railroad figures engine whistle toots cost about two-thirds of a cent each in fuel. It costs more than $15,000 a year to whistle on the run from Dallas to Houston alone. How minutely are costs figured in other businesses or industries? What does it cost in man-hours to figure costs? Does such research really help?

Little matches are big business. "Gopher" matches are given away by an estimated 257,000 companies, at the rate of 250,000,000,000 a year! So many of them are given away for promotional purposes that the average American spends only thirty-one cents a year for matches. Is a special kind of wood needed in a match? A special kind of paper in "gophers"? How are they made? How many different kinds of matches are there?

More Americans are buying now and paying later. Consumer credit runs to about thirty billion dollars. Is this credit getting out of hand? Should the trend be watched with any alarm? Get the opinions of credit managers, bankers, and others.

Yesterday's stores kept most of the merchandise hidden in drawers, cabinets, and boxes—far out of reach of customers. Today's displays are accessible for all. What are some of the effective ways of attracting attention? Are certain locations in a store better than others? What part does correct lighting play in increased sales?

Some folks say young job applicants nowadays are too concerned with vacations, days off, sick leave, retirement, bonuses, pension plans, and other "non-work" phases of a job. Interview a job counselor or personnel director. Are applicants more interested in jobs or what the company has to offer in the way of bonuses? What are good tips for job seekers?

Every state government has an office charged with the responsibility of seeing that scales are accurate. Every consumer wants a full fifty cents' worth of hamburger for his money. Most of them don't know, however, who keeps the scales accurate, how often they are checked, or what percentage of tested scales are off. Do scales that weigh wrong usually benefit the consumer or the merchant?

How many different magazines are for sale at the biggest news-

stand in town? Which sell best, week in and week out? How many requests are made for a magazine not in stock before the newsdealer
tries to get it? Which magazine sells fewest number of copies regularly? Are general sales less now than before TV? Do people buy and
read more newsstand magazines in winter than in summer?

Is nature losing out to science? "Straw" brooms are made of plastic, "rubber" place mats are made of plastic, "sponges" are now chemi-
cally made. Ask local grocers how much sales of natural items have
dropped in the face of this test-tube onslaught. Are some natural products still better sellers than their plastic counterparts?

What is scrap paper used for? Lots of service groups collect scrap
paper for charity. But we seldom see it after it's hauled from our door.
How is it re-used? Do the different grades of paper in magazines and
newspapers make any difference in the way it is reconstituted or what
it is used for in the future?

Everyone has heard of a "bull" or a "bear" stock market, but how
many really know what the terms mean? Your readers will enjoy a
feature on how the stock market works. Local brokers will be glad to
tell you how they help investors. How do they make a purchase for a
client? A sale?

How does a book publisher know how many copies of a first edition to print? How does he decide which manuscripts to "gamble"
on? What percentage of manuscripts submitted are published? How
are new books advertised? Has book reading increased or fallen since
radio and TV became popular?

What about wood pencils? In an age of atomic power, jet pro-
pulsion, and color television, are people using fewer wood pencils? Ask
your office supply man which colors sell best. Are pencil sales seasonal?
Are ball point pencils making inroads in wood pencil sales? Why are
some round and some hexagonal? Do those with bigger erasers sell
better than those with small erasers? Have costs gone up?

Credit cards in many kinds of business now enable more people
than ever before to "buy now and pay later." One of the services makes
it possible to eat in any of several hundred places, sign the check and

list a credit card number, and be billed later. Any folks you know use one of these cards? Are they used mostly by traveling men? How are they used for tax computations? How many other kinds of goods and services make use of the credit card technique?

The amount of money people save is a reflection of business conditions. Let your banker tell you how the amount folks save, and the regularity with which they save, is indicative of current business trends. Do people save most in good times or bad? Is this slogan true: "It's not how much you save that is important, it's how often"? Who decides the rate of interest to be paid on savings accounts? How often is it paid? Why is there no interest on a checking account?

One resident of a good-sized town was amazed that he couldn't find an American flag for sale? What about your community? Who sells United States flags? How great is the demand? Are more sold before Memorial Day than at any other time? What's the price range in flags? What materials are used in most of them? How many firms manufacture flags?

A Wisconsin store uses an unusual contest to stimulate interest in its annual "Circus of Values" sale. Children are invited to paint their faces and enter a Kiddie Clown Face Contest. To what extent do your stores use events as aids in their merchandising programs? Which have been successful? Are certain types of events to be avoided?

Some businessmen use clever ways to impress employees with certain ideas. You've probably seen these signs, "No One But the Boss Can Work in This Office More Than 60 Hours a Week," and "If You Love to Work, You'll Have a H—— of a Good Time Here." Make a collection of these sayings. Ask the bosses if they get results.

A Pennsylvania furniture store sold more than 50 per cent of its walkouts (customers who look at merchandise and then walk out without buying) by sending salesmen to homes for follow-ups. What are your stores doing to solve the walkout problem? Find out some of the main reasons for walkouts—inadequate selection of merchandise, prices, personalities of salesmen.

New machines have always been distrusted—until the facts were known. Not so many years ago, people wondered about the acceptance of the automobile. When dial telephones were introduced, many people feared that employment would be cut. Instead, expansion of the industry was so great that the number of telephone operators increased 79 per cent from 1945 to 1955. What about the many new automatic machines being introduced today? Will they affect employment? Processes? Wages?

One of the jobs of the Better Business Bureau is to ferret out shysters. What methods do BBB men use in finding unethical business practices, and in warning other businessmen and potential customers? What are some of the unusual schemes used by unscrupulous retailers and salesmen? How is the Better Business Bureau organized to fight these schemes?

How often have you heard someone say, "If I worked in a candy store I'd eat all the time"? But do persons who work in such stores, or at candy counters, really eat more candy than others? Ask the girl behind the counter what kinds of candy sell best, year in and year out. Are some candies seasonal? Do new candies come into the market very often, or do most folks prefer to stick with established favorites?

Everyone likes to hear stories of unusual epitaphs. Got any in your cemetery? Ask local dealers about the kinds of monuments most people prefer. Where does the stone come from? How are inscriptions cut into the stone? Has your dealer received orders for unusual stones or inscriptions? How many persons pick out their monument while still in good health?

Many stores are concerned with traffic blocks caused by customers who thumb through magazines on display racks. Ask local grocers and druggists how they cope with the problem of the page-flipper.

The scrap metal and rag business has boomed in recent years. But many people are still unaware of the size of the industry. Ask a local junk dealer where he gets old metals, how he can tell value, and who he sells it to. Is his business seasonal?

An automobile dealer in Kenyon, Minnesota, was still active in the operation of his business when he was ninety-three years old. There are probably some men in your town who are making use of their years of experience despite the fact that they are long past the usual retirement age. Everyone past fifty will be especially interested in an elder citizen's viewpoints on leading an effective and useful life in later years.

United States employees get a break. Some thirty thousand firms are spending an estimated $800,000,000 a year on recreation for employees, in the form of athletic, social, and cultural activities. What are some of the activities in large or small concerns nearby? Do they improve work by improving morale, or do companies do it simply because everyone else is adopting the practice?

Automobile companies solicit ideas from employees and from the public. Yet they say only one idea of each thirty thousand submitted is both new and useful. How do big concerns sift through the thirty thousand ideas to find the one that's good enough to be adopted? With that ratio, is the practice worthwhile? What are some advantages of soliciting ideas from others? What are some automotive features that have come from these ideas?

Coin-operated vending machines are now found in theaters, railway stations, offices, and many other places. You can get everything from a foot massage to a whiff of your favorite perfume merely by dropping in coins. How many items can be obtained from the machines in your community? What are some of the most popular items?

A Philadelphia businessman summed up his success secret in four lines: "Early to bed, early to rise, work like hell—and advertise." Talk to a number of successful businessmen and get their philosophies. What gives them drive and ambition? What do they consider basic in making a success in business?

Do your Business and Professional Women sponsor a banquet for their bosses? If so, find out what many of the girls consider qualifications of the perfect boss. Make your story a "Do's and Don't's for Bosses."

Stockholder meetings are being emphasized by many business organizations as an integral part of their public relations program. How are these conducted? Are executives present to answer questions? Are the meetings held in different cities? What are some of the ways in which companies are keeping in closer touch with their stockholders?

Find out from a good salesman in one of your town's best stores what techniques he uses for attracting buyers. How do modern sales techniques differ from those of earlier years? How has modern advertising changed sales methods?

Are business morals getting better or worse? Dr. Albert Edward Wiggam thinks they are getting better, mainly because of rising ethical standards and laws that enforce high standards. Are the cutthroat days over? Ask a number of your leading businessmen.

Despite the growth of suburban shopping centers, downtown business districts still enjoy important advantages. What are your downtown merchants doing to keep business? Lowering prices? Providing parking facilities for customers? Carrying larger lines of merchandise?

Maybe you've noticed it: an up-to-date grocery store of today offers five thousand or more items for sale, compared with about one thousand items fifteen years ago. What are some of the newer lines? Are grocerymen planning to add even more lines of merchandise? Do additional items mean more problems?

Businessmen are going back to school. Not just to attend short courses, but to visit museums, libraries, and learn more about liberal education. Chances are that some big organization in your community is sponsoring such a program. Are skills enough for success in any field? How important is self-expression—in letters, speeches, and in group situations?

A colonel, so the story goes, upon being transferred to a new command, found stacks of old documents, so he wired headquarters for permission to burn them. The answer came back: "Yes, but make copies first." How do modern filing clerks operate? How do they know what to save and how long to save it? Show modern methods of filing and the forms which are used.

Time after time, public opinion polls have shown that many people have ideas about profits that are directly contrary to the facts about profits. For instance, some think that all of the company's profits go into the pockets of owners. Interview a high official of a large business and ask: How much of the profit is paid in dividends to stockholders? How much to pay the cost of growth and expansion?

About 68 per cent of customers drift away from a store because of indifference on the part of the store and its employees, an expert reveals. Do stores in your city take customers for granted? Or do they make a special effort to keep in touch and offer special services to old-time customers?

There's a story in the largest fruit wholesaler in your city. From what states or countries does the fruit come? What are the most popular items locally? When are certain fruits in season?

Does your community have twin brothers who are engaged in a successful business? If so, how are decisions made? Plans for the future? How they started? On what do they disagree?

Six southwestern states produce most of the natural gas that is used in forty-three states. How does it get into those forty-three states? What is "natural gas"? What are its advantages and disadvantages as a fuel? How is it produced?

More windowless buildings are being constructed. Some girls employed in such a building in Long Beach, California, tired of looking at bare walls, so they started putting up interesting pictures. Result? Everyone—buyers, office boys, sales persons—are happier. How have some of the windowless buildings in your city solved this problem? How have some of the flat walls been livened up?

How is a song, article, or trademark copyrighted? What laws govern copyrights? How do modern trademarks work in protecting a product—and the consumer? Compare trademarks of today with the "hallmarks" of the English guilds.

Stress in the lead of your story the names of new streets and ask readers if they know their location. Then find out from delivery boys and others who must know the town how they keep up with names of new streets and new additions. Do some streets have two names, an old one and a new one? How is a person employed to make deliveries taught the names of all streets?

What motive has the businessman who wants his son to continue in his business? How many boys wish to take over their father's business? How many succeed? Contact a number of businessmen who represent the second or third generation of a family in the same business and see what they like about their activities.

What's happened to the country store? Is it still a gathering place for people of the community? Have automobiles and paved roads caused most of the stores to close? What kind of stock does today's country store carry compared with one of yesterday?

Mobile phones in automobiles are now in general use, but chances are a lot of your readers don't know how they work, what the charges are, and how far they will reach. Your telephone company will be glad to give you the details.

The lost and found department at the telephone headquarters building in St. Louis gets more earrings than anything else, usually a single earring. Check the biggest store in your town for unusual lost items. What is done with money or merchandise that is never claimed? What are items most frequently lost by men? By women?

Businessmen go to market once or twice a year. What do they look for? How do they anticipate trends in business? Is the trip a pleasure or a chore for most? How can they guard against over buying? How far in advance must purchases be made? Are delivery dates important?

A date to remember: August 26, 1868. That was when the typewriter was patented. Can some veteran secretaries recall the introduction of typewriters locally? Show improvements in typewriters, their many uses. And you might tie in the number of students enrolled in typing classes in your city (business college, high school, and college).

What were the first jobs of some of the foremost businesswomen of your community? What business training, if any, did they have? Do they feel that they have equal opportunities with men? What are some of the satisfactions of their work?

Some people believe that "charge customers," rather than "cash customers," have a preferred status at stores. Interview the credit manager of the largest store. Ask him about collections, the place of credit in the nation's economy, how he decides the amount of "carrying charges," and whether women buy more than men on credit.

To what extent do your businessmen and other leaders believe in the contents of special letters which attempt to give forecasts, show trends, and state opinions? Information in the letters is often contradictory. How many types have subscribers in your community? Is the material of great value to readers in making decisions?

What are some of the rackets which are old but are still fooling people? What are some of the newer ones? What precautions should be taken in buying anything from a stranger? Talk to the manager of the Better Business Bureau in your city.

Buses
A Texas bus driver solved the problem of what to do about riders who won't move to the rear of the bus. He put up this sign: "Standing room in the front of this bus is reserved for henpecked men and women over thirty." How do your bus drivers handle this problem? Joke with passengers? Bawl some of them out?

Cabinet Shops
Almost every town, no matter how small or how large, has one or more cabinet shops. What is made in the shop? Do people want more built-ins today? What types of woods are most frequently used? Describe the operation of modern woodworking tools and machines.

Caddies
Like the old gray mare, caddying isn't what it used to be. Find several and ask about their ambitions, their trials and tribulations, famous folk for whom they have caddied, and why they enjoy their work.

Cafes

A restaurant owner in Lansing, Michigan, announced a free meal for any patron who can pronounce his name—George Pappavlaho-dimitrakopoulous! What promotion stunts have the restaurants of your city used? Which have been most effective?

Candidates

Locate someone who has collected candidate cards as a hobby. What are the different types? Most unusual? The oldest? Have cards changed much through the years? Do many use pictures of the candidates?

Candy

What are the biggest sales dates for candy? Halloween? Christmas? Mother's day? Easter? What age group buys the most? Do many elderly persons enjoy candy? Interview a candy store manager and also a salesman in a drug store or a checker in a supermarket.

Carnivals

The next time a carnival comes your way, interview one of the women barkers. Some possible questions: How long has she been in show business? Why does she enjoy carnival life? What makes a good barker? Does a barker travel all year?

Carpenters

Styles in house construction change. Interview an old carpenter or two and get their views on changing styles of architecture, how labor-saving devices help them, how many more kinds of material are used today, and other angles.

Catalogs

Merchandise catalogs may be the butt of many of a comic's jokes, but they are still a vital part of American selling. The story of the catalog, from inception to sale, would be an interesting one. Do big companies print their own catalogs? What's the cost to the company? Are mailing lists confined to those who have previously made purchases through earlier catalogs? Who takes the pictures, writes the copy, and does the layout work?

Celebrations

Miss Dorothy Babb, a teacher at North Texas State College, sat down and figured that in her adult life she'd spent $1500 on bridal and baby showers and wedding gifts. She decided it was time that she and other spinsters had their inning. As a result, the mayor proclaimed August 15 as Old Maid's Day. Merchants donated free corsages, free movies, free shampoos, free transportation, and a tea. Anything like this in your community?

Celebrities

Does your city have any fan clubs? Who are the celebrities— crooners, movie stars, TV personalities? Are most of the fans teen- agers, or are some of them middle-aged and elderly people?

Cemeteries

Every now and then, for special reasons, a body is removed from one cemetery to another. What are some of the reasons? What are some of the legal aspects of the procedure? And what have been some of the oldest bodies which have been removed?

Does your community have a cemetery association? If so, find out its purposes, its officers, and its activities through the years.

Does your city have a potter's field? Who pays the burial expenses of strangers who die without any identification? Best slant: unusual or mysterious cases.

In all likelihood, there's a small community near you where the residents gather for one day each year and clean up the cemetery. Find one and then do a story showing how long the event has been ob- served, what is done during the day (lunch is often served), and who sponsors it.

Censorship

Are some public meetings of your city closed to newsmen? When are closed meetings justified? Give the viewpoints of both the report- ers and the public officials who believe that restrictions should be placed on some meetings.

Chamber of Commerce

A secretary-manager must be a versatile person. For one thing, he never knows what a new day will bring forth. Interview your local secretary and find out: What does he like most about his work? Does he receive any strange requests? What does he consider the city's most important projects?

Chauffeur

Are chauffeurs really like those portrayed in movies and in books? What are the duties of a full-time chauffeur? Do fewer families use chauffeurs than used them a few years ago?

Checkrooms

How often do mixups of apparel occur at check rooms? Does your community have a memory expert—like the man at the National Press Club in Washington, D. C., who remembers what each person checks without using any tags or other identification? Do look-alikes—men's hats, for instance—cause mixups?

Child Care

Some parents may not agree with the Bicycle Institute of America when it says that children three and one-half years old are not too young to learn to ride a bicycle. What do most parents feel is the best age for bikes? What about wagons? Do parents base such decisions on their own childhood experiences?

What should a young child do when a stranger offers him a ride? Is it safe for parents to allow their children to attend the movies alone? Get the answers to these questions from judges, ministers, social workers, teachers, policemen, child psychologists, and others.

Childhood

Psychiatrists find that more men than women have the wish to "return to childhood." Are women more interested in their immediate environment than in their past? Which live more in the future—men or women? Do many regret decisions of the past?

Children

The normal child usually "Gives out like a siren" when he makes his first visit to the barber shop. How can parents overcome the fear of the barber shop in the child's mind? Listening to dad's electric razor? Playing barber? Offering him a treat after the visit to the shop? Do barbers have any suggestions?

A sandbox—one of the oldest and most fascinating of children's playthings—is a must, declares Dr. Dorothy V. Whipple. What kind of sand is best? Should the box be placed in the sun or in the shade? How about a few sand toys? Are there new ones being manufactured? Should the sand box be inaccessible to pets? For answers to these and other questions check with physicians, youth workers, and mothers.

"Today's children receive an automatic, unearned allowance, and as a result they think it is something that may be had for nothing," a noted psychologist declares. What is the average allowance received by children of various ages? Are some children required to do some work for their allowance? Do many of them believe that money is something to be spent and not earned?

Did you see the cartoon of the weary mother-hostess who decided to end her little boy's birthday party by giving a prize to the first child who went home? Are some of the tried-and-true games still played at kids' parties? What are some of the newer ideas? Activities? Refreshments? Invitations?

Every now and then you hear of a child who is an expert cook. Ask the youngster how long he or she has been cooking. Get the favorite recipes. Do the kids use their cooking ability at summer camps?

What's being done to assure glasses for children with poor eyes? The Better Vision Institute estimates six million school children have uncorrected visual defects? Many schools have regular eye inspections. Do young people see their optometrist as often as their dentist? How can parents tell if their children should have an eye examination? Does one of your civic groups sponsor a sight conservation project?

Yesterday's youngsters had to pitch in and help with the chores around the house and barn. How many children help in the home today? Do mothers require enough? Have labor-saving appliances reduced the amount of work required to keep house?

Children of all ages like pioneer tales of the past. So every now and then run a story on the history of your city or county. Look up old trails and roads, ruins of historic buildings, and other spots of interest.

Most children outgrow their shoes rather than wear them out, a noted pediatrician states. How should children's shoes be fitted? How can mother and dad tell if Junior's shoes are correctly fitted? Are soft shoes harmful to children's feet?

Does your city have any large and unusual doll houses? Who makes them? Have some of them been used by several generations?

Two young burglars—age five and six—who tossed a brick through a barber shop window in Chicago and scooped up $37.34 in change were given a strange sentence—six months without ice cream. What are some of the unique punishments meted out to kids in your community?

Is it wise to spank a child? Is there a more effective method of punishment? H. D. Haygood, a psychologist, once said, "If spanking sets up fear or hatred of the parent and is done in anger, it is bad. But if the child understands this punishment is the natural consequence of his behavior and it is not done in anger, spanking may not be destructive, but other methods are far better." What do parents think?

"Best parents show love or disapproval wisely, spontaneously, unthinkingly, immediately and solve the child's problem without hesitation," declares Dr. Benjamin Spock, a child specialist. How do attitudes of parents affect children, particularly the young? Is it wise for parents to worry and feel that they have made the wrong decisions? For answers, interview a child psychologist.

Good teachers rarely have discipline problems with children. How do they keep the kids interested? Get some tips from teachers and then pass them along in a feature for parents.

Do kids often get into trouble and become unhappy because they feel that they are not loved? Does love mean more to a child than to an adult? Psychoanalyst John C. Thurrott says, "For a child to have no love is death. Children should receive love as the normal course of things." Get the views of social workers, family life experts, child psychologists and others.

Who has the most adopted children in your community? Did

the foster parents come from big families? Here's another slant: Find out some well-known persons in your community who were adopted children.

Chiropodist

What's happening to people's feet? Since people walk less, are their feet weaker? Which sex experiences the most foot trouble? What are the most common feet ailments? Are flat shoes worn by young women injurious to their feet? Best source: a chiropodist.

Choir

Does your city have a church choir which gives a number of out-of-town concerts? Or one which often goes on a tour? If so, interview the director about the membership of the group, the types of music which are most popular, and his rehearsal methods.

Christmas

Package-wrappers who seem to have ten thumbs are envious of the work done by department store professionals. How long does it take to learn to wrap a pretty gift package? What is the most unusual package local employees have worked with? The smallest? Largest? How much does Christmas gift wrapping increase the usual load?

The Christmas season is bad-check season in lots of towns. Check with authorities to see what stores get the most bogus checks. Are they usually for small amounts or large? What percentage of checks are made good? How does a "hot check artist" work? How can storekeepers be alert for bad-check writers?

Christmas shoppers often assure themselves of a miserable Christmas by inadvertently setting themselves up as "pushover" victims of thieves. News slant—get precautions from a local policeman. Typical ones: do not leave Christmas packages unguarded in unlocked automobiles, watch your billfolds and purses, and do not lay a package down unguarded.

A twelve-year-old Cleveland boy's name was drawn at a Christmas program sponsored by merchants. He came to the stage and then asked the chairman to pick another number, and another boy won the bike. It isn't necessary to be grown up and fat to play Santa Claus.

Watch for human interest stories, especially those centered around children.

Personal experience feature: Get a job as salesman in a big department store during the Christmas holidays. Then describe your experiences—the tragic and amusing—in a feature story.

Sometimes Christmas is written "Xmas," because "X" is the Greek equivalent of "ch" and stands for the word "Christ." Many folks think it wrong to use the abbreviation. Get some comments.

Legend has it that before the crucifixion the berries of Christmas holly were white instead of red as now. Find out the favorite decorations in your community, where they are obtained, and the many ways in which they are used.

The Christmas seal has become an annual institution and offers at the Christmas season an opportunity for rich and poor alike to help in the fight against an ancient enemy—tuberculosis. Get the local slant on how many seals are sold, who does the mailing, what percentage of the people respond, and how far ahead the sales are planned.

The hanging of the mistletoe and the burning of the Yule log are two of the most ancient customs which have come from our pagan ancestors. Do any local families or groups have a log-burning ceremony? Is mistletoe as widely used as it used to be?

Everyone likes Christmas music. Interview some person who knows something about hymnology and get the history of the old tunes; then show how they will always be popular.

December 25 is the anniversary of many important events in world history, although none begin to compare with the birth of the Christ Child. George Washington and his army crossed the Delaware River on Christmas day in 1776; Charlemagne issued his proclamation as emperor on that day in 800; William the Conqueror was crowned in 1606; Columbus' ship, *Santa Maria*, was wrecked in 1492; Captain Cook discovered Christmas Island in 1777; and Nashville, Tennessee, was founded on Christmas day in 1780. What important events have taken place in your city on December 25?

Watch for any unique projects sponsored by the Salvation Army during Yuletide. In many cities the organization exhibits a huge Christmas tree and holds a lighting ceremony. Then a string of lights is added for each one hundred dollars received. Funds are used to purchase food baskets for the poor.

There are Scandinavian, French, and ancient Egyptian legends which claim to have given the Christmas tree to the world. What kinds of trees are preferred in your community? Where do they come from?

In rural Norway the women bake a year's supply of bread at Christmas time and store it. How much baking is done in your community? Or do most women buy their cakes and bread at bakeries? Get a few grocers' opinions.

Proper and dramatic displays of merchandise in store windows during Yuletide has become an art. Where do stores get their ideas? What display ideas have attracted the most attention? How many weeks in advance are ideas planned?

How Christmas is celebrated in other lands makes an interesting feature. Interview persons of various nationalities in your community. Be sure and see if any of the groups observe Christmas here as they did in their native land.

Christmas is usually the year's biggest day for telephone operators. What preparations are made in advance for the big rush? What suggestions would operators make to callers? What are the peak hours?

Many persons like personal photographic Christmas cards. Interview a photographer and ask what kind of photograph is best, how handwritten greetings can be added, how much time should be allowed from the time the picture is taken until the cards are mailed, and the approximate cost.

Your local library will probably arrange a special exhibit of books telling of the life of Christ during the holidays. What is the oldest book? The newest? Which book through the years has been the most popular?

Be on the alert for any unique projects sponsored by churches during the Christmas season. In one church, for instance, the members decided that instead of the usual wife-husband gifts they would donate the amount usually spent to the building fund for a new church.

Fires can spoil the Christmas season. So why not interview a safety expert or a fire chief and get a list of "do's" and "don't's" which should be known by anyone who has a Christmas tree.

Do school children still take part in the same kind of Christmas program which their parents enjoyed when they were young? Interview a veteran teacher and ask about any innovations through the years.

It's amazing to know the number of handmade presents which are given by children each year. Check with school teachers, directors of youth handicraft groups, and others for a good story.

Check with record shops and see what types of selections are most in demand. Are some of the old selections like "Silent Night" as much in demand as some popular song of the moment with a Yuletide theme?

Postmen of the United States totter under a mountain-high load of one and three-fourths billion cards every Christmas. Do a story on the types of cards—some are inexpensive while others are elaborately lithographed in many brilliant colors. What types sell best?

Timely feature: Get the recipes for ten different kinds of Christmas candy made by local experts.

Is Christmas over commercialized? Get the comments of both religious leaders and leading businessmen and then let the reader make up his mind.

Even criminals usually receive a good meal on Christmas day. Find out what your local jail plans to serve for the main meal on Christmas day.

Does your community sponsor a Christmas lighting contest for homes? If so, find out some of the more unusual displays. Are they original?

Christmas eve feature: Get a story on all of the people—policemen, firemen, nurses, telephone operators, and many others—who must remain on duty Christmas eve or Christmas day.

Shoplifters are usually very active during the Christmas season. How do stores guard against them? How can a shoplifter be detected? Where do they try to hide the merchandise?

There's always a story about the groups which go caroling during the Christmas holidays. Are the singers mainly young people? What are the numbers most frequently requested? How does each group decide whom it will sing for?

How shy are men shoppers? Interview a lingerie saleswoman and get her comments on the ways in which she has learned to help shy men shoppers during the Christmas season.

The street festivals of Italy and Spain had fireworks at Christmas time. Do kids in your community shoot fireworks? Have city ordinances been passed which prohibit the sale of certain types within the city limits?

Many groups now pool their funds (which were formerly used to buy presents) and give them to worthy groups or individuals. Find out what's happening in your community.

How do local merchants know what types of toys to stock for Christmas? One year most of the boys may want cowboy pistols and the next year they may want big toys. Do merchants just guess in ordering what they hope the kids will want?

It is reputed that the first Christmas card, as we know it, was dispatched in 1845 by W. C. Dobson, one of Queen Victoria's favorite artists. What kinds of cards do people prefer today? Do many people compose original verses or sentences? Do elderly people prefer one kind of card and young people another?

Christmas cakes, iced cookies, and other goodies are survivals of the old custom of giving confectionery gifts to the senators of Rome. How many local folk give food as gifts?

Your community has several men with big hearts who always act as Santa Claus for various affairs. How long has the oldest one been playing this role? Why do the men enjoy it? What are some of their most interesting experiences? Do they furnish their own suits?

Does your community observe a "Burning of the Greens" ceremony? Christmas trees and other shrubbery are burned in one huge fire. What is the origin of this ceremony? Who sponsors it? Are prizes given for those who bring the most trees?

Old but always interesting: describe the Christmas rush at the post office. Do most people still mail their packages too late? To what extent are part-time helpers used? Are many packages poorly wrapped? And always gets the views of a veteran postal employee who can recall incidents—amusing and tragic—from the past.

Swindlers and high-pressure salesmen step up their efforts during the days preceding Christmas. Check with your local Better Business Bureau and get a list of some of the schemes which have been worked on hapless people year after year.

Watch for names of children born on Christmas day. Occasionally, when a child is born on Christmas, the parents name it Noel, Christina, or something in keeping with the holiday.

After-Christmas business story: How many shoppers used their credit privileges? How many paid cash? How did sales compare with those of the previous year? Were more expensive presents—furs, automobiles, television sets—bought this year than last?

Church

Most denominations disfavor the use of women as clergymen. Which denominations of your city allow women to preach? Do they feel that women can fill a unique role in the ministry? What are some of the denominations which limit the roles of women in religious work? Why do officials of these groups feel that women should not preach?

116

A Presbyterian minister in Indiana, concerned lest his congregation be depleted by traffic accidents, distributes cards that read, "We believe in predestination . . . but drive safely—you might hit a Presbyterian." Have your local pasters, in their public relations activities, created or done anything unusual or clever? In advertisements? Letters? Church bulletins? Direct mail? Are they using more effective public relations techniques in their activities?

Billy Graham was once criticized for budgeting $133,000 for an all-out evangelical campaign in Scotland. One of his spokesmen answered, "You don't reach the largest number of people possible in an age of television, radio, movies, and automobiles by having evangelists slip into the town and address one or two people." What is involved in the pre-buildup for a big revival? Publicity? Music? Special services? Committees?

One church honors a family whose members are most active in Sunday School. Check with pastors and you'll be able to do at least one feature and possibly a series on this angle. Which family has given the most years of service? Which is the most versatile in talents?

About 1,500,000 men and women are needed to teach the Sunday school classes. Many are loyal and dependable. But there is a terrific turnover in most churches. Why? Do some people shirk because they think some theological expertness is expected? Do some steer clear of children's classes? Pastors and Sunday School superintendents can give you some comments which will add up to a good feature.

Dr. Albert Schweitzer, who completed three doctorates before he was thirty, gave up a promising career to serve his dark-skinned fellow men in the African jungle. As the whole world knows, he became a medical missionary. By looking around, you will find ministers in your city or state who gave up promising careers in other fields of endeavor to dedicate their lives to church work. Why? When did they make the decision?

With more than 250 religious bodies in this country, almost every one of the religions of the world is practiced by at least a few Americans. How many different denominations in your community? Oldest? Youngest?

In our nation of more than 160 million people, we have more than 294,000 churches. And of these, more than 40,000 have been built since the end of World War II. Look around and you will probably be amazed at the number of new churches which have been constructed in your city or county in the past five years. How does this total compare to construction figures of the previous five years? What types of architecture are most popular?

Often you hear of a minister who also serves as a teacher. Many times, he helps to relieve a teacher shortage. Find one and see how he performs the double duty of clergyman and teacher? Does he enjoy his classroom duties? Had he ever taught before?

Modern circuit riders are the scores of ministerial students who serve churches on weekends while studying at theological seminaries. The dean can tell you of one who has an unusually long distance to travel for his weekend sermons. When does the young minister prepare his sermons? Do his out-of-town duties interfere with his studies? Tell of some of his experiences.

Lee Hastings Bristol, Jr., with the help of a friend, has composed words and music for a children's hymnal. Why? He felt that many standard church hymns didn't "say anything" to children. Get the comments of choir directors and church youth leaders and see what they think of the idea. At what age should children be taught about old hymns?

A ministerial alliance is usually more than just a committee of preachers. Find out some of the activities of your local group. Does it sponsor a religious census? Union services—like a Thanksgiving service? Back-to-church movements?

Pastors are learning to write like reporters. Ministers and other church workers are receiving tips on newswriting at news clinics being sponsored by various denominations over the country. Who teaches the courses? When are church events news? How should news releases be prepared? Does church news interest a great number of readers?

Today there are approximately 295,000 churches in the United

States. Architecture of many denominations has changed quite a bit. Who decides on church architecture? Are there ever disagreements between architects and church governing boards? What faiths use approximately the same type of building design they used years ago?

Do a survey and find out how many charter members of local churches are still active. Get the oldsters to reminisce about the past history of their churches, pastors they have known, and special programs and activities.

Where does a minister find ideas for sermon topics? Reading? Travel? Observation? Experience? What are some topics which usually bring the most favorable comments?

Choir music library: From your oldest and largest church, find out how many anthems are kept in the music library? How many new ones are added each year? What are some of the oldest and most popular numbers? What determines choice of anthems each Sunday?

What congregation in your city has the best attendance record over a period of years? What percentage of its members attend regularly? How do the minister and church officials keep the attendance at such a high peak? What are some of the principal factors which keep people away from church? How can churches counteract competitive appeals and influences?

"64 Million Americans Do Not Attend Church." That's a headline in a magazine. Why do many people fail to attend? What do pastors consider a good attendance percentage of their people Sunday after Sunday? How are pastors attempting to interest those who either attend irregularly or not at all?

More and more eating places—cafes, restaurants, diners, coffee shops, and cafeterias—are placing cards with three types of grace on their tables. Do waiters feel that many persons use them? Are many cards taken? Do many folks—with or without the cards—say grace before meals when they are eating out?

Every city has a variety of church publications—newspapers, bulletins, news letters, and pamphlets. Has the number increased? Are they slanted to different age groups? Do the editors feel that their publications have high readership?

Dedication of a new church is always worth a feature. What former pastors will attend and take part in the program? How many former members will attend? How much has the church grown in membership since it was started? Who are some of the laymen who have occupied high offices in the state or regional organization?

The Jewish New Year, or Rosh Hashana, is described by Jewish authorities as the "annual day of judgment when all creatures pass in review before the searching eye of Omniscience." New Year's day and the day following are observed as holy days. Because of the design of the Jewish calendar, the beginning of the new year moves from September to October 5. Describe the various ceremonies and show their origin.

Surveys show that about seven out of eight children stop going to Sunday School before they reach fifteen years of age! How are youth workers in churches trying to "bridge this gap"? To what extent does the Sunday School attendance of youngsters depend on the church-going habits of their parents?

"Many modern parents are using Sunday Schools and churches as nurseries for their youngsters on Sunday mornings and the parents never attend services," a speaker declared recently. Is this true in your community? How do churches encourage the attendance of parents with their children at Sunday School and church?

Protestants totaled 27 per cent of the church-going population in 1925, while today they make up about 35 per cent. One factor in their growth has been the increasing emphasis on personal evangelism. How do your local churches train workers in personal evangelism? What qualities are necessary for success? Are ministers depending more and more on laymen to spearhead the visitation program?

At one time a statistician reported that the average churchgoer contributes a yearly average of $41.94. How does this compare with the church members of your community? What percentage of the members tithe? How do most people prefer to contribute—weekly, monthly, quarterly, or annually?

Some twenty-three thousand pastors join the spiritual force of the churches each year, to replace those who have retired or died, and to meet the demands of increased memberships. Interview ministers of different denominations and ask them, "Is your church training enough young men for the future of the ministry?"

Methodist tie-in: John Wesley was born on June 28, 1703. Use this date to publish a story on the growth of Methodism in your county or city—new churches, new activities, prominent laymen, and unusual projects.

Christian Education Week is now observed by many churches in September. See how it is emphasized in the churches of your community? What are its aims? Who sponsors it? Do leaders feel that church groups have emphasized adult activities and forgotten the importance of Sunday School and other Christian education programs?

Tithing among church members is on the increase, leaders of several groups declare. What about the churches of your city? How many denominations stress tithing? Is the practice observed by people of all ages?

Interview an aged minister and get the highlights of his career, how many sermons he has delivered, where he served longest as pastor, and his favorite Bible verse.

Circus

Date tie-in: Phineas Taylor Barnum, great American circus owner, was born on July 5. If the date is out of season for a circus to come your way, you might interview a former circus employee, and get the recollections of persons who remember the shows of the old days.

Elephants used to do much of the heavy work in moving a circus, but trucks now do most of it. Horses and elephants usually walk from the rail siding to the circus lot. Are elephants used to move the heavy poles or to do any other special tasks? Do a feature from this angle the next time a circus comes to town.

Citizenship Day

Formerly known as Constitution Day, Citizenship Day is observed on September 17, on the anniversary of the signing of the Constitution of the United States. Does the constitution meet the needs of modern society? Should parts of it be revised?

City Government

How are the public papers and documents of your city protected? Where are they stored? Does anyone ever consult them? For how many years have records been kept?

Peg for feature on city manager: On April 2, 1908, the city council of Staunton, Virginia, elected Charles E. Ashburner as the first "General Manager." The city has published a booklet, "The Origin of the City Manager Plan in Staunton, Virginia," which will be sent upon request.

A child visiting the Columbus, Ohio, zoo had her pocket picked by a friendly elephant. She asked the Columbus city council to reimburse her $5.60. Other city governments have had similar unusual claims. How are they handled? Talk with municipal attorneys, city managers, and councilmen.

The official key to Washington, the nation's capital—which all visiting dignitaries get—is made in the District of Columbia jail. Do your officials give a key to the city to celebrities? If not, are they named to an honorary office, given certificates, or honored in some other way?

Civic Affairs

Dr. Anne Gary Pannell, president of Sweet Briar College, says that men are so busy today that "much of the civic responsibility falls on women." Do women in your city keep the museums and art centers going and work on the civic and charity drives? Do some of them have positions once held by men?

Citizens of Moline, Illinois, spearheaded by the East End Businessmen's Association, sponsored a Gripe Night. Two topics were barred: personalities and politics. Result? Answers to a lot of questions. Does your community sponsor a meeting where everyone is urged to "get something off his chest"? Does your chamber of commerce use a questionnaire or any other method of getting suggestions for community betterment?

What is the outlook for your community just as the New Year comes into view? Get comments from ten community leaders. Be sure that those chosen are representative of various groups and interests.

Civic Clubs
Are there still some Babbits in service clubs? Do some people still believe that many men join civic clubs mainly to help their business prestige? Show how many men have been active members of service clubs for twenty or thirty years. Interview a few old-time members and get their philosophies.

Civil Defense
How active is your community in civil defense? Have classes been held in rescue work, fire control, and other important topics? Do officials believe that they can best get public co-operation by building their pleas on the basis of terror? Are most people apathetic toward the whole idea?

Classifieds
Want ad in the Dansville, New York, *Breeze:* "Farmer, age 38, wishes to meet woman around 30 who owns a tractor. Please enclose picture of tractor." What precautions do newspapers take to prevent amusing ads like that one from appearing? What are some of the funniest ones which have been run?

Cleaning
Cleaning is big business, particularly in cities. There are firms which will clean one room or every room in a skyscraper. What about the window cleaners? Workers who specialize in floor cleaning?

Clocks
Does your city have several outdoor clocks? Do some of them have chimes? What is the oldest clock? The newest? To what extent do passersby rely on them? Can they be seen both day and night?

Clothes
Men who lead active social lives are lucky if they live near Wash-

ington, D. C. For just $13.50, they can rent pink Bermuda shorts, a navy blue sport coat, and a flashy sport shirt for a weekend. How widespread is the practice of renting clothes for special occasions? Is it confined to large cities? What styles and types of clothing are most in demand? Do men rent more clothes than women?

Americans are enjoying more leisure time. As a result, our wardrobes are growing because of the needs for sports and other leisure time activities. What percentage of clothes sold today are for sports or leisure time activities? Who buys more—men or women? How will sports clothes of the future differ from those of today?

Many folks joke about laundries tearing buttons off men's shirts. Is this just a joke? How do modern laundries handle this problem? What precautions are used in handling various garments and fabrics?

Find an old-time tailor and you'll find a good story. Get his comments on current fashions. Do many people still prefer tailor-made suits? Do styles go in cycles? Are modern fabrics as durable as those of years ago? How can you tell a good fabric?

The average American woman currently buys more than four dresses a year. How does this compare with sales in your community? What age woman buys the most dresses? How many women seek their husband's advice in buying dresses?

A Kansas man appeared at his twenty-seventh wedding anniversary wearing the same suit which he wore at his wedding—and it looked as good as ever! How long does the average man wear a suit? How many suits does the average man purchase in a year, or in five years? Are today's fabrics as durable as those used years ago? Ask the veteran tailor or salesman.

Sports shirts now outsell business shirts two to one. Is this because men have more leisure time? Or is it just a trend toward casual dress? Leading haberdashers will have some interesting comments for you.

"What's Holding Back Men's Clothing Sales?"—headline. What motivates the ordinary man in buying clothes? His wife's insistence that he needs a new suit? A special occasion? How many suits does the average man own? Are men afraid of new styles in clothes? Do most men get their wife's approval before buying a suit? An experienced haberdasher will be good for some interesting comments.

Clubs

How many people feel like the columnist of the *Pratt Tribune* of Pratt, Kansas, who wrote, "We've got too many organizations in this town. It wouldn't surprise us to see on somebody's tombstone: 'John Doe, clubbed to death.'" How many organizations does your community have? Has the number grown in ten years? How many are active? What are some of the newer ones? Ask several prominent persons the question, "Do you think we are over organized?"

Coffee

Many folks believe that coffee is harmful. And others think that they drink too much, a survey showed. How many cups of coffee does an average person drink each day? Do more men than women drink coffee? Do those who enjoy it believe that they drink too much?

Coins

The financial panic of 1837 so depleted the supply of small coins that many businessmen issued their own. They were known as "hard time tokens" or "Jackson cents," and often carried the maker's advertising message. Find out if any local coin collectors have any of these in their collection.

In Uganda, Africa, a sixty-two-pound ivory tusk sold for a thousand cowrie shells. A cow was worth 2,300 cowries. A bride sold for only two! What are some other units of exchange that have been used as money in other parts of the world? Consult your encyclopedia.

In 1786 the Congress authorized the mill as a coin. However, no mill has even been minted by the federal government. But lots of other coins have been struck. What metals are coins made of today? How do they differ from earlier metals? What coin is in greatest circulation today? What's the story of rare coins? Why are they rare? Some states have coined mills for use in collecting sales taxes. Are such coins recognized by Uncle Sam?

Collections

Today's professional bill collector uses a smooth, psychological approach rather than yesterday's raucous methods, say members of the American Collectors Association. If there's a member in your city, find out how yesterday's unethical bill collector is becoming rare, and the differences in collecting techniques between yesterday and today.

College

A student pledge to a college fraternity usually goes through a period of hazing and horseplay before he becomes a member. In the last few years, however, many fraternities have abandoned "Hell Week" in favor of "Help Week." Now the pledges work on constructive projects—building playgrounds for orphanages and summer camps for boys, and cleaning up community centers and old folks' homes. Who picks the projects? How many hours are spent in completing them? Do groups ask the boys for help?

Thales, the Greek philosopher, looking at the stars and falling into a well, has been a popular picture of all college professors. Are they really absent-minded? Talk to the president or some other high administrative official of a nearby college and find specific instances of how professors contribute much to life and society—through research, surveys, experiments, and other means.

Students passed out candy and cigars to faculty members at Idaho State College as a part of "Be Kind to Faculty Week." And they did it just before final exam week! Do you know of a nearby college or university in which students polish the scholastic apple in this or similar ways?

Every university yearbook editor chooses a theme for the publication. Where does he get the idea? What themes have been used in the past? How have yearbooks changed through the years? Are they still as popular as ever?

Every university and college has an unusual student club. Find one at your local college and show why it was organized, its objectives, and its activities for the year.

Columnists

Leonard Lyons, once accused of gathering his material the easy way, replied that it required about fourteen hours of work to find enough items for his daily column. Where does a local columnist get ideas? Does he keep a file of material for use on dull days? Do many readers disagree with his comments? What topic or topics excite the most interest?

Community Chests

Americans have big hearts. Each year they give about three hundred million dollars to united community charity drives, community chests, and similar activities. Are people becoming more generous? What are the best appeals? Does the per capita gift decline as the number of appeals grow? What are the best times of year for charity drives?

Communications

The longest telegram on record was sent by Canadian football fans to one of the players of the Montreal Alouettes. It contained more than 44,000 words, was 306 feet long, and had nearly 22,000 signatures! What unusual telegrams can your local office manager remember? How does he take care of peak loads during holiday seasons? How is a telegram actually sent? Have telegrams played any important roles in history-making events?

The job of laying the first transatlantic cable was successfully completed in July, 1858. However, it broke, and the Civil War prevented further work on the cable. The first permanent cable was stretched from Ireland to Newfoundland in 1866. How many cables now stretch across the Atlantic? Has cable use been supplanted by radio? How are inspections and repairs made? What is the source of greatest "wear" in such a cable?

A hot-tempered housewife in New York was found guilty of refusing to yield a country telephone party line when a volunteer fireman tried to report a fire. If you have party lines in your community, find out how emergency messages are handled. Do most people cooperate?

Community

What has happened to the itinerant fellows who sharpened knives and scissors? Can you find one to interview? If so, ask him why he likes to travel, the kinds of people he meets, and if people use knives and scissors in the home as much as they once did.

To what extent is the national anthem used at school assemblies and other programs in your community? Write your story so that it can be released on September 13 or 14, because the "Star Spangled Banner" was written on these days in 1814.

Give your readers a glimpse-of-life story about some group in your area—an Indian tribe, a German settlement, or a Chinese district. Show how the group maintains certain traditional ceremonies and beliefs.

You've read thrilling stories of community efforts—the fight for better schools in Arlington, Virginia, the struggle for decent housing in Baltimore, Maryland, and the fight against crime in Gary, Indiana. Be on the alert for the same kind of community-wide self-developed effort—its problems and results. Who are the leaders? What are the obstacles? And how did people feel when it was all over?

Concerts

Notables of the concert stage are very particular about all of the arrangements concerning their appearances—dressing room, stage lighting, programs, and other factors. Find an individual who has booked celebrities through the years and ask about special requests from the stars. Any impossible requests? Are famous folks really prima donnas?

Confederate Memorial Day

Some states of the south observe Confederate Memorial Day, which was first observed in Mississippi. Through the efforts of President McKinley, a plot was set aside in the Arlington National Cemetery for the burial of the Confederate dead. Is this day observed in your city or state? If so, who participates? Or was it once observed in your region?

Conservation

Soil conservation planting of pine trees is boosted by many youth groups in Tennessee and other southern states. What is being done in your state? How many trees have been planted? What varieties? Is your timber supply being used faster than new forests are being grown?

By jumping back through the years—by reading, and interviewing certain persons—you can write an interesting feature on the early game laws. Did the old-timers practice conservation? What body made the first laws? Are some laws about the same as they were when they were passed?

Contests

A Des Moines woman won the $1,500 first prize in a newspaper's puzzle contest. But then people began to bother her with anonymous letters and telephone calls. Some were trying to sell her something. Unsolicited articles came in the mail. If you have a contest winner nearby, ask him or her: Was it worth the trouble? Did many screwballs bother you? Any amusing experiences?

Controversies

Chances are if a subject is interesting enough to be controversial, it's interesting enough for feature material. How do local folks feel about liquor advertising on radio and television, about state or federal aid to parochial schools, about college fraternities and sororities, about universal military training, about teen-age marriages? Or there may be a controversial local issue lively enough for a feature.

Conventions

Many a state delegation, when attending a national convention, wears a special uniform or insignia. And the delegates may also give away samples of some product for which the state is famous. What souvenirs do your state delegations give away at big meetings? Do they wear any sort of special attire? Do they take along some musical group which may be unique or different?

A convention of women may add more to a city's scenic beauty than an all-male convention does, but city officials prefer the men— because they spend more money and take fewer towels. Are lady conventioners likely to get into as much mischief? What is the average amount of money spent by men conventioners in your city? Women delegates? Which prefer heavier meals? Hotel officials and convention specialists with your chamber of commerce will reveal some interesting angles.

All types of machines and gadgets are being used by speakers at conventions. Designed mainly as possible cures for the platform paralysis which threatens both amateur and professional speakers, the new devices are mainly to prompt the orators. By covering several large conventions, you can get enough material for a feature on "speakers' aids."

Corporations

Corporations nowadays are realizing the importance of stockholder relations. Some of the nation's biggest companies hold meetings in several different cities each year, to increase active participation. What other techniques are used to maintain and improve relations between the executives who operate a big business and the people who own it? Ask the public relations director of a corporation what devices he uses. How successful has he been?

Cotton

Less than a century ago, the American cotton industry was dumping millions of dollars into rivers and streams each year. At that time cotton gins disposed of "waste" cottonseed in nearby bodies of water, or left it to rot. How has this "useless" cottonseed come to be the basis of a four-hundred-million-dollar industry? What qualities make it suitable for such products as food or gunpowder? Interview a cotton expert in your town, or a chemist.

Fashion comes to the farm in feedbags made from colorful cotton fabrics. More than 125,000 of these emptied containers are converted annually into attractive wearing apparel and household accessories by budget-conscious housewives. For a story, talk to your county home demonstration agent.

Cotton, traditional queen of summer fashion, has blossomed into a hardy perennial for year-round wear. How did designers discover the versatility cotton offers for exciting cold-weather styling? What are some of the "winter cotton" fabrics?

Courts

A Florida man, sentenced for an auto theft charge, asked the court to sentence him for "enough time to learn something—about four years." Ask an old judge or court reporter for some of the unusual reactions and comments voiced by persons when their sentences are given.

Some courts accept confessions recorded on tape—others do not. A Detroit woman won her divorce on the tape-recorded evidence that her husband had used "vile language" to her. Check with local judges and lawyers and see how they feel about taped evidence.

A New York man failed to appear in police court on a traffic charge and forfeited his bond. He left seven Bibles, valued at $150. Your police court judge can tell you what other unusual articles have been put up as bond. Are many unclaimed?

Does your city have a girl court reporter? If so, ask her about her early experiences. What have been some of the most interesting trials? How many witnesses are gripped by fear and thus find it hard to talk?

A prospective juror in St. Louis was asked, "You say you work at the brewery. What is your capacity there?" and the man replied, "Oh, about five bottles." Talk to court reporters, judges, and others and find out some of the amusing things which have occurred in the courts of your city.

Court House

There's always a drama or two around the court house. How many people come seeking information? What are some of the unusual requests made at their various offices? And show how county officials are besieged by canvassers in religious, civic, community, and other types of drives.

Are dogs used by your sheriff or deputy sheriffs in trailing escaped prisoners? If so, how were the animals trained?

Crafts

One of the attention-getters in the old days was the carved ship in a bottle. Do men still whittle such things? Have power machines reduced the work done by hand? Interview teachers of industrial arts.

Creativity

"Prosperity tends to impoverish us creatively," Alex Osborn reminds us, "whereas hard going tends to enrich us." Is there any truth in the Horatio Alger rags-to-riches pattern? You can get an interesting angle on this topic by getting comments from veteran teachers. Are poorer children likely to be more creative? Is hardship always a handicap, or can it be a stimulant? Does a student who works at some outside job, for instance, gain experience which may make him more original and ingenious?

Have a small fraction of the world's peoples made possible most of civilization's advances? Stephen Visher says that "The most creative one-tenth of men are 1,000 times as valuable as the average tenth and 1,000,000 times as valuable as the least productive tenth." Who are some of the most creative folks in your city? Are people as creative today as ever?

Credit

A housewife in Memphis, Tennessee, finally received a watch which her husband selected as a Christmas gift eleven years before. Could any of your local stores equal this record? Do customers often purchase something on the layaway plan and then forget about it? How long do most stores hold merchandise?

How do business firms of your city speed up collections from "slow-pay" customers? By letter? Collection stickers on statements? Telephone calls? How can credit managers speed up collections and yet retain customer good will?

Crime

A Philadelphia reporter who covers the federal building received a post card from a former federal court attendant now in the penitentiary. It said, "Thanks for the excellent story—hope to see you soon—wish you were here!" Do judges and other court officials ever receive letters and post cards from prison inmates who were sentenced in their courts? Are some of the inmates grateful for the leniency shown in their sentences?

Citizens often forget that detection of criminals and their arrest is a teamwork affair, with several law enforcement agencies co-operating. Show the setup in your county: how the city, county, state, and federal enforcement officers often work together. And explain how prisoners are returned from other states.

"Banks," FBI Chief John Edgar Hoover once wrote, "are an almost irresistible attraction for that element of our society which seeks unearned money." Does your bank have any protective alarms? Are employees taught what to do in case of a holdup? How hard would it be to rob a local bank?

Have local officers used marked money in solving crimes? If so, has the plan always worked? If not, what went wrong?

How are suspicious deaths investigated in your city? Under what conditions should physicians encountering deaths under certain circumstances notify authorities immediately? What are some cases in which the circumstances are not clear cut?

Every community of any size usually has some type of unsolved murder. Find a number of these and combine them into one story. What was the unique, unsolved problem of each one? Are officers still attempting to find the murderer or murderers?

Seventy per cent of the car thefts of the nation are of the "joy-ride" type. Would that percentage apply in your city? Are the "joy-riders" mostly kids? Do they usually damage the cars? What are some of the reasons for the thefts in this class?

Thieves became supermen in stealing two anvils from a shop in Tennessee. What have been some of the largest "hauls" made in your city? Do modern thieves use trucks and other equipment in their big jobs?

Several thousand murders pass unrecognized in the United States each year, some authorities say. Responsibility for this failure to bring criminals to justice is laid directly on the coroner. More states are replacing coroners with medical examiners. What happens in your community when a person dies under unusual circumstances?

Thomas McGuire, a Boston policeman with an uncanny eye and

a memory for figures, is among the nation's best in recovering stolen cars. He and his patrol car partner recovered 250 stolen cars in two years—mainly because of McGuire's memory for figures. What is the average number of cars recovered each week or month by your local police? What system of trying to remember the license numbers of stolen cars do they use?

More and more cities sponsor some type of training program for their policemen. What are the subjects taught? Are they urged to correct the old conception that police are big bullies who bawl out everybody? How do policemen keep up with new techniques in crime detection?

Describe a typical day for your local chief of police. Show some of the day-to-day duties which may be unknown to most people. How did he become interested in law enforcement? Describe some of his unusual experiences.

In Tampa, police closed their books on a case of suspected murder after they got word from the FBI that the bones they had discovered in a trash pile belonged to a prehistoric Indian. Through the years, what are some of the stories connected with skeletons which have been dug up in your community? How is the age of the person estimated by experts who examine the bones?

Crops

Corn and tobacco are the only two crops that are indigenous to the United States. Where did all the others come from? What is the history of some of the favorite "American" foods that came from other countries? Sources for comments: county agents and instructors in agriculture at high schools or colleges.

Crop reports are issued regularly by statisticians of the U.S. Department of Agriculture in your region. How are the reports compiled? To whom are they sent? How many years have records been kept? How does weather affect crop conditions?

Custodians

Wastebaskets collect many strange items. A night janitor for a Dallas building said that he often finds overshoes and umbrellas in wastebaskets—placed there to keep the drippings off the floor. On other occasions, even a set of false teeth and a check got in the wastebaskets, but both were recovered. Talk to the head custodian in a large building and find out what has been lost or recovered in wastebaskets.

Customers

To what extent do customers return goods to stores? Who returns the most—men or women? Are all clerks taught how to handle returned merchandise? What age group is hardest to please?

Customs

It's not every day that customs inspectors at the border find an attempt being made to smuggle diamonds into the country in the heel of a man's shoe. But customs men have to deal with countless folks who try to bring in less important goods without paying duty on them. What are some of the excuses? Some of the unusual hiding places? Some of the unusual items? How long does it take to train a customs man to do his job well?

Are any vestiges of earlier social customs still apparent in rural neighborhoods near you? What's happened to the husking bee, the quilting party, and the house or barn raising? What are the chief social activities among farmers and farm families? Build your story on the then-and-now angle.

Dancing

Arthur Murray, noted dance teacher, once said that a married man usually enjoyed dancing with another woman, rather than his wife, because "his wife is likely to criticize her husband's dancing." Interview members of a dancing club and get their views. How many enjoy the newer steps rather than the older ones? Do they consider dancing a good exercise?

How long does it take a new dance to catch on in your city? Do the young people usually lead the way? Do the old dances, like the waltz, still interest a lot of people? Has the showing of so many dancers on TV started any trends in dancing? Instructors at dancing schools can give you the answers.

Dances aren't just dances. Many of them tell a story. Interview a dancing instructor and find out the differences in the dances of various nations. Are most dances following older tunes or the newer ones? What are some of the dances which are quite old but which retain a consistent popularity?

Television fans recently saw a lady of sixty-six years who dances "every night of the week and twice on Sunday." Who is the oldest square dancer in your community? How long have some of the club members been dancing? Seek comments from dancers answering the question, "Why do you like to dance?"

Dates

Writer Walter Lippmann decries the current practice of timing and dating. He notes that some morning newspapers hit the stands the night before, afternoon newspapers are published in the morning, March magazines come out late in January, fall and winter clothing is in store windows in summer, bathing suits are advertised in early spring, and so one. The practice of keeping ahead of the competition by "out-dating" them would make a good feature.

Death

What is the suicide rate in your city or county? How does it compare with other cities or counties? What is the chief reason for self-destruction? More men or women? Average age?

Debt

How much debt can you afford? Do you feel that you owe too much? What is a sound debt capacity on your income? Get tips from a number of credit experts and find out how much money a person can safely afford to owe.

Defense

Have you done a story lately on your local armory? When was it built? What units have served in wartime? Describe some of the equipment. How has equipment changed?

Dentists

One of man's oldest and most universal health problems is the cause of tooth decay. Why are some people completely "immune" to the bacterial disease known as dental caries. Approximately ninety-nine out of one hundred persons in the general population, dental authorities estimate, are susceptible to tooth decay. That other lucky individual is apparently resistant to the same decay process. Why? Have scientists been able to isolate the substance or bacteria? How is it formed? Local dentists should have something interesting to say.

One out of every seven people in the United States has never seen the inside of a dentist office, says an American Dental Association report. How often should an adult visit his dentist? A child? What can happen to the condition of teeth during delays?

Making a playhouse out of a dentist's office—and trying to convince the youngster that it's all just a game—is a ridiculous approach to child dentistry, an expert declares. Should children be treated as little adults? To what extent can dentists use psychology when working on children?

University of Minnesota scientists found that many women in their fifties and sixties and even many in their seventies had conditions of the mouth that were considered unsatisfactory for good mastication. Do women in these age groups neglect their teeth? What are some of the reasons for them to visit their dentists? Should some of them follow carefully planned diets?

Dial Phones

Wonders are taking place in the world of dial phones. Will all telephones eventually be operated so that there will be no need for operators? Will the new dialing devices cause more wrong numbers? Talk to an electrical engineer and find out how the new telephone "brain centers" operate.

Dictionaries

Dictionaries are being published in many sizes. Who are the biggest buyers—students, secretaries, teachers? Do newer ones show newer words and their meanings? Tie-in date: Samuel Johnson, English author and dictionary maker, was born on September 18, 1709.

Directories

Old, but always good: Any time a new city directory or telephone directory is published, you can do a story showing who is listed first

(Mr. Aabba led in one city) and who is listed last. Other angles: persons who bear names of celebrities, the longest name, the shortest name.

Discipline

"Discipline is the whole basis of society, and it is needed," an expert says. Do children want discipline and freedom, too? What are some "don't's" for teaching discipline? Could many disciplinary problems be solved through explanation rather than punishment? Combine the views of parents and teachers in a story.

Divorce

A woman in Oklahoma filed for divorce fifteen minutes after her marriage. When do most divorces occur—Five years after the wedding? Ten years? More? Get some comments on the divorce rate from a judge who has presided at many divorce trials.

Dogs

It's ten to one that your community has at least one unusual dog. It may be a mongrel known to everyone. How old is it? To whom does it belong? Can it do any tricks? Has it ever done anything unusual?

You'll get a lot of favorable reader reaction with this story: first aid for pets. What are some of the basic practices for good health? And what are some practices which might damage the health of pets? What about the amount of food required for various sizes and ages of dogs and other pets? Experienced veterinarians will know all the answers.

Interview a veteran judge of dog shows. What are his favorite breeds? Did he always have a dog as a youngster? What are the most difficult dogs to train? What are some of the characteristics he looks for in a dog?

Check with your city attorney and see if your city has any special laws regarding dogs. Are some of them out of date? Have some of them been the basis of cases in court? Is there an ordinance regarding the operation of a kennel within the city limits?

Life at the dog pound. What are the most popular breeds sought by people who adopt dogs? How many canines are picked up each year? Interesting experiences of helpers.

An inspector for a gas company in Arkansas uses a pedigreed English bloodhound in searching for escaping gas in the lines which feed seven towns. Use of dogs has proved more economical than mechanical devices. Are dogs used in any unique ways in your city? Your veterinarian should know.

An Ohio dog was given a thirty-five dollar funeral. How often do pet lovers have funerals for their dogs, cats, or other pets? Where are the pets buried? In what special way? Your veterinarian will know the answers.

Do-It-Yourself

Where do the "do-it-yourself" folks get the know-how for various jobs? Magazines? Books? Relatives or friends? Newspapers? School training? Special courses? Self taught? Here's another angle: How many adults have taken up some activity which they used during their younger days?

Drama

Is the American theater on the wane? How many plays are presented each year in your community? Does your community have a Little Theater? Is drama emphasized in the schools, the colleges, or the churches of your city? Does drama have something "different"— even in a day of TV? Comments of a drama teacher will give you a good story.

Don't overlook the public interest in the child actors of your city. Mention some of the outstanding ones and the productions in which they have appeared. Are their parents former drama students? Do they have professional ambitions for their children?

Dreams

How truthful are dreams? Would it improve a person's character to study his dreams? Dr. Calvin Hall recommends it in his book, *The Meaning of Dreams*. He tells of a tribe in Malaya which teaches its children about dreams, and whose adults guide their lives and government by their dreams! What do psychologists believe is revealed in dreams? Is daydreaming to be encouraged?

Here's one kid's dream that came true: A sixteen-year-old youth found seven hundred dollars in checks stolen from a dairy, so as a reward the president gave him all the ice cream he could eat in a year. Has any kid in your community received an unusual reward for a noteworthy act?

Drivers

Is safe driving due chiefly to the driver's skill? The Iowa State Traffic Laboratory revealed that the driver's emotions and attitudes about safety, speed, traffic laws, and other drivers are about as important as his mechanical skill. Localize these findings by quoting your chief of police, the head of the safety department, or teachers of driver training.

Driver Training

About one-fifth of public high school systems in the United States provide programs for driver education. What is done in your school system? How many students complete the course each year? Is it required? Are boys or girls better drivers when they are learning? What is the hardest thing to learn?

Drives

Someone has said, "I can remember back to the good old days, when charity was a virtue and not an industry." Are all successful charity drives organized nowadays? What about companies that do nothing but organize campaigns for worthy charities? Do organized drives net more than unorganized ones? What are some examples of successful charity drives?

To stir up rivalry, an organization often divides its members into two groups—Indians and cowboys for instance—when seeking funds or new members. How does this produce results? Why do people like the competitive element? Is it partly because everyone likes to be on the winning side? Check your chamber of commerce secretary, the head of your community chest, and others who must direct campaigns.

Driving

A Pennsylvania expert says it's murder in some cases for parents to try to teach their children to drive. A survey in that state shows home-trained youngsters were involved in three times as many traffic accidents and violations as those who had formal driving training. How does school or commercial driver training differ from most home training? Why is it better? How widespread is high school driver training?

Who says men are better drivers? A recent traffic survey shows that 37 per cent of women drivers tested made improper signals before turning, but 58 per cent of the men made improper signals. Ask traffic officers their opinions of drivers. Do women drivers have particular traits that differ from those of men? Do women react differently from men in heavy traffic or in near accidents?

Many hot rod clubs have an intensive safety program within their own organizations. The Ardmore (Oklahoma) Slowpokes fine a member 50 per cent of his traffic fine if he's convicted on a violation. What are similar groups doing around the country? Is the practice helping to counteract unfavorable publicity usually given hot rodders?

Druggists

Are you sometimes shocked when the druggist tells you the price of a prescription which he has filled for you? Why are some drugs higher than others? Why are so many modern drugs limited to prescription? Are many drugs expensive to manufacture? Talk to your pharmacist and you'll get a story which will have tremendous interest.

Almost ten thousand new drug items have been introduced since 1939, according to Food and Drug Administration records. And more than half of all drugs now being used by physicians and hospitals were unknown fifteen years ago. How does the modern druggist keep up his stock? What are some of the old drug items which are still in demand? Does an article about the curative power of a new drug in a magazine bring in a lot of prospective customers?

Early Birds

Your town has a few early birds. Who are they? Do they feel that they can do their best work early in the day? Give your story an amusing angle by getting their answers to the question, "Do you think everybody should get up earlier?" Do they really believe in the "Early to bed and early to rise" philosophy?

Easter

Bill Morgan, religious news editor of the *Oklahoma City Times,* did a Good Friday feature in this way: with the help of a university of religion, he superimposed a map of ancient Jerusalem on one of Oklahoma City. Thus the map showed how far Christ would have traveled from late Thursday evening until He went to Gethsemane.

Eating

A survey shows that about 19 per cent of the people of this country eat outdoors more than once a week during the summer, about 17 per cent eat outside weekly, and about 12 per cent every two weeks. Why do people enjoy eating outdoors? Has this rather new interest resulted in the sale of barbecue equipment and similar merchandise?

Education

Surveys show that unusually bright youngsters are happier when they are put in classes made up exclusively of children of their own mental caliber. What is being done about the extra bright children in your town? Is there any way they can be taught more, in less time, or do they have to be held back to keep them with the others? It's an important question in education. What do teachers and school administrators think about it?

Most colleges offer a wide variety of scholarships. How many does the college nearest you give? What is their total value? How many new scholarships are given each year? Do some grants or scholarships require unusual qualifications?

Athletes have to take their lumps sometimes in the classroom as well as out on the field. They're generally accused of being sub-par scholars. How about those in your town? Check with school officials to find how athletes rate with other students in class work. How many graduate? Go on to college? How much does sports take away from time that could be devoted to study?

Harvard offers scholarships to youths with the name of Murphy or Baxendale, and to boys who happen to live along the Chicago, Burlington and Quincy Railroad in Iowa! There may be similar unusual scholarships available in a college or university near you. Institutions of higher learning will be glad to supply you with all the facts of scholarships and grants.

Thousands of adults are enrolled in correspondence courses. What are some of the most popular courses? Average age of most students? Do many of the students want college credit, or do they just take the courses for fun or to improve their skills?

A well-known psychologist says girls are better in English, spelling, writing, and art; boys are better in arithmetic, history, geography, and science. What do local teachers think about such a statement? Although boys and girls may differ in particular talents, aren't abilities about equal on the whole?

Signatures that can be read only by someone familiar with them may be the sign of the successful executive, but poor penmanship can be a bad thing. One midwestern telephone company says it has lost as much as fifty thousand dollars in a single year because operators wrote so poorly that calls couldn't be properly charged. Do big companies have a course in legible writing for employees? What other examples can you find of the importance of clear writing in business?

A few years ago men enrolled in home economics courses were something of a rarity. Not so now. Lots of courses in home economics have one or two men in them. Why do they take such courses? Talk to them, and their teachers. What part of home economics is most popular with male students?

Lots of sports fans don't know the expense involved in putting a team on the field. Let your high school or college coach tell you the price of equipment, uniforms, training facilities, grounds upkeep, and ticket distribution. How big is the team's cleaning bill? How fast does equipment wear out? What about changes in sports style? Football helmets used to be leather, now they are plastic. Jerseys were long-sleeved and heavy, now they're short-sleeved and light.

Where do medical schools get the cadavers and skeletons they need to train doctors? Do popular prejudices keep some schools from getting enough? How many cadavers does a big medical school need each year?

College enrollments are increasing. What percentage of your high school graduates go on to college? Do most of them pick local schools, or do they go out of state? How many more high school graduates go to college now than went ten years ago?

Authoritative economists find that a college education is worth about $100,000 more than the cash value of training acquired by the average high school graduate. By using this angle you can get some excellent comments which will cut the number of "drop-outs" in your local system.

People today are flocking to movies—movies which show them how to step up their skills and abilities. How are movies being used as training aids in companies, stores, and institutions of your community?

There's always a story on the reformatory for girls in your state. How have teaching methods changed since the old days? What are the average ages. Ask the superintendent, "Do girls of today face more temptations than girls of yesterday?"

If you have a girls' school in your community, then you can tie in the birthday of Emma Hart Willard, pioneer in education for women, who was born February 23, 1787, in Berlin, Connecticut. Have beliefs regarding women's education changed through the years? Are women now specializing in fields of work once dominated by men?

How do you measure if a person is well educated? About forty thousand Michigan citizens voted it this way: (1) grammar and pronunciation; (2) ability to meet people; and (3) ability "to say what he means." Ask eight or ten persons what they consider the marks of the educated man.

Do we keep some children in school too long? Harvey Lehman, a psychologist, says that the big urge to create comes between eighteen and twenty-five, when enthusiasm runs high. Nearly all great achievers began doing important things in these early years. Should a person know what career he is going to follow before he is twenty-five? Is he losing time if he makes the choice later?

A West Point education for one man costs the government

$24,000. Localize this by finding out what it costs your city to educate a child from the first grade through high school. Or what it costs to provide four years of education to a college student.

Parents worry about schools. Many wonder if their children are getting a good education. Writers for *U.S. News and World Report* went to Europe and found that pupils over there learn more, work harder, and play less than in United States schools. Do parents think that their children work hard enough? Are teachers demanding enough? Interview parents and teachers.

Elections

Elections are a vital part of American life. Local election officials will be glad to tell you about the extra work necessary at election time. Who prints the ballots? What precautions are taken for voting secrecy? How long are ballots kept after an election?

Do a flashback story showing some of the turbulent elections of your county and city in past years. What were some of the most exciting? What were the issues? Who were the personalities? What types of situations bring the most voters to the polls?

Electricity

Thomas A. Edison first lighted a lamp containing a carbonized thread element on October 21, 1879. Use this date as the peg for a story about your local electrical system—its history, progress, and plans for the future.

What percentage of the farms in your county receive electric service? How much has the average annual use of electricity increased on farms? What are some of the newer uses for power on the farm?

The trend toward "electrical living" continues. How many types of electrical appliances are found in the average home? What is the most common? The rarest?

Dangerous occupation: trouble-shooter for the power company. What special precautions must he observe? Has he had any narrow escapes? Does he mind being called out of bed to repair broken lines during a night storm? Would he prefer another assignment with the company?

Electrocutions

How do men and women face death in the electric chair? "All men face death in the chair bravely," a veteran executioner stated, "because they want to show how courageous they are." The warden of your state penitentiary will reveal some of the sidelights of the condemned person's last few hours. What do they talk about? What advice do they give for those who may be contemplating lives of crime? How do they feel about death?

Elevators

An elevator operator who tired of wags saying, "I'll bet you have your ups and downs," now uses this answer: "It isn't the ups and downs that get me—it's the jerks." What are some of the amusing questions asked by passengers? Are some people afraid of being caught between floors? What are some of the safety precautions which are observed? Do operators tire of their work and change to other jobs? What are the qualifications of a good operator?

Employees

Appreciation for the work and devotion of a loyal employee is being shown by many companies after the person has been with the organization for ten or fifteen years. Instead of presenting a button or a badge, some companies now give watches or other presents. Do companies in your locality follow the plan of giving presents to an employee upon his retirement or after only a few years of service?

Southwestern Bell Telephone, like many other large organizations, gives its employees the A B C's of good public speaking. Sessions combine speech techniques, making speeches, and a diagnosis of the talks. How long does it take to get over the fright period? Are women better speakers than men? Is the training required for employees in certain categories?

Employment

How much of a stigma is attached to being discharged from a job? In the complexities of modern business life, what about the automobile worker who is laid off with thousands of fellow workers? What about the public official who loses his job in a patronage switch? Talk to personnel directors and others concerned with the work records of job applicants. What importance do they attach to being fired? Is the reputation of the former employer taken into account?

Older women seeking employment must have confidence in themselves, advises a bulletin of the Women's Bureau of the U.S. Department of Labor. What unique advantages does a mature woman have as an employee? How can she make the most of her background and maturity? Get suggestions from personnel directors and employment office heads.

Employers are setting higher requirements for college graduates that they add to their payrolls, one large insurance company reports. Are most graduates hired only after interviews? Approximately how many persons are employed after campus interviews by company representatives? In what fields are college graduates especially needed?

Surveys show that one out of four women with children under eighteen is now employed outside the home. What are the main types of work? How do they organize their home schedules? Do they find time to take part in church groups, clubs, and other activities?

How steady can a job be? Are there individual employee responsibilities in addition to company factors and changes in the general economic stability? How does the weather and other factors affect employment? Interview men and women high in management for the answers.

More than 50 per cent of the elderly employees in twenty companies are more dependable than younger ones, according to a survey. What about the production records of the oldsters? Absenteeism? Query a number of personnel directors and ask them in what ways some of the elderly employees are more reliable.

Here's one boss who used tact: He called in a man to fire him and said, "Son, I don't know how we're ever going to get along without you, but starting Monday we're going to try." In what ways do supervisors, directors of personnel, and others notify employees that their periods of service are near an end? Letters? Interviews?

Handicapped persons are engaged in a wide variety of worthwhile and interesting occupations. It is heartening that many employers have changed their attitude toward hiring the handicapped. Look around your community and write a series on people who are doing amazing jobs even though handicapped. Be sure to give the main philosophy of each person.

How many firms and organizations object to secret marriages? Do many firms have strict rules regarding the employment of married women? Or do most married women prove to be competent and stable workers? For interesting comments, talk to personnel directors or officials of employment agencies.

Engineers

About 88 per cent of the nation's 625,000 engineers are employed by private industry. Do they receive as much recognition as those working for the government? Why has industry employed so many engineers? What have been some of their major contributions? How many women enter engineering?

Women are quickly moving into jobs once reserved for men. For instance, there are now about 6,500 women engineers, compared to 730 in 1940. You'll probably find women engineers in your community. What type of work are they doing? Any special hazards in their duties? Why did they pick engineering as a career?

Evangelists

Evangelists depend on vocalists or other musicians to help them. Interview an evangelistic musician and see which songs are most popular. How does he feel that music helps in the success of the meeting? Interesting experiences in his travels will give you anecdotal material.

What advance preparation is made before an evangelist visits your city? What are the functions of the various committees? How is interest built up in the months and weeks preceding the revival? What are the duties of the advance man?

Exhibits

Exhibits and displays have been with us since Bible days. In the Book of Esther we find that King Xerxes of Persia (519-465 B.C.)

"shewed the riches of his glorious kingdom and the honoir of his excellent majesty many days, even an hundred and four-score days." Who arranges a big exhibit in your city? What are some of the problems? What are some of the newest trends in exhibits? More animation? Sound? Color?

Experiences

Riverboat captain J. W. Menke got a telegram in 1925 that read: "Most anxious to get in touch with your boat. Please wire details of summer itinerary." Menke had never heard of the woman who signed the telegram, Edna Ferber, so he filed it and forgot it. If he had answered it, Miss Ferber's *Show Boat* might have made his boat immortal. Can you find other stories of near misses in claims to fame?

Experts

When the light on the speaker's stand went out, members of the Dallas Electric Club—composed of electrical engineers and contractors—rose confidently. They traced wiring, inspected connections, and tore into the lamp base. Then a hotel employee discovered the bulb had burned out. Have any of your local experts been stumped with a simple problem?

Express

The pony express started on April 3, 1865. And even though it survived less than two years, the express became the subject of hundreds of frontier novels and movies. Use the date as a peg and explain modern methods of carrying the mail and express.

Two spotted woodpeckers, shipped from New York to St. Louis, pecked a hole in their shipping box and escaped. How many birds and animals are handled by express? Do some require special food? What was the largest handled? Smallest?

Expression

Peter Drucker reminds us that "in very large organizations, whether it is the government, the large business corporation, or the army, this ability to express oneself is perhaps the most important of all the skills a man can possess." That's why many firms issue correspondence manuals and encourage employees to attend company-sponsored public speaking classes and to improve their self-expression in other ways. Look around you, and you'll find a company or business organization with such a program. Tell it dramatically, and you'll have a good story.

Fabrics

Many of the newer fabrics do not lose their crease or shape in rain. Does this mean less business for cleaners? Will the day come when a garment may be manufactured with a "permanent crease"? Is special care important for the newer fabrics?

In this day of varicolored fabrics, a flashback story on the old ways of making dyes from roots, berries, and other products of nature would be of interest. Good bet: Interview an Indian woman on some of the old-time methods of dyeing—what they used; if the processes were the secrets of a particular tribe.

Fairs

Your fair association—whether county or state—has a story behind it. When was it started? What were some of the early problems? How are affairs of the association conducted? Special problems, like the weather. How much have fairs changed since the early days?

Fame

Where are they now? Who? Eight or ten of the notables of your community or state ten or twenty years ago. Select persons who were prominent or featured in headlines and show their present-day activities. Have their philosophies of life changed?

Families

A former portrait photographer in Washington, D. C., now makes a good living making and photographing family coats of arms. He found lots of people were interested in their family tree! How many persons in your area are concerned with their genealogy, their coat of arms, and the origin of their family names? Can anyone you know trace his family back more than two or three generations?

It's almost unheard of now for members of a family to spend the evening together—doing something as a family. Could families spend more time together? Could they play games and enjoy other simple forms of pleasure? Comments from pastors, leading citizens, and even some young people should make a readable story.

Ethel Barrymore, the great American actress, revealed in her autobiography that she "had a strong urge to belong to someone." And she stated that "it is characteristic of my family that we never talk intimately to each other about important things—never." What is happening in family circles today? Are members of a family as close as the families of yesterday?

Chances are that at least one family in your city has reared a large number of adopted children. Interview the husband and wife and ask if they can recall some of the incidents in rearing the children. At what ages were the children adopted?

Practically every county has at least one family musical group—a quartet, an instrumental trio, or a similar organization. Find a popular one and then find out how many engagements the group fills each year. Is everyone in the family a musician? Do Mother and Dad play with the kids? How long has the group been playing together?

Tolstoi said, "All happy families are alike; unhappy families, unlike. Each unhappy family is unhappy in its own fashion. The things that make marriage happy are few and simple—similar backgrounds, likes and dislikes, and philosophies of life." What makes a happy family today? Are the elements any different than they were in grandfather's day? Ask a family life expert or minister.

Less than a third of American families say grace at meals, a Gallup Poll reveals. Is the practice on the increase? What are churches doing to encourage prayer at meals? Do children or adults usually offer grace?

Who decides things in most families? Mother? Dad? Children? Or do all join in voting on matters which affect the whole family? Family councils are increasing in number. Interview members of families which have them.

Farming

"The Old Gray Mare Ain't What She Used to be"—on the farms.

How far has mechanization gone on the farms of your county? Do farmers mechanize because they find it difficult to hire farm laborers? Do many farms still use horses and mules? Best source for answers: the county farm agent.

No one doubts the effectiveness of the law of supply and demand in setting prices. Everyone seems to favor the good old free enterprise system. Yet when farmers vote on acreage allotments and support prices, they invariably cast their ballot for tight controls that mean guaranteed good prices for what they grow. Most rural areas vote several times a year on different allotment and control measures. It's a good time for interviews on how farmers feel about such legislation.

Who is the most successful young farmer in your region? Best source: your county farm agent. Find out about his program, his methods, and his philosophy of farming.

It's always news when a farmer develops something new or different, whether it's a well cover or a gate. Try to get a picture to use with the story.

Interview a brand inspector and find out how modern cattle thieves operate. How many brands are there in your territory? What are some of the oldest?

Agriculture experts have learned that hens in cool houses eat more and lay better. As a result, coops are kept cool with ventilation, insulation, and even the use of sprinkling systems. Do experts think it possible to breed a heat-resistant hen? How many years would be required? What facilities would be needed for developing a stock which will show a tolerance for heat?

Are farmers superstitious? Do some of them plant their crops because of certain superstitions? Or do most of them rely on suggestions of experts?

Plan to do a local story on plants to be published March 7. Luther Burbank, plant wizard, was born on that date in 1849. One angle: unusual plants which have been developed by horticulturists of your county or state.

The average farm hand's working day, once extending from sun-up to sundown, is now about eight and one-half hours, thanks to increasing mechanization. To what extent do farmers and their wives work together on certain projects? What is the farmer doing with an increase of leisure time?

The iron plow, which was invented by Charles Newbold in 1793, speeded up farm work. Today there is a school of thought which believes that land can be plowed too much and too often. How has the cultivation of land changed since the invention of the plow? How do modern farmers plow their land compared to the ways of their grandfathers?

How many veterans have returned to farms they left, or started their own? Is this a new experience for some of them? Were some too optimistic about farm life? What channels of assistance are open to farm veterans? Do most of them stick it out or quit after a short time? Best source: your county agent.

Modern farmers may have all sorts of mechanized equipment, but many of them still plant potatoes by the light of the moon. How prevalent are such legends and superstitions today? Is there any scientific basis for some of the beliefs? Talk to county agents and vocational agriculture teachers.

Do you have any successful women farmers in your community? Do they do it largely without any masculine aid? What is their past experience? How have farming methods changed? What are some of the jobs they feel they can perform better than men?

Fathers

Dad is so busy being a big shot in business that he doesn't devote nearly enough time to his kids, Philip Wylie reminds us. Are most fathers neglecting this opportunity to be companions to their children? Do mothers give more time to their children than do fathers? Do many fathers try to give at least several hours a week to their children?

Do new fathers still give cigars to friends upon the birth of their children? Is this the custom in the men's clubs of your city? Do most of the fathers buy quality cigars? The cigar store proprietor can probably give you some amusing slants on the custom.

Cigar Day: The Cleveland Hill Teachers Association in Buffalo, N. Y., petitioned the school board for one day's maternity leave for men. Should a new father be given a holiday upon the birth of a child? Even if a father works on that day, does he accomplish much?

Federal Agencies

Nation's Business reports that "while our population was doubling, government employment multiplied eight times; government payrolls multiplied twelve times; government expenditures multiplied seventy-one times." What does the average citizen think of these figures? Does he think there is too much waste? Too many agencies and bureaus?

Feet

Women's feet now average a full size larger than twenty-five years ago. And nine out of ten adults have some sort of foot trouble, chiropodists point out. Interview salesmen for women's shoes and ask if most customers insist on shoes too small for them. Does the practice of wearing flat shoes cause women's feet to become larger?

Fences

An alert Missouri reporter did a bang-up feature on the unusual fences in his city. So why not look around your city and find out the oldest fence, the newest styles, why many people like fences, and the types of locks used on some of the gates.

Field and Stream

Do fishermen outnumber hunters in the nation? In 1954 they did, 17,867,922 to 13,997,155. How does that percentage apply to your county or state? What percentage of the fishermen are women? How many women buy hunter's licenses?

Films

Color films are favored four to one, according to a survey made by the Association of National Advertisers. Furthermore, the survey revealed that the average business film lasts five years or more. Check with business leaders of your city and find out how films are being used more and more in management, training, sales, and other areas.

Two or three studies seem to indicate that "slow" children learn more from educational films than "bright" children? Is this true among children in the schools of your city? Talk to the person in charge of visual aids.

Football coaches often exchange films before their teams meet in a bowl game. Does each coach devise special plays for the big game in addition to those shown on the films or those seen by scouts? How are films analyzed by coaches in setting up defensive patterns against the opposing team?

The king of beasts has been greatly lionized, says Al and Elma Milotte, who have taken so many films of wild animal life. Do you have a photographer of wild life in your community? What has he observed in making films of animals? Does he take special precautions?

Does your city have a film council? Usually, such a group previews and evaluates new films, and it may also have a film library. If your city does not have such group, see if your school system has a committee to evaluate and select films for use in classrooms.

Finance
For as little as $300 a year, a university finance professor says, the average head of a household can have an individually planned savings program, adequate insurance coverage, and the assurance of a substantial net worth at the time of retirement. What is the main thing in a retirement program? Who should plan it?

Fine Arts
Millions of dollars worth of paintings, sculpture, and other works of art had to be moved to safety during World War II. Others were moved by military leaders to spots where they could personally enjoy them. How many of those art objects are still missing? Were many actually destroyed in the fighting?

Fire Fighting
Did your town once have a horse-drawn fire department? If so,

get in touch with retired firemen or other oldsters who can recall what happened in the old days. How were the horses trained? How fast could they pull the fire wagons? At what age were old horses replaced?

Does your fire department make regular inspections of fire extinguishers in public buildings, stores, and other establishments? If so, how often? Do persons in a building know how to operate an extinguisher?

Just how does a firebug operate? How does he start a fire? How can an investigator find clues in a pile of ashes? Does an arsonist prefer a certain kind of building? Is he likely to be more active certain days of the week? Your fire chief can give you slants on the firebug.

What do people try to save when their homes are on fire? Pets? Sentimental objects like photos? An experienced fireman can relate stories, some tragic and some humorous, about happenings in this realm.

Gone are the days when the fire chief had the only red car in town. Because of the flashy trend in auto colors, the Milwaukee fire chief decided to use a plain white car. But he decided to keep the traditional red for fire trucks. Is your fire chief ignored when he speeds to a fire? Does he still drive a red car? Has he thought of painting it another color?

Today's fire fighter is trained for two major tasks: fire prevention and fire fighting. What is involved in fire prevention? Are regular inspections made of buildings? Do firemen give talks at schools, civic club meetings, and other places? What percentage of fires are caused by carelessness?

Does your fire department have a board of strategy? If so, what are the objectives of the group? Does it study changes in industrial and commercial structures to see if any new hazards are involved? If hazards are found, does it advise the industries of such hazards and of how fires may be attacked if they occur?

Do-it-yourself fire fighting is deplorable, says the fire chief of East Moline, Illinois. "Don't be embarrassed to call for an investigation by the fire department, if you smell smoke or even suspect a fire," he said. Use this idea as the peg on which to get suggestions from the local fire chief.

Fireplaces

Benjamin Franklin, annoyed at the fireplaces of colonial America, wrote, "They almost always smoke if the door be not left open. . . . A man is scorched before, while he is froze behind." How are modern fireplaces built? What percentage of the new homes in your city have fireplaces? Do some of the older homes still have fireplaces in the bedrooms?

Fire Prevention

Does your community elect a Miss Flame as a part of Fire Prevention Week? If so, what are her duties? Who chooses her? How does she help stress fire prevention?

There are 1,150 fires in United States homes every day. Nine out of ten are caused by human carelessness. And every year twelve thousand Americans die in fires. Get a list of specific precautions from the fire chief. Summarize by showing the total loss caused by fires in your community in a year.

Does your community sponsor a poster contest for kids as a part of Fire Prevention Week? If so, is it limited to certain grades? Who are the judges? Are the winning posters exhibited? Then humanize your story by interviewing the winner. Where did he get his idea?

With a great increase in the use of power mowers, more people keep gasoline. What are its dangers? What is the best type of receptacle? Where should the receptacle be kept? What precautions should be kept in mind in its storage and use? Your fire chief has the answers.

Fire Stations

In some cities, visiting officials and dignitaries are sometimes housed in fire stations. Who decides? List some of the guests who have stayed at fire stations. Are some given meals in addition to rooms?

Fish

Raising tropical fish is an absorbing hobby. It is the focus of a one-hundred-million-dollar annual business of dealers, importers, breeders, and equipment manufacturers. Today there are approximately two hundred amateur societies in the nation. If there's one near you, find out: What is the lure of tropical fish? How much do certain species cost? Is the hobby an old one? How does a person get started? Where can you buy tropical fish? How do you start an aquarium? What do you feed the fish?

Fishing

Fishermen who are inclined to rest and spin a yarn or two can sit on a special "Liar's Bench" in Sarasota, Florida. Your local group may not have a special bench, but you can round up a number of tall tales related by fishermen. Are some of the stories told, dropped for several years, and then told again?

Do loud noises and talking disturb fish, as some fishermen believe? That's just another fish story, experts say. Can fish hear? In what way are they sensitive to movements about them or reflections in the water? Get experts to tell of any unusual incident showing a little-known characteristic of fish.

Bullfrogs are considered fish by California law. Therefore, an angling license is necessary in that state to catch bullfrogs. Are there any frog hunters in your region? What is the best way to catch them? The best time?

Look around and see if you can find a woman who lives near a fish pond or river in your community and sells fish. What kind of bait does she use? What are some of her biggest catches? Why does she like outdoor life?

Do a story on the oldest fishermen in your community for publication on August 9. Anniversary angle: Isaac Walton, the "Father of Angling," was born on this day in 1593. Do the aged fishermen still use the same kind of tackle and lures they did years ago? Why do they enjoy fishing?

Flag

Francis Bellamy, author of the pledge of allegiance to the flag, was born May 18, 1855, at Mount Morris, New York. Flag Day proclamations naming Bellamy as the pledge author have been issued by governors of at least forty-five states. To what extent is the flag salute used by local organizations? By schools? Do most people actually know the words, or do many of them mumble along with the audience?

Floods

Damage by floods in America totals between $200,000,000 and $500,000,000 each year. How do floods start and gather momentum? What can man do to prevent them and control them? An expert conservationist can give you facts and comments which will make a fascinating story.

Florists

Florists are greatly concerned about the practice of including, in death notices, the suggestion that friends contribute to a memorial fund "instead of flowers." How are florists counteracting this practice? Best source: state or regional florist association official. Or, without mentioning the obituary angle, you might show the many new ways of using flowers for everyday and special occasions.

Flowers

How many varieties of wild flowers are grown in your state or region? What is the rarest? Are there more or fewer varieties than a few years ago. Good sources: high school or college science teacher or competent local naturalist.

A teen-ager sent his girl her first orchid with this note: "With all of my love and most of my allowance." What are some occasions on which a boy sends the first corsage to a girl? Are they shy in giving the order? Do boys prefer certain kinds of flowers? Your florist will give you enough comments for an amusing story.

Folk Songs

Your region, like many others, probably has its own folk songs. Have some of them been recorded? Have others been passed from one generation to the next just by singing them? Who is the best-known folk singer in your region? How many old songs does he know?

Folklore

Your community is a combination of people, influences, and

things. The log cabin, for instance, came to us from the Swedes; the branding irons of the Southwest came to us from Spain, via Mexico; and segments of our music originated in Africa. Best bet for a story: interview a local history teacher, sociologist, or a student of local folklore.

Food

Why is French cuisine acknowledged by many as the most savory in the world? The secret is in the delightful and imaginative use of sauces. How can sauces enhance the flavor of dishes? What are some easy-to-prepare standard sauce recipes? How can economical dishes be glamorized with sauces? Sources: chef, home economics teacher, or housewife who is known for her cooking ability.

Americans drink millions of gallons of coffee every year. How much of it is served in your town's busiest cafe or restaurant on a cold winter day? How much do coffee sales fall off in summer? Do fluctuations in the price of retail coffee affect consumption noticeably?

Doctors say too much weight means too much work for the heart. That means some folks have to diet, and that's easier said than done sometimes. Talk to men and women who have successfully lost pounds by dieting. Does it work for everyone? What methods are best? After a dieting "spree" of several months, how hard is it to keep weight down?

Menus at fashionable eating places used to be printed in French. Now, although "soup du jour" is still a pretty common term for the day's soup special, most menus are in English. Why the change? Is there a psychological difference between the languages when it comes to food? Most persons think there is a relation between the language in which a menu is printed and the price that is charged. Is such thinking justified?

The world's heaviest eaters, according to the United Nations statistical yearbook, are the Irish, who average 3,500 calories a day. The United States, with 3,210 calories per day per person, is well down the list. Do many people pay much attention to the number of calories in their meals? Ask dieticians about the suggested calorie intake for different types of persons.

In twenty years, shrimp consumption has risen from 150,000,000 pounds a year to over 240,000,000. Ocean perch, virtually unknown in America two decades ago, is now being consumed at the rate of 200,-000,000 pounds a year. Write a story showing how fish is packaged, preserved, and processed.

The favorite recipe at the Lime Rock Inn near Salisbury, Connecticut, is Old English Kidney Stew. But eating places don't have to date back to 1720 to feature special foods. Even the corner beanery can have an extra fine way to cook and serve beans. What are some of the favorite recipes of restaurants in your area? Does the recipe have an age or method of preparation worth telling about? Or is it a guarded secret? How often is a special item on the menu asked for by new patrons?

Here's an interesting feature idea: Ask six or eight men to discuss "The Dinner I'd Love To Come Home To." In each instance, give the complete menu and note anything special or unusual, even in the way the man would like to have the food prepared.

How do customers buy meat? A survey was made among members of a consumer panel for a national magazine, and the results showed that 67 per cent selected their own meat. Interview a veteran butcher and get his comments on the meat-buying habits of his customers.

About one-fourth of all food eaten in the United States is fresh fruits and vegetables. Fruits and vegetables, mostly fresh, provide over nine-tenths of our Vitamin C, about two-thirds of our Vitamin A, a quarter of our iron, about a fifth of our carbohydrates, and 7 per cent of our protein. Check on the sale of fruit and vegetables in your community. What are the biggest sellers? Do fresh fruits and vegetables continue to sell well in spite of the competition of processed foods?

In days gone by the family gathered around the dining table to eat three times a day. It was more than a time of enjoying good food—members of the family exchanged experiences. How much time does the average family spend around the dining table today? In many instances, does each one prepare his own snack and eat alone? Do dieticians deplore the passing of the leisurely old meal with its attendant enjoyment?

Groucho Marx once bought a frankfurter and said, "Give me the bottom one—I'm always for the underdog." Are hot dogs still as popular as they were? On what occasions are they sold in your community? Do some drive-ins feature them? Are teen-agers the biggest consumers?

Does anyone make sorghum in your part of the country? Describe each step in the process—how the juice is squeezed from the sorghum cane, how it is boiled, and when it is finally ready. Has one family used the same method for generations? Who buys most of it—tourists, stores, or friends?

If a person is over forty-five, odds are one to four that he will be on some kind of diet before he reaches his next birthday. What are some present-day diets? Special diets? Is it difficult to stay on a diet? Talk to several dieticians and medical specialists.

In the average American family budget, food accounts for 30 per cent of the outlay. Is this true in your city? Does it vary from month to month? Does the average family try to stick to a certain amount for food each month? How many housewives have little or no idea about the amount spent for food each month?

Experts say that today's homemakers can spend as little as ninety minutes fixing breakfast, lunch, and dinner for a family of four. Take this idea and do a flashback: interview a few old-timers and show how much time women used to spend in cooking. Do some of the elderly ladies still prefer some of the old-time methods?

Dieters, take notice: the color of your dining room walls may be increasing your appetite. Yellow, orange, or orangy-pink walls can make you want to eat more, says an expert on paints. Soft green and soft gray won't stimulate your appetite. And charcoal gray or deep brown can take away all desire for food. Do restaurant and cafe owners take these ideas into consideration in their interior decorating? What do paint salesmen think about this?

Frequently the most popular cuts of meat are the most expensive. But there's no more food value in a filet mignon than in a less expensive cut. Let an experienced butcher give you the facts of best buys in meats. Pass the information along to the housewife in a money-saving feature. Another point: find where the various cuts of meat come from on a beef, hog, or sheep.

Timely summer feature: Food poisoning outbreaks increase during the summer. Potato salad, coconut cream layer cake, and lunch meat sandwiches are among the foods often involved. Talk to public health officials and get their advice on (1) preparation and care of food, and (2) precautions which every person should remember in his eating habits.

Men do one thing better than women: they eat a better breakfast. A survey revealed that 44 per cent of the men and only 29 per cent of the women over twenty-five eat a well-balanced breakfast. What do local men prefer for breakfast? Do working girls eat a bigger breakfast than housewives?

Run a story on the favorite recipes of eight or ten grandmothers. Have some of them been used in the family for many years? What do grandmothers think of all the emphasis on box mixes?

The man of the house used to say, "What's cooking for dinner?" Now he asks his wife, "What's thawing?" Do women can as much food as they used to? You might get an elderly woman to compare cooking methods of today with those of fifty years ago.

Do men or women have more dislikes in food? Which is the more critical, not only of the item but of how it is prepared? What are some foods most disliked by men? By women? For answers, talk to a cafeteria manager or several waitresses.

Does the housewife pushing the grocery cart really know much about food prices? Does she know a bargain when she sees one? Does she know how to pick better quality food—vegetables and fruit, for instance? Are most women buying food just thinking of the next meal or two rather than being concerned about prices?

There's a story behind the oldest cookbook in your community. When was it published and where? Do some of the recipes call for ingredients no longer used? Did any of the recipes call for alcoholic beverages? Have some of the recipes been used by the family owning the book for years and years?

More than one-fifth of the nation's families own a home freezer. Turn the clock back and show how food has been preserved through the years. Interview some old-timers who can remember when the family butter supply was suspended in the well to keep it cool.

Football

Who handles the microphone at the football games? Do certain persons or groups try to get free publicity over the public address system? What types of announcements are prohibited? Who determines the policy regarding announcements?

Forest Fires

With increased travel in forest areas of the nation, foresters and other interested citizens are greatly concerned about fire damage. With the help of Smokey the Bear, thousands of campers and travelers have been taught better outdoor habits. What is being done in your area? Check with your state forester or commissioner of conservation, or write the U. S. Forest Service, Washington 25, D. C.

Here's an alibi given by a man arrested for starting a forest fire: he had a small fire in his back yard; a rabbit ran through it, caught on fire, and dashed into the woods, thus setting the woods on fire. Talk to a forest ranger and find out some of the strange alibis used by folks who are questioned about starting fires.

Fraternal Groups

Try this: do a story on the origin and history of the emblems used by the fraternal groups of your city. And with each description, you can give a few facts about the achievements and objectives of each organization.

Fraternities

Many school systems have bans against the organization of fraternities and sororities. Does your school system permit social groups? If not, do some students organize social groups which have no relationship with school life?

Freaks

In 1896 the famous Barnum and Bailey Circus exhibited a "horse-less-carriage"—an automobile—as a freak. What modern-day machines, inventions, or objects, now misunderstood by many, are likely to prove as necessary as the automobile? Is anything new—whether an idea or an invention—likely to meet public acceptance?

Fruit

Do a story on the most successful fruit raiser in your region. What are some of his problems? When did he start? How is fruit carried to market? What was the greatest crop year? Are people eating more fruit?

Fund Raising

Your city has one champion fund-raiser—and he is usually sought by many groups. What are his secrets? Why is he so successful? Does he think that there are too many drives? What caused him to become interested in this work?

Funerals

In less than a century, the funeral director has changed his title from "undertaker" to "mortician" and finally to "funeral director." How did the profession grow? How much education or training is required to receive a diploma? Is there a shortage of experienced funeral home employees?

Mark Twain once remarked that a community can be known for the funerals it holds. To what extent have funeral services changed through the years? Are some of the funeral customs ancient? What are some of the problems which a funeral director faces?

Do Indians follow any unusual custom at their funerals? Have they gradually changed their burial practices? Is Indian music used at modern funerals? Get the views of an old Indian, a government official who works with Indians, or a teacher who has a knowledge of customs.

Furniture

Now you can rock away your troubles. Thomas E. Saxe, Jr., has organized the Sittin' Starin' 'n' Rockin' Club. It's purpose: to bring back the quiet, peaceful, rhythmic squeak of the old-fashioned rocking chair. Check with furniture dealers and find out about sales of rocking chairs. How many people still prefer them to modern chairs? Are many homes without rocking chairs of any kind?

The young homemaker—or even the older one—faced with the task of furnishing her home, finds herself dizzy with furniture terms. What are the most popular styles of furniture? Will early American blend with modern furniture? Is veneer furniture inferior to solid? How can you select good upholstered furniture? How can luxurious and practical furniture be selected?

Manufacturers are offering "super size" bedding. Sheets, blankets, and beds are tailored to the new 82½-inch mattress, six inches longer than the old standard type. What percentage of people are tall enough to need extra long beds and sheets? Do they find in their travels that hotels and motels have beds large enough for them?

About 80 per cent of the antique furniture in America is a fake, declares Gordon Obrig, one of America's pioneer home furnishers and industrial designers. What precautions should be observed in buying antique furniture? Is a dealer willing to put on the bill of sale the approximate age and source of the antique? Are a lot of worms getting credit for holes they never made (hot copper wires are sometimes used to give a table a worm-eaten appearance)?

Design in furniture has undergone some revolutionary changes. Talk to an old-timer in the business and ask him what he thinks of modern furniture? Does he prefer the older patterns? Are modern chairs, for instance, more comfortable than the ancient ones? What styles will always be in demand by the majority of buyers?

Games

Nine million Americans play chess. It is one of the oldest games, and one of the few that can be played between two persons who do not understand a word of each other's tongue. Actually, luck has nothing to do with the outcome; the better player always wins. And experts point out that, contrary to popular notion, it is easy to learn. What unique talents are required? Is chess as popular as it has been? What nation has produced the best players? Do more men than women play?

What are the favorite games of firemen, policemen, and others who often have time on their hands? Give some of the champions, of both yesterday and today.

Check with local stores and find out the names of the most popular games. Are some more popular in summer or winter? Do certain games have followers among all ages of persons? Have certain games always been rather popular?

What makes a game "catch on?" Why is it that one type of game —bridge, for instance—is popular year after year? What are some games which enjoyed a brief popularity and then were forgotten?

Gems

Small wonder diamonds are expensive! In a typical diamond mine, only one in thirty-five million parts of the material mined is diamond. What's the rest? What's the story of mining and processing the world's best known gem?

General

Close to 90 per cent of the United States' supply of chewing gum is made by three American firms. How about the sales of chewing gum in your city? Is the bubble gum fad still going strong? Do people who are trying to quit smoking switch to chewing gum?

Why not write a story about the blind and handicapped who ask for donations in the business district? What is their philosophy of life? When are people most generous? Does weather affect the size of gifts?

Unknown to many persons is the jargon of printers. Talk to a veteran printer and get some of the more interesting phrases and explain their meaning, how they originated, and how they are used.

Has your county ever engaged in any boundary quarrels? How were they settled? Have some of the boundary lines been changed? Any evidence of old markers?

How many people follow the adage, "Early to bed, early to rise"? Has television made a difference in the time at which most people retire? Do old-timers think that most people stay up too late?

Wilfred Funk declares that in the arsenal of anti-social traits, tardiness is probably the most selfish one of all. Do most people take pride in being on time? How do employers feel about this trait? School teachers?

Dr. Walter B. Pitkin, author of *Life Begins at Forty* and other books, says it's a mistake to conceal an error because it may come out of hiding some day and bite you. When should you admit your blunders? News slant: get comments from local leaders and see if they think Pitkin is right.

Millions of greeting cards are sold each year. And you can get one for almost any occasion—happy or sad. What types of cards are in greatest demand in your town? What are the biggest seasons for selling cards? How many different types of stores now handle greeting cards?

Today psychologists and educators bear the glad tidings that intelligence can be increased by as much as 10 to 20 per cent. Take this fact and tie it in with a story about evening classes, adult education centers, hobby classes, and other activities.

Ghost Town

In its heyday, the late 1870's, Bodie, California, had a population of twelve thousand and was known as the roughest, toughest of all the rip-roaring gold-rush boomtowns in California. Today two people live there. Can you find a ghost town in your region? How many persons live there? Describe its activities during its boom days. What caused its decline?

Gifts

Solicitations form the major headache in most communities. The mounting number of appeals for charitable, health, welfare, civic and other causes is felt in every community. It is getting more difficult to get persons to serve on soliciting teams. How are heads of your local groups handling this problem? Do they depend, for the most part, on the same people year after year? What incentives do they use to attract people for volunteer work?

How many gifts are exchanged, particularly at Christmas time? Do men or women lug back the most gifts? Do most men know the right sizes for their wives? How do store managers regard the exchanges?

What do people seek when they buy gifts? Something different? Foreign-manufactured articles? What are the main seasons for gift buying? Do women or men buy more gifts? Can a buyer for a gift shop predict what will become a popular item? What are some items which seem to retain their popularity year after year?

Girl Scouts

Senior Girl Scouts, fourteen to seventeen years old, use their Girl Scout activities to explore and "sample" quite a few career possibilities. This sampling is based on training followed by volunteer service. See how many find their careers in this way.

You can usually do an interesting story on a father who is an active leader in the Girl Scouts. Did his daughter cause him to become interested?

On March 12, 1912, Daisy Gordon met with ten other young girls in Savannah, Georgia, and organized the first patrol of Girl Guides, which later developed into the Girl Scouts. Daisy's aunt, Mrs. Fuliette Low, who was acquainted with the Boy Scout program in England, suggested that the girls meet. Use this date the next time you do a historical feature on the Girl Scouts of your community.

Girls

High school girls primp and worry more about clothes than college girls, Mary Ryon states in *Science Digest*. Only 15 per cent of college girls refuse dates because of not having the "right" clothes. At what age does a girl really become clothes conscious? Do high school girls make some of their own clothes? Are they influenced by styles worn by TV and movie stars?

Glad Hander

In the care and feeding of celebrities, Grover Whalen of New York is America's unchallenged expert. He describes his experiences in the book, *Mr. New York*. Who handles the bigwigs who visit your city? Do arrangements often go haywire? How does the weather affect events? Are there a few people who always "crash" some official receptions?

Glass-making

The glass industry in America began in 1609 at Jamestown, Virginia, where eight Dutch and Polish glass blowers sent over by a London firm began making crude glass articles for the settlers. How have glass production methods changed through the years? What is the principal ingredient? What is the temperature of molten glass?

Glass-making, which was started by Virginia colonists in 1609, is said to be the first colonial industrial undertaking in America. You might use this fact as a peg if you do a story on a local glass plant. How have methods of manufacture changed through the years? How does the demand for certain products change from time to time?

Gold

King Midas, with his talent for turning to gold all that he touched, cannot compete with the golden touch of modern research. The glitter of gold is seen on dresses, shoes, tablecloths, place mats, upholstery, drapery fabrics, and other items. Get a story on the "golden look" from one of the buyers in a department store.

Golf

Do you have a trick shot golfer in your state or community? If so, how did he become interested in this phase of golf? Where has he given exhibitions? Is he a consistently good golfer, or do his score cards indicate the ups and downs of the typical player?

An avid golfer recently claimed to have played on more than one thousand different courses, in nearly every state in the union. There's probably a man in your local golf club who has played a lot of courses, in widely separated places. How about a story on well traveled golfers, both in the distance they go to get to other courses, and in the miles they walk after they get there.

A California sporting goods shop advertised, "We sell everything a golfer uses except profanity, and if you use our goods you won't need that." Interview your golf pro and get his slants on human nature as revealed in golfers. In what ways does a golfer reveal his feelings and attitudes in his game? In what ways does golf help a person psychologically?

Gossip

Almost one hundred years ago a telegraph line, attached to trees, was set up between Virginia City, Nevada, and Placerville, California. In time, the wire became loose and lay on the ground like loops of trailing wild grapevine. During the Civil War, when telegraph lines were used by troops they were dubbed grapevine telegraphs. In those days, reports via telegraph were often false and conflicting. So, the name, shortened to grapevine, became synonymous with the spread of gossip and rumor. How do rumors spread? Who starts them? Good sources for answers: psychologists, sociologists, and experts in mass communications.

Government

Most folks are unaware of the many safeguards provided by agencies of government. How many tests and safety features are provided in your municipal water system? Trace the path of a glass of water from well, river, or lake to home spigot. Show the series of tests made, the purification steps taken, and the safety factors considered. Interview the water superintendent, mayor, or city manager. How soft is the water? Or how are hard water sources treated to make the water softer?

Supplies for offices and buildings used by the federal government cost about two billion dollars a year—and include everything from apple butter to blow torches to eggbeaters. What are some of the other unusual items in the more than two hundred thousand Uncle Sam buys each year? Is any progress being made toward simplification of buying procedures?

What's in a name? Probably there's a good opportunity to substitute a set of initials. Quiz your readers. Do they know the words in back of letter sequences they see every day? Ask them about FCC, ROTC, AEC, AAA, REA, FTC, TVA, and others. How many remember what NRA stands for? HOLC, WPA, PWA, CCC?

How many people are concerned about the federal debt? Does your community still seek federal funds for varied purposes? Do some federal projects compete with private business? Get the views of bankers and high officials on the possibility of reducing the national debt.

Campaign tactics have changed much since the days of the stage coach and covered wagon. Long campaigns were necessary because a candidate could be seen and heard by only a few hundred or a few thousand voters at a time. Now the candidate must have a successful TV personality. What makes a good TV political personality? Looks? Charm? Showmanship? Speaking ability?

It was only a few years ago that the federal government got the War of 1812 off the books, with the death of the last pensioners who were related to survivors of that war. Are we still paying for the Mexican War? Contact the Bureau of the Budget in Washington.

Franklin Pierce, the fourteenth president of the United States, went through his entire term of office without making a single cabinet change. But it's a different story with most presidents. How many men have served on all the cabinets of all the presidents? Who served the shortest time? Who served under the most presidents? What unusual stories of cabinet life can you dig up from almanacs, encyclopedias, and other reference books?

An Oklahoman has a collection of buttons, badges, and banners of yesterday. Among them are the following slogans: "Our Hero, Col. George Dewey," "16 to 1," "Liberty Loan Volunteers," "Bread and Butter for Bacon and Beans," "William Jennings Bryan, Our Next President," and "The Man of the Hour, Woodrow Wilson." Chances are that someone in your community has a similar collection. Even a list of the slogans will give you an interesting story.

One losing candidate for public office submitted his expense sheet which showed that most of his funds were used to buy cheese and crackers for himself during the campaign. If your city or county requires candidates to itemize their expenses, then look over a few after the next election for a story.

Fire and police departments continue to train their employees at regular intervals. What provisions are made for this continuing training where you live? Do policemen, deputy sheriffs, and firemen attend sessions at home, at the county seat, or at the state capitol? Do heads of departments attend annual meetings for idea exchanges?

There are national associations of all kinds. How about your city manager, mayor, librarian, county assessor, dog catcher, and health department supervisor—do they attend the regular meetings of their national or regional professional associations? What other methods do they use in keeping up with late developments in their fields?

Are there old-timers in your town who were once members of the state legislature? Get their views on modern legislative methods. How does present-day campaigning compare with earlier methods of luring voters?

Nearly all states have official flowers, birds, trees, songs, flags, and emblems. How many of your local folks know what they are? What is the origin of them?

Grades

Try this: If your school system isn't too large, get the names of high school seniors who have come up to their final year in high school with straight "A" grades. More boys or girls? Which high school (if you have more than one) has the most? How many students had all "A's" except for the grade in one course? Are most of the honor students active in school affairs?

Grandmothers

A grandmother can be a heaven-sent blessing or she can be a pain in the neck, declares a columnist. Ask a number of grandmothers, "What are your responsibilities to your daughter-in-law, son-in-law, grandchildren, and others?" "When can you give help without interfering?"

Gratitude

When John Rowell of Rutland, Vermont, helped two women in distress by removing their abandoned automobile stalled on a railway crossing, all he got was a "thank you" followed by the comment, "You shouldn't have done it. The car was getting old anyway." How grateful are people today? Is ingratitude too prevalent?

Gravestones

Charlie Starr of Ovid, Michigan, ordered his own gravestone. Has this ever been done in your city? If so, did the person write his own epitaph? What were his reasons for ordering the stone?

Guns

Some historians say that the use of guns dates back to 1346, when firearms were used for the first time in the Battle of Crécy. Someone in your locality has a collection of guns or knows enough about types of guns to give you a better-than-usual story.

Habits

Americans don't "say it with music" any longer, they say it with greeting cards. Some four million cards are sold each year at a cost of more than $350,000. Of course the big greeting card events of the year are birthdays, anniversaries, and holidays, but cards are available for some five thousand other occasions. What are a few of these "other occasions"? Are some cards favorites year after year? What unusual types of novelty cards are popular?

It's a popular notion that women like men who smoke pipes. But is it true? Make a poll of women. Do they prefer that their men smoke pipes rather than cigars and cigarettes? Or do they care? If they admit they like pipes, find out why? Fewer ashes on floor? Aroma? Appearance? Expense?

Halloween

Residents of Circleville, Ohio, celebrate an annual "punkin show" each fall. Prizes are given for the largest pumpkin, the largest pie (a five-foot one holds the record), and other special events. Does your community observe Halloween in a special way?

Handicapped

The Twentieth Century Club of Twin Falls, Idaho, saw to it that polio patients did not lose out on learning by paying the salary of a teacher for them. Has any individual or group in your community done something unique for handicapped persons or someone who is ill?

What is being done in your state to help severely disabled job seekers? These include the cerebral palsied, paraplegics, hemiplegics, the blind, and the more severe cardiacs. Most of them have probably undergone rehabilitation and are ready for employment. Your state employment office and agencies like the division of vocational rehabilitation can furnish figures and stories showing how many persons have capitalized on their calamities.

Hand-shaking

The grip power of your hand, if you're an average man, is between 60 and 130 pounds, and, for a woman, between 30 and 70 pounds. Does a public official increase the strength of his grip by using his hand more? Are there secrets of shaking hands without suffering from soreness afterward?

Handwriting Experts

How is handwriting analyzed by experts? One expert says, "Handwriting is brain-writing. An expert forger has to write backward to keep from revealing his personality." How are the experts in crime detection trained? Cite some of their most puzzling cases.

It's said that Napoleon's handwriting was so poor that sometimes his letters were mistaken for maps of battlefields. Some of this country's top literary figures write poor longhand. What correlation is there, if any, between a "good hand" and intelligence? Teachers can discuss trends in penmanship in recent years.

Happiness

Fifty-seven per cent of the people think they are fairly happy, 38 per cent consider themselves very happy, and only 4 per cent are convinced that they are unhappy, a national opinion poll revealed. Are most people fairly happy? What would make some of the unhappy ones happy? Are some persons neutral on the subject?

Headaches

Americans swallow about fifty-three million aspirin every day, which means that one out of every three persons in the United States has a headache or is feeling less than tiptop. Do modern folks have more headaches than their forefathers? Does the stress and strain of life today boost the consumption of aspirins?

Health

The average American today loses teeth at the rate of four-tenths of a tooth per year between the ages of fifteen and sixty-five. Before thirty-five, decay is the prime cause of tooth loss, while beyond thirty-five, the major factor is disease of the gums and supporting tissues. Get additional comments from officers of your local dental society.

Care and transportation of the sick and injured is a major problem in many localities. Well-meaning spectators often do the wrong thing when someone is injured. How many persons in your community have taken a Red Cross first aid course? Have all ambulance drivers passed a course in first aid? In the event of a major catastrophe, how many trained persons could be obtained in your community?

A national magazine really stirred up comments when it published an article, "Our Boys—Are We Raising Them Too Soft?" About 52 per cent of the letter writers agreed with the article's accusation. Forty-eight per cent were in sharp opposition. Get the comments of draftees, mothers, fathers, physical education instructors, and others.

Most leaders try to keep physically fit for their jobs by exercising in one way or another. John Adams fished and rode horseback. Thomas Jefferson tried to ride daily. John Tyler fished and hunted. John Quincy Adams, so the story goes, used to take a morning dip in the Potomac. Dwight Eisenhower enjoys golf. How do your city or state leaders shed the cares of their jobs? What are their favorite forms of recreation? Are some of the leaders more or less spasmodic in their leisure time activities?

Many ailing folks ask pharmacists to prescribe for them. Under what conditions can druggists suggest remedies? What are they forbidden to do? What are some drugs and preparations which they cannot sell without prescriptions? Are these practices governed by city, county, state, and national laws? Can a pharmacist do something in an emergency which he could not do otherwise?

If you are going to a doctor for the first time, try to make it easier for him and yourself by bringing an outline history of your medical life, a columnist advises. What should the history contain besides ailments and operations? Is he interested in other doctors who have treated you? Get suggestions from a number of doctors and then compile a list of suggestions for a feature story.

"Beware of quack cancer treatments," warns Dr. Charles E. Horton of Duke University. "There is no secret cure." He completed a study of sixty-four cancer patients referred to the university after treatment by quacks. Why do people go to quacks? Are they poor and ignorant? Fearful? Looking for a miracle worker? Are some of them in hopeless stages?

Four per cent of the nurses in the United States are men. Why did they decide to become nurses? Where were they trained? What special qualifications are essential? What are modern working conditions? In what special fields are men especially needed? Is the need for male nurses likely to become greater?

A research organization in Chicago reveals that on a comparable basis, men account for 70 per cent of the prolonged absences in industry and women for only 30 per cent. How does this compare with absences due to sickness in your community? Are minor illnesses the cause of most absences? Do doctors believe that women can resist disease better than men?

Muscular fitness tests were given to European and American children. Results showed that 57.9 per cent of the American youngsters tested failed one or more of the tests given, but only 8.7 per cent of the European children from similar urban and suburban communities failed any of the tests. Should children who lack muscular fitness get more exercise? What kinds of exercise? Do our kids ride too much? Do they watch too many contests instead of playing themselves? Get quotes from doctors, physical education teachers, and others.

Is there a doctor in your community who has served on the state board of health or in a similar capacity? What were his responsibilities? Term of office? Interesting experiences? What were some of the advancements made by the board during his term?

Obstetricians say there is a growing number of requests for fathers to be present at the delivery of their infants. What is the policy of your hospitals? How do mothers feel about this policy?

Is there such a thing as brain food? In the old days it was a common belief that fish was a so-called brain food because it is rich in the mineral phosphorus. Can the right diet help to promote a keenness of mind? Find out what health experts think.

Not your number of birthdays but the youthfulness of your various organs is the true measure of your biological age, according to an article in the *Journal of Gerontology*. Ask local health experts: Which are the most important of the organ systems? Are the heart and blood vessels more important than others?

The life span in this country has nearly doubled since 1879 and is now approximately sixty-seven years. What part have preventive health measures played in this extension of life?

Average daily food consumption per person includes one egg, about one and one-half pints of milk, about one-half pound of meat, fish, or poultry, more than one and one-half pounds of fruits and vegetables, about one-half pound of bread and cereals, and one-third pound of sugar and other sweets. Check these figures with local dietitians, cooks, cafeteria and restaurant owners, and others.

While winter holds sway, millions of Americans have their annual bouts with the common cold. Others suffer from serious respiratory conditions. How about writing a story titled, "Good Hints for Winter Health"? Get suggestions from city, county, or state health officials on ways to "weather the winter."

The American mother today has better than 999 chances out of 1,000 to come through childbirth safely. Interview several obstetricians and let them tell you of the many advances made in their procedures. Contrast some of the old practices with modern ones. What percentage of babies are born in hospitals compared with the number ten or twenty years ago?

In our country today there are twenty-five million men and women who are overweight, five million of them seriously so. What advice do doctors give to overweight folks? Should they exercise with moderation? Cut out all rich foods? Eat often and in smaller amounts?

"A stooped posture often means lack of sleep," an expert on health declares. How much sleep does the average person get? Do older people sleep more than younger people? Do people sleep more in the winter than in the summer? Does the average person think that he gets sufficient sleep?

Parrot fever (psittacosis) usually increases as parakeet fanciers increase. This type of fever is sometimes fatal. Among its symptoms: headache, fever, dizziness, back and stomach pains, and delirium. Check with state and county health authorities on the danger of this fever and how it can be avoided.

Only a small percentage of the population bothers with annual physical examinations. Why? Laziness? Afraid the doctor might find something wrong? How much does a thorough one cost? How can you tell when you're getting a good one? Can your family doctor recommend a good diagnostic clinic?

The first tuberculosis sanitorium was established in February, 1885. Use this date as a peg when doing a feature on your local or state tuberculosis association. Point out how the number of deaths from TB has decreased through the years.

"The measure of man's inner civilization," Curtis Bok once remarked, "is his ability to loaf creatively." Should modern man slow down a bit? Should he learn to relax? Does he push himself too hard? Doctors will give you interesting comments.

More and more health agencies are using sound movies in their educational programs. What types of film are the most popular? Are certain films restricted to certain types of audiences? Do the films really show results in terms of improving health conditions?

Here's an idea for an amusing feature—one which will be read. Ask quite a few people what they do to go to sleep at night. Do they read, listen to soft music, take exercises, drink warm milk? And find out the number of hours each believes necessary for a night's rest.

Many new uses of blood and blood products have been discovered by medical science. Here are some story possibilities: (1) uses of whole blood; (2) uses of blood plasma and other blood derivatives; (3) blood needs of your community; (4) the American Red Cross blood program; (5) interview doctors for a feature on dramatic local cases in which blood was used.

The average person has three colds a year. How do you catch colds? Are you more likely to catch cold in a city or in a rural area? Has medical science made much progress in finding either causes or cures?

Aching backs bother many persons today. What causes them? Poor posture? Sagging? Lack of fresh air? Lack of exercise? Ask a physical education teacher, "How can people avoid aching backs?"

Ulcers are thought by many to be the exclusive possession of men, but women are rapidly catching up, Dr. Joseph Shaiken points out. Is this because doctors can discover ulcers more easily than formerly? What are some of the factors which are causing the increase in both sexes?

The round, roly-poly boys are the jolly boys and make the best providers, a psychologist believes. Is it true that "everybody loves a fat man"? Does he have to watch his weight and general condition more than a string-bean type? Is the athletic type the most desirable? Get the comments of health experts.

"Most of our fatigue is mental, not physical," a noted physician declares. Why do we get tired? How is our bodily feelings tied in with our moods and attitudes? Does boredom cause fatigue? Seek the comments of health authorities and psychologists.

Is there a well-known mineral spring in your region? Is the water bottled and shipped? How many visitors come to the spring? What are the chemical elements in the water? How old is the spring? Who discovered it?

Fathers-to-be are welcomed at certain sessions of prenatal clinics. What are some of the subjects covered? Do more women than men attend? Who conducts the sessions?

About nine million Americans are mentally ill (more than one out of every seventeen). How many hospitals are adding psychiatric units? Is there a shortage of psychiatrists? Are enough nurses being trained? What is your state doing in treatment of the mentally ill?

The hundreds of thousands of dollars spent each year by cities, towns, and villages for ragweed eradication "might as well be thrown down the drain," officials of the American Foundation for Allergic Diseases state. Hay fever and other allergy diseases afflict more than seventeen million Americans. Should sufferers take shots before the season starts? Get some comments from allergy specialists.

Are there hidden disorders which make some people accident-liable? Some medications, for instance, may cause dizziness, muscular weakness, or lack of co-ordination. Should your family doctor advise you when you have medical factors that can make you especially liable to accidents and remove them?

A radiologist is an M.D. who is an X-ray specialist. How does he serve as a consulting physician? Show how he can look at an X-ray film and interpret what he finds there. Also, explain how he knows the structure of the body and how different diseases affect it.

Did you know that you can get severe skin irritation without touching poison ivy, poison oak, or poison sumac? When is danger of poisoning greatest? Talk to health authorities and list some of the precautions which should be kept in mind.

Needed: a motivating force to make men strive for slimness. That thought has been expressed by Dr. James M. Hundley of the National Institute of Health. He pointed out that there are about twice as many fat men as fat women. How have some local people handled the problem of obesity? What are some of the amusing stories which can be related by men who have reduced?

About five hundred thousand deaths are caused annually in this country by physical deterioration resulting from hypertension. Should more people be lazier? Does a person who relaxes accomplish more? Do too many people push themselves in everything, including their relaxation? Good source for answers: a doctor who is a diagnostician.

A New Jersey man has donated 250 pints of blood to the Red Cross in the past thirty years. Who holds the record in your community? Do some of the same people always respond to appeals? Give the philosophies of those who donate regularly.

The life expectancy of a new-born child is years longer now than it was fifty years ago. Write about medical progress in terms that can be easily understood by your readers. Which diseases still pose the greatest problems for medical science? Are annual campaigns to help heart disease, tuberculosis, and other diseases really paying off for most Americans? Your doctor will know and will be happy to pass the word along for your story.

Bodily aches and pains decrease markedly when you are relaxed, Dr. Edmund Jacobson declares. By combining statements from local people who are qualified to comment on this statement, you can write an excellent feature.

Unknown to many are the activities of the health department personnel of your city. What violations do they watch for? Do staff members receive complaints from citizens regarding health violations by business establishments? Do health officials conduct classes for food-handlers and other workers?

Now we have a Better Breakfast Month. What has happened to the old-fashioned breakfast? Why have people quit eating such large breakfasts? Diets? Rather sleep than eat? Do health specialists urge that people eat larger breakfasts?

Heat

An aircraft company has gone to the sun to achieve super high temperatures for testing materials. By means of a solar reflector, temperatures as high as 8,500 degrees Fahrenheit can be created. Who has the hottest job in your town or city? Check factories and manufacturing plants, especially places where there might be blast furnaces or similar equipment.

Heroes

Who are some of the most decorated veterans of your county? Where do they keep their medals and other decorations? Have some of them served as officers of the American Legion or other veterans' organizations? Current slant: get their views on United States preparedness or the lack of it.

It was in April of 1904 that the Carnegie fund was established for rewarding acts of heroism in times of peace. Have any local folks won the Carnegie award? What were the circumstances?

Have TV and movies changed youngsters' admiration of the old-time heroes and heroines in favor of more modern ones? Get the opinions of history teachers or teachers in the elementary grades. What does a youngster admire in his heroes and heroines?

Every kid has at least one hero. But rather than writing a story from the children's angle, ask ten or twelve men, "Who was your hero when you were a child?" And be sure and find out why each person admired his hero.

Highway Construction

Have you done a recent story on highway construction in your county? How many old, narrow highways are still being used? What are some of the construction problems in planning for the future? Show how costs of construction have skyrocketed.

History

Most states have historical societies that try to preserve the cultural heritage of the state. How do such organizations work? Do they publish magazines or pamphlets? Do they operate museums? How much help do they get from unpaid helpers and unsolicited contributions? Which states have good historical societies?

Hobbies

A Norfolk, Virginia, man says he's won awards in twenty-five hundred contests in the last thirty-two years, for a take of twenty thousand dollars, seventeen trips, five automobiles, and a college course in business! Can you find a "professional" contestant in your town? Will he reveal the secrets of his success? Is it hard work, skill, or luck that wins contests?

About two million home handy men work at shops in basements

and garages. But there are certain dangers which should be avoided. What about inflammable liquids? Dressing properly? Keeping tools out of the reach of children? Do machines have guards? Get the answers from an experienced worker.

Puzzle fans and the types of puzzles which they enjoy will give you a story idea. What are some of the newer puzzles? Are some old types still popular? Why are some folks fascinated by puzzles? Are puzzles for kids big sellers?

What's the story on stamps? Not stamp collecting, but the stamps themselves: their design, printing, and distribution. How many stamps are used every day in the United States? How much of a nation's history can be followed in the stamps it has issued? Your local stamp expert, hobbyist, or dealer will have some interesting answers.

Mrs. Karl E. Mundt, a senatorial wife in Washington, once created the unusual hobby of collecting barbs from the pens of Washington society writers. Odd? Maybe. Do you know some person who collects unusual clippings of people, events, or ideas? Find out why, and how long the person has been collecting the information.

The science of spelunking (exploring caves) has been widely publicized. But few people know any spelunkers. Got any you can use for feature stuff? How does cave exploration differ from, say, mountain or jungle exploration? What dangers are involved? How do explorers keep from losing their way in the darkness of deep caves?

Not all youngsters collect stamps, earn merit badges, or save odd-shaped bottles. Take the hobby of one thirteen-year-old boy in Pontiac, Michigan: making brass knuckles, blackjacks, and lead nickels. Young folks' hobbies aren't often this bizarre, but there may be some youthful hobby fans near you with interesting spare time activities. Discuss the educational advantages of constructive hobbies for children.

Phil C. Grimm of Cuba City, Wisconsin, has collected about 570 penny banks. Do people still hide money in crocks, jars, and bottles? Are kids who start saving with penny banks likely to start savings accounts at banks later?

M. A. Scott of Ottawa, Kansas, built a fifteen-hundred-piece miniature carnival with three hundred animated figures. Completion time: five thousand hours over a period of seven years. Can you find someone in your community who has completed a similar project over a period of several years? Was it done mainly for fun? Does it have any commercial value?

Chances are that some person in your community collects candidates' cards as a hobby. If you can find someone who collects them, ask him about his oldest cards, how today's card differs from those of long ago, and how many years he has collected the cards.

Do you know of a person who collects bottles? If so, find out from what states and countries the bottles came. Why is the person interested in bottles? Are fewer products being sold in bottles? Were some of the older bottles blown by hand?

Despite the precautions taken, humorous headlines pop up in newspapers. Know of anyone who collects them? Get the best from his collection, and the resulting feature will have a wide appeal.

Pieces of driftwood, in unusual shapes, are used in homes, stores, and other places as decorations. Who finds the originals? Who paints them? Is the idea spreading?

Have you considered the possibility of a story on local persons who collect bookplates or books containing bookplates? Look for unusual designs, the oldest and newest, and other angles.

More than eighty thousand amateur radio operators in America communicate with each other and with amateurs in other countries. Any local operators? Interesting conversations with others far away? Are they prepared to help the nation in time of an emergency?

Many great men have collected significant things in childhood. Darwin not only collected insects, but classified them. Franklin was always prying into the cause of things. Faraday invented things as a child. Ask the opinion of teachers who have taught long enough to have observed children in the schoolroom and also in later life.

Americans of all ages spend $824,000 a day on their hobbies of model making, says the Models Industry Association. What kind of model enthusiasts do you have in your community? How long have some persons been interested in the same hobby?

Does your community have a collector of dime novels? If so, what are some of his oldest? What do the covers look like? What are considered some of the rarest of the old novels? Which ones were most popular in their day?

Hoboes

What's happened to the old-time hobo? Does he now travel by automobile? Check with officials of relief agencies, police, and any mission or similar agency which might provide meals and room.

Holidays

Flag Day is June 14. But many times folks don't remember it, and it's sometimes hard to find a flag on Flag Day, even at meeting places for patriotic organizations. Have people forgotten the struggles that went into the history of the flag? Or is it lack of proper promotion and advertising?

What are the principal holidays observed by the people of your state? Interview state historians, prominent citizens, and state officials for their opinions. What dates are observed by most public schools? What dates form the basis for special ceremonies? Are too many holidays just "days off" rather than a time for observances?

New Year's Day has possibilities for many local stories. Here's an easy one to write: ask the president of the chamber of commerce about his plans for the year. And as a part of the same story, review the progress of the city during the year just ending.

Groundhog Day, which is observed in February, is always good for a story. What about the hibernation of a groundhog? Do any still live in your region? How many people still believe in the "shadow story"?

February 12 is Abraham Lincoln's birthday. How will it be observed in your community? Talk to history teachers and get their evaluation of the "Great Emancipator." And ask ministers about Lincoln's religious views.

To remind forgetful merchants in Oak Park, Illinois, that flags should be displayed on Memorial Day, Independence Day, and Flag Day, a local radio station offered one free spot announcement to any firm showing the American flag. How do other communities rate in the flag-waving department? What excuses do merchants have for not displaying flags on these and other patriotic days?

How did the rabbit come to be associated with the Easter season? And what does a rabbit have to do with the traditional Easter egg? Are there other Easter traditions that are peculiar to certain parts of the country?

The White House gates are opened to children each year during the Easter season for the traditional "egg rolling" celebration. What is egg rolling? Where did it start? Do you roll 'em down hills or on the level? Are there any egg rollers in your neighborhood?

Many folks feel that parades of fashion finery on Easter aren't in keeping with the spirit of the occasion. What's the consensus in your neighborhood? Where did the fashion parade idea originate?

A Bible class in Wilkinsburg, Pennsylvania, picked the dandelion as the appropriate Father's Day flower. The reason: "The more it is trampled on the more it grows." Are there special Father's Day observances in your town? How do some big families honor their Dad? What's the history of Father's Day?

America's unknown soldier was buried in Arlington Cemetery November 11, 1921. Ever since, the grave has been under constant guard by a select group of soldiers. How are men chosen for such duty? What are their special instructions? How bothersome are tourists?

Probably every one of the nearly fifteen million men who were in service June 6, 1944, can tell where he was and what he was doing when he heard the news that the Allies had made an amphibious landing in France. And chances are good that there is a man nearby who was there. Get in touch with American Legion or V.F.W. posts for talks with men who lived a chapter of world history.

On January 1, following his first inauguration, President George Washington opened his home to receive those who wanted to call on him. The custom has been abandoned in recent years. What open houses are now observed among officials in your city or state? What are the origins of the New Year's Day open house?

October 12 is Columbus Day. Is the day observed in your local schools? Do children regard Columbus as much a hero as some of their modern heroes? Ask teachers if children are eager to read books and stories about Columbus.

How does your community observe Armed Forces Day? Will it have a parade, speeches, open house at the armory or military installation, radio and TV broadcasts, or a flyover? If you have a military installation in your city, find out if it will send men and materials to other cities for the day.

Decoration or Memorial Day is observed in most states on May 30. What is its origin? Does any group in your community sponsor its observance? Does your local observance have any unique aspect? Talk to old-timers and see how the observance has changed.

How many holidays does your community observe? What are some local holidays which are different from the national ones? Have observances changed much through the years? Do you still have orators who speak at the Fourth of July event?

Home

Thousands of Americans can now move their homes to any part of the country. They live in mobile homes. Talk with trailer residents in your community. They will be happy to tell you the advantages of the trailer home. Most folks are unaware of the many conveniences available to the trailer family, through more complete facilities in the trailers themselves, better accommodations in many cities, and other advances.

More and more home designs include dens. How does the den

rate in popularity with local builders and homeowners? If homes have dens, is the living room still used, or has it become, like the parlor of earlier years, a place just for entertaining?

The refrigerator, with its trays of ice cubes, has just about made a forgotten man of the ice man. But there are still enough of them to tell you the problems they face. How much harder does an ice man work in summer than in winter? How many pounds of ice does he carry on a busy day? Is he tired of "ice man" jokes?

There are now more than twenty-five million American home-owners, compared with about fifteen million in 1940. How much has home ownership increased in your community or state? Do real estate men predict that the total will continue to grow? Give some reasons for the increasing total.

How many new homes have dining rooms? Would many families prefer an extra bedroom or another room instead of a dining room? Get some comments from local home builders.

Never before has a nation been so concerned with odors. We are deluged with deodorants of all kinds: for the body, the kitchen, and the bathroom. Interior paint can smell like cookies while drying; artificial "fresh bread" smells are incorporated in the manufacture of the bread wrapper; newspaper inks can be scented with perfume. How great is the sense of smell in buying? Ask leading retailers how it's possible to increase sales with smells?

Do many persons still own grandfather clocks? Are they ever purchased by young couples today? Local jewelers should be able to tell you approximately how many are found in your community.

By inquiring around, you may find a house with historic wall-paper. If you do find such a house, describe the paper designs. Are they copied for modern homes? What did the wallpaper cost at the time of purchase? Talk to a local dealer in wallpaper and get his comments on how the designs and patterns have changed.

Your region probably has several homes of dignitaries of your state that have been restored as shrines. List any outstanding relics.

Show the number of visitors annually. Tell how the upkeep of the home is financed.

About 70 per cent of American homes today are painted white. Next in popularity: gray (8 per cent), cream (5.5 per cent), and brown-tan (5 per cent). How do these figures compare with colors in your city? Do people follow fads in house colors? Why do so many still prefer white? Show some of the popular colors of the moment.

The increase in the number of electrical appliances has caused overload dangers in the electrical systems of many homes. Electricians will be glad to give you tips to pass on to homemakers: tips about safety, the added convenience of extra appliances, and so on.

Home Life

What makes a happy home? One authority states, "I believe that only one ingredient matters; the rest may vary. That ingredient is the right state of mind. It is an attitude which depends not on one member of the family; rather it is a sense of mutual cooperation, of 'togetherness'. It begins in the heart." Get the comments of ministers, sociologists, family life experts, and well-known parents.

The man who can "do-it-himself" gets all the publicity. But some suspect there are more who *can't* "do-it-themselves" than there are who can. What about a feature on mistakes in the do-it-yourself world: the man who can't saw a right angle in trying to build a house for Fido, who can't lay a level stretch of sidewalk, who can't add a room easily, inexpensively, and in his spare time, and who can't paint as well as a professional painter!

There's no doubt about it: "It takes a heap of living to make a house a home." And families who have moved to a new house will be among the first to admit it. Talk to folks who have moved from one home where they had lived for years into a new house. How long did it take to feel the new structure was "home"? Is there a relationship between family happiness and long-time residence in one home?

A writer once devoted an entire newspaper column to can openers, the old versus the new. He told how his forty-two-year-old can opener had outlived all the newer, shinier ones that had come and gone. There's probably a similar story in every house in the block. What old appliances are still giving dependable service, after years of use? Are folks willing to put up with a little inconvenience in order to keep a serviceable appliance they know will work?

Horses

Alice Bonneville of Northridge, California, is one of the few lady saddlemakers in the nation. In her early days she made smaller pieces of leathercraft—wallets and coin purses. Then she took lessons from an old-time saddlemaker. Who makes saddles in your region? Are most saddles tailor-made to specifications of the buyers? To what extent are they hand carved?

Riding trail, like any kind of horsemanship, has to be learned even by people who can perform beautifully in show rings, bridle paths, and on polo fields. How can a rider learn to negotiate rough desert and mountain trails? To what extent must the rider have confidence in his horse? Should a beginner go over the same course again and again before trying a new situation? How should the novice be taught to ford streams? To follow a trail that leads along the side of a steep hill or mountain?

Hospitals

For the most part, conditions at mental hospitals have vastly improved in recent years. Find out about new methods of treating mental patients, the new strength of public support and understanding, improved finances, and such information.

Because of wonder drugs and advances made in medical science, the average stay in a hospital is much less for certain types of illness than it was ten years ago. Check with the hospital administrator on pneumonia, for instance. What is the average stay for some typical cases?

About how many hours does an intern work? How many patients does he see on an ordinary day? Who makes out his schedule? To whom is he responsible? How does he work with the more experienced doctors?

Does your hospital have a "cheering section"? Do individuals or groups bring flowers, mend clothing, run errands, bring gifts, or perform other chores for patients? Has any one person established a long record of service? Any unusual requests from patients?

Does your local hospital have plaques honoring different persons? If so, who were the people? Who presented the plaques? Were some of the plaques hung at special ceremonies?

The American Hospital Association was founded in 1898. How much has the demand for hospital services increased? What are some of the many services offered by the modern hospital? Describe some of the newest equipment and tell what it does.

You'll find a top-notch feature in the emergency room of a hospital. Some angles: unusual cases, how cases are handled, special equipment available, and the goings-on in a busy night.

What are the boom months in births at your local hospitals? What is the record month? Among the new babies, what is the proportion of boys and girls?

Whole blood is vital in saving lives—even in peacetime. Many persons are justly proud of their record of donations. Your Red Cross chapter can tell you what local folks have been most generous in blood contributions. Who has given the most? Over how long a period of time has he made donations? Are blood bank collections used mostly on the local level? Or is it national and international?

An expanding field for volunteers is in mental hospitals. Check with your local Red Cross chapter and with the administrator of the nearest mental hospital to find out what is being done by volunteers.

Don't worry too much about what you say when coming out from the influence of anesthesia, an expert declares. "It is mostly babbling and doesn't make sense," he says. What is the first question a person usually asks as he comes out? Do some patients have delusions after an anesthetic? Do they have a loss of memory? Pop these questions to an anesthetist.

Mental hospitals sponsor dances, parties, and other social events for many of the patients. What is the value of these activities? Are certain events sponsored for certain groups? What is the philosophy behind many of the newer techniques of helping the mentally ill?

Hospitals, while ministering to the ills of mankind, must be operated on a sound financial basis. Interview the business manager of the local hospital. Do most people pay their bills promptly? How many patients carry some kind of hospital insurance? How do hospitals handle emergency cases? Through relatives?

Hotels

How does a hotel clerk or manager size up people? Can he tell the inexperienced traveler from the much-traveled person? Does it pay him to be a good judge of human nature? Can he tell a "deadbeat" when he sees one?

Guests at one New York hotel can now enjoy special sound effects, by request. A homesick Texan, for instance, missed the sound of the oil field pumps, so the manager arranged to play a record with these sounds on it. What do your hotels do to make their guests "feel at home"?

What are the duties of the hotel maid? How long does it take to clean an average size room? How many does she clean every day? Do guests often leave clothes and other belongings behind? Is the maid required to report everything she finds to her superior?

Are your local hotels bothered by "souvenir hunters"? How much silverware, towels, blankets, and other articles are taken away each year? Do hotels recover some of the goods? If so, how?

Hotel detectives pride themselves on being able to spot an undesirable. How do they do it? How long does it take to become a good house detective? How does it differ from ordinary police work? The house detective in a big hotel can provide you with lots of feature material.

Hotels have stepped up their community relations. Check with managers of your hotels and find out what they have done to attract tourists, build business, and help the community in other ways.

Up-to-date hotels provide a variety of special services for travelers. Many, for instance, provide baby-sitting service. Check with a number of hotels or motels and see what new services have been added.

You've heard that patrons often carry towels and other articles away from hotels. Give this story a different switch: What do guests often leave behind in hotels? Do they usually call or write for them? Are valuables sometimes forgotten? What are employees instructed to do when they find articles in rooms?

Hotels, like many other types of business, often urge their guests to give suggestions and criticisms. How many guests respond? What do most people complain about? What pleases them most? How is the information used by management?

Housing

By 1976 the United States must build almost two million new homes a year to accommodate its expanding population, experts say. Part of the need stems from the fact that in the next twenty years some sixteen million homes will become substandard. What will be the housing needs of your city? How many homes will become substandard in ten or twenty years?

A host of young married couples in Philadelphia banded together to remodel a slum area. What groups or organizations have done anything similar in your region? If slum areas have been abolished, then that's another story.

An official of the U.S. Housing office says that more than "1 out of every 10 homes in this country are rock-bottom slums." What is your city doing for slum prevention and slum elimination? How do slums and housing problems lower the social and economic level of whole communities?

Human Nature

It's easy to spot a well-informed man. His ideas coincide with yours! How true is this kind of statement? Do people prefer to associate with others who hold similar views. Interview a couple of long-time friends and see how their interests and ideas are similar. How do they differ?

Too many people quit looking for work when they find a job. Do many people today look for easy jobs? Is salary or wage the first consideration? Get comments from workers in employment offices.

Human Relations

This is a great day for amateur psychologists. Psychologist Alex Magoun says that most people know they are ignorant of chemistry and physics, yet parents, teachers, and bosses generally think they are experts on human behavior. Are people reading too many books and magazine articles on psychology? Can the science ever reduce to tangible factors? Good source for comments: a university or college psychologist.

"Don't try to understand the way people act only in terms of what you see," a psychologist says. And then he adds, "Look also for aims and causes." Is there usually only one basic cause for a person's behavior? Or many? What causes a person to act as he does? For interesting comments, talk to psychologists, supervisors, or anyone who is skilled in dealing with individuals.

What is the surest way not to get along with people? Try to improve them, says J. Worsham in his *Art of Persuading People*. What should we do? Take people as they are? Never call attention to their mistakes? How do supervisors handle this problem? When are reprimands necessary, and how should they be given?

Is there one sure way of appealing to all persons? Henry Van Dyke said, "There is one thing in which all men are exactly alike— they are all different in intelligence, education, ambition, leadership, and response to blame or praise." What are some tested ways of getting the co-operation of others? What are some ways of "rubbing others the wrong way"? Get the comments of two or three persons who are skilled in human relations.

Hunting

Farmers and ranchers in many states are urged to use "Hunting By Permission" signs rather than the "No Hunting" variety. In some places the signs are furnished free to landowners through sportsmen's clubs and game rangers. Do many landowners in your region refuse to permit hunters to use their property? What is being done by sportsmen? Talk to a game ranger.

Hurricanes

Why are girls' names used for hurricanes? Shorter? Quicker? Help reduce confusion for weather observers? Get the story behind this practice from the federal weatherman.

Husbands

Most American women are more interested in having a good-tempered husband than a faithful one, although they wish he were more romantic, a national poll reveals. Ask a group of young women what qualities they would like in their husbands-to-be? How high do they rate faithfulness in desirable qualities?

Illness

"Illness doesn't mean the same to all persons," Dr. Theodore Watters, a psychiatrist, believes. Certain families "favor" certain types of illness, he says. Is it unusual for a physician to find a person who has no desire to get well? Do members of the same family often go to a doctor for the least little thing? Do some people resent being sick?

Improvement

So you want a better job? That's a live topic. Paul W. Boynton, supervisor of employment for Socony-Vacuum Oil Co., Inc., gives this answer: "Just one rule—do everything you have to do better than you have to do it." Actually, there's no magic formula for promotion because circumstances differ. But you can whip up a lively feature on this topic by getting the advice of employers, supervisors, and heads of business concerns. Just ask them, "What are some of the main factors you consider in making promotions?"

Income

"Of all the places we've lived," John Newton Baker reminds us, "the very worst was just beyond our income." How many people live within their income? How many have no hope whatever of staying within their income? Does the average person expect to be in debt for most of his life?

Indians

Indians have more holidays than their white brothers, and fewer ulcers and nervous breakdowns. Most holiday celebrations and dances are open to visitors, and there's a story in each. There are Indians in every state but one: Delaware. That means there's an Indian feature story near you, particularly at holiday time.

Industry

Experts say we need an expanding economy. We certainly have an expanding consumer population. Some seven thousand babies are born in the United States every twenty-four hours. Each baby will consume 515 pounds of food, at an approximate cost of $120, its first year. Manufacturers and business leaders should have plans to meet the multiplying demand for the necessities, and the luxuries, of life. What ideas can you find among big businessmen for coping with increased demand?

Another facet of our expanding economy: In the years 1950–55, Americans bought more than two electric appliances for every man, woman, and child in the country.

Union men claim reading racks full of company-distributed material in industrial plants constitutes a form of brainwashing. Executives say it's part of their program to explain the corporation to their workers. What about the employees themselves? Get a sampling of opinion on reading matter put out by the company. Do workers read all or most of the pamphlets and magazines? Do they feel that they are being unduly influenced? Do they feel better informed about company policy after reading house organs?

Many kids no longer have any trouble answering the question, "What does your Daddy do?" Many firms today urge that kids come to the plants on certain days and see what their fathers do. Some of them may be allowed to perform some of the simpler tasks. Why is it important for kids to know what their dads do? How many firms follow this practice in your community? Do the kids have lunch at the plant or are they served refreshments?

Initiation

A polio-stricken editor was initiated in his Bellevue, Iowa, home by telephone into Sigma Delta Chi, national journalism fraternity. Has anything like this been done in your community? Ask company officials if any similar ceremony has been performed through the help of telephone facilities.

Insects

Man will always have to fight insects to survive, E. O. Essig, entomologist, says. One housefly would produce—in one summer—191,000,000,000 descendants, if all lived. What are some of the current battles being waged against insects by health authorities? By agricultural department experts?

Instruments

What kind of wood is used in rulers, slide rules, and other precision instruments? How is it treated? How are the instruments marked for accuracy? Your local expert on wood should know the answer.

Insurance

Approximately 40 per cent of the life insurance in force with more than one thousand companies of the country is group or term insurance. Do most of the businesses and institutions of your city have some kind of group insurance program? What percentage of the employees are covered?

Ever stop to analyze those four thousand words, more or less, that make up your life insurance policy—why they are there, what they mean, and why they are in that style? Get an insurance expert to explain what must be considered in writing a policy.

One of the big stories of business development of the past decade has been the spread of group insurance. What are some of the factors behind this amazing development? What are some of the types of group insurance?

Can you qualify for life insurance? Few can say "No" today. Out of every one hundred applicants, ninety-seven are now accepted. Practically no occupation is a barrier any more, and certain types of heart disease, cancer, or tuberculosis are no longer a bar to insurance. Check with insurance officials for a story showing how practically everyone can have life insurance.

Do you have to die to win from life insurance? No, that idea went out a long time ago, and today more is paid each year to living policy-holders than to beneficiaries of those who die. Get a story on the "living" uses of life insurance and how it has changed from a generation ago.

Are there any college honor graduates in your area who were launched on a specialty career by insurance benefits which paid their college costs? Thousands of students are in universities today because of insurance planned for this specific purpose.

People used to "buy" life insurance. Now most of them seek the services of insurance counselors in the planning of family financial programs. What services do most companies render? How have services expanded?

Intelligence

Is intelligence (not scholastic standing) a major factor in success? Dr. G. H. Estabrooks, psychologist of Colgate University, made a study and found this: given the minimum ability to enter into a specific career, a man's success depends more on his interest, readiness to work, additional study, and other factors. How do bosses of your community rate intelligence of job applicants? Do they believe other factors are more important?

Is it true that "genius is akin to madness"? Havelock Ellis, British neurologist, could find only three geniuses in all history who could be called "insane." And psychiatrist J. Adele Juda studied 294 "distinguished" German scientists, writers, artists, and musicians and found more than two-thirds mentally "Well-balanced." Local angle: Talk to high school teachers and see if the exceptionally bright student is usually normal in most areas of living.

Jail

Do prisoners write many letters? Are their letters read by an officer? Is incoming mail inspected? What are some of the undesirable items addressed to prisoners?

Are religious services conducted in the jails of your city on Sunday? If so, by whom? Are prisoners usually receptive? What is the nature of the services?

Jewelers

Is there such a thing as a "lucky" stone? What are some of the common superstitions concerning gems? Are opals a source of misfortune? Do buyers object to certain stones because they believe that they might cause trouble? Try a veteran jeweler for comments.

Many owners of diamonds often wear imitations of their real stones, particularly at times when they might be held up or on occasions when they might lose them. Without giving names of owners, find out from local jewelers about how many persons have imitations. Can owners always tell the genuine stones from the imitations? To what extent do unscrupulous persons try to sell imitations as genuine stones?

Heavy earrings, when worn for a long time day after day, can pull the lobes down and may even split them, Dr. H. L. Herschensohn warns. He suggests that if women want heavy earrings, they choose those which look heavy but are very light. Localize this tip by interviewing an ear specialist.

Jobs

Why do most people choose their jobs—because of security or opportunity? If opportunity, what kind? Do security or opportunity rate along with salary? If the salary of two openings is about the same, what causes the person to choose one over the other?

Who has the most frustrating job in your city? Some who have chances to help others but for certain reasons are unable to? Someone who must say "No" to all requests? Or someone who is caught in a situation in which he hardly knows what to do. By handling with a light touch, this feature can be outstanding.

Joiners

A Rhode Island man received publicity by revealing that he carried forty-three types of membership cards in his billfold. How many does the average man carry? Are some of them out of date? Which ones does he consider the most important?

Juries

Who is excused from jury service? How are jury rolls selected?

Do most citizens try to get out of jury service? Should citizens welcome the opportunity to serve?

Do women make as good jurors as men? William Marston found that women made more notes, were moved less by passionate, sentimental oratory, and studied evidence more carefully. Would local judges agree? Also, get the opinion of several women attorneys.

Juvenile Delinquency

Morrie Gallant reminds us that "One way to curb delinquency is to take parents off the street at night." Do adults leave the kids at home too much at night? How many mothers and fathers actually plan family affairs at home at night?

Kindergarten

There's always a live story in the kindergartens. Visit one and see how the kiddies are taught. What are some of their activities? Why does the teacher prefer to work with children of this age group. And for smiles, ask the teacher to recall some of the cute sayings of the children.

Labor

In many cases organized labor has been slow to accept mechanical aids that will reduce the number of men needed for a job. Yet today, with modern techniques, practices, and instruments, there are more persons employed than ever before. You can build a good feature around this fact. Talk with labor leaders and industry representatives. Show how labor-saving devices affect the economy. Show the new jobs that are available now that did not exist a few years ago.

Labor Unions

Five labor unions in Oklahoma City joined in finishing the interior of a medical foundation building free. Labor groups are stepping up their community relations activities. Check with officials of your local groups and do a roundup story.

Labor Day

Peter J. McGuire, then president of the United Brotherhood of Carpenters and Joiners of America, suggested setting aside one day of the year in honor of labor in 1882. It is always observed on the first

Monday in September. How is the day observed in your city or state? Has the type of observance changed through the years? Summarize the activities and achievements of labor groups for the previous year.

Land

Property owners in this country own their land outright, but ownership is not absolute. It is still subject to the right of the state or federal government to take the property for certain essential uses? What are these? Does "taking" mean more than actual possession? How can property be condemned? What determines adequate compensation for property?

Language

Every day most Americans use words and phrases with whose origins they are not familiar. What do we mean when we say "spitting image"? Why are policemen called "cops"? Where did the phrase "pay through the nose" originate? How about "up to snuff"? Check reference volumes in your library for these and others.

Businesses are hiring teachers and setting aside time during work hours for their employees to study foreign languages. This is particularly true of those which have outlets and offices in other nations. Are language classes encouraged by any firm in your city? If so, are the classes required of certain employees?

Ihor Sevcenko, language teacher at the University of Michigan, deplores the fact that too few students in this country study the Russian language. He believes that we have a fear of public opinion against anything Russian. What does your high school or college language teacher think of this observation? And ask a few citizens if they believe that this situation is due to a certain fear.

College slang, like everything else, has changed through the years. Interview several veteran professors. Ask that they recall some of the campus slang of their day. How did some of the expressions originate? Are some of the terms still in use?

Such abbreviations as i.e. (that is) and e.g. (for example) are used in English printing. Why do we use them? What are their origins?

There are others: *sic*, viz., etc. Are these abbreviations used less now than in earlier years? Why?

Laundries

Monday isn't "blue Monday" to laundry owners—that's the biggest business day of the week. They would like to have more people send their clothes on other days. How many people send their laundry on Friday? Are certain periods of the year busier ones than others? Has the increasing sale of sports clothes meant more business for laundries?

Laws

Failure to practice the Ten Commandments is the reason thirty-five million laws have been passed during recorded history, a sociologist declares. Would the Ten Commandments solve most of the major problems? Get the comments of several ministers, judges, and police officials.

Every day someone somewhere proclaims "there oughta be a law" for or against something close to his heart. If you are located in the capital city of your state, find out some of the strange proposals which legislators have suggested through the years.

You've heard people say, "A person claiming the privilege against self-incrimination under the Fifth Amendment, or under a similar provision of a state constitution, is guilty or else he is lying." Is this true? Is inference warranted? Does a person condemn himself? Does it depend on the nature of the question which is asked? Or on the nature of the tribunal which subjects the person to questioning? Seek the opinions of lawyers and judges.

A California judge sentenced two men to jail for forging $236 in bad checks, although neither of them could write! The judge gave a stern warning to the man the two illiterates had persuaded to write the checks. Similar unusual cases in the administration of justice make good feature stuff. What problems have beset the judges in your town or county? How did they handle them?

An Arkansas law governs two trains that meet at a crossing. It says neither shall proceed until the other has passed! There may be less classic laws on local statute books, but chances are you can find plenty of outmoded laws and ordinances if you'll look. A collection of them would make interesting reading.

A Boulder, Colorado, man proved a point when he said certain legal forms are too complicated. In a few hours time he found thirty signers to a petition that read, in fine print at the bottom, "Signers are to be publicly hanged by the neck until dead, in the courthouse square." What about it, don't people read what they sign? Talk to lawyers, real estate men, and others who deal with lengthy documents folks have to sign. How many read them through? How many see a lawyer? How many ask questions about some part they don't understand?

You'll find many an interesting yarn by getting the records of the early-day courts held in your state. What were the cities in which court was held? Major offenses? Types of punishment? What trials attracted the most people? Who were some of the judges and other court officials?

Why are so many judges so far behind schedule? Have the complexities of modern life increased the amount of litigation? What percentage of the cases come from broken marriages? Would extra judges solve some of the problems? Are some trials too long? To what extent do politics enter the judiciary? Get the views of judges and lawyers.

Who is the youngest judge in your region? Tell of his legal career. What are some of the most colorful trials over which he has presided? Get his comments on the prevention of crime.

Do most people have wills? What is the value of having a will? What are some of the unique ones? Interview several judges and attorneys.

The system of trial by jury, as old as Anglo Saxon justice, is coming under the eye of "reformers" who feel that something should be done about it. Are juries too generous in granting damages in lawsuits? Are jurors swayed by emotional issues? How can the system be improved? Get the views of judges, lawyers, and citizens who have served on juries.

Lawyers

If your county has an active bar association, do a story showing its history, its leaders, and its activities through the years. Does it sponsor special programs through the year?

Laymen have little idea about the vast amount of preparation which attorneys must make before a trial. Do a story which shows how a lawyer prepares for a case, what he encounters, and the many sources he must use.

Did you read about the plaintiff who took a tape recording into court to prove how loudly his neighbor's dog barked at night? Talk to a veteran judge or court clerk and find out what unusual types of evidence have been introduced in court. What types of evidence are forbidden?

Today there are more than fifteen hundred city, county, and state bar associations. What are some of the activities of your city or county group? Is it emphasizing the public relations services of the profession? Is the local program tied in with the national objectives? How old is the local group?

Richard Husband, in his *Applied Psychology*, says that one eminent lawyer classified all witnesses into five personality types. What are typical types of witnesses? Must the lawyer be prepared to deal with many types? Does he make advance preparation? What type makes the best witness? The poorest?

Does the bar association of your city or county have a legal aid service which provides free advice for persons who feel unable to pay the costs of legal services? If so, what are the principal kinds of requests? What was the most unusual?

Leadership

"The trouble with being a leader today," a newsletter published at the Pensacola Air Station reminds us, "is that you can't be sure whether people are following you or chasing you." How far can a leader be ahead of his group—in ideas or action? Can he be too different from his followers in their thinking? Here's a good source for some interesting answers: a former politician.

Do you have to be a go-getter to be a leader? Do some positions demand a rather quiet but creative type of leadership? Does the general public prefer a dynamic leadership? For answers, query a psychologist.

Leap Year

The Greeks consider leap year unlucky for marriages. So they usually marry in record numbers in the last days of the year preceding leap year. Is this true in your county? Will records in the court clerk's office verify this?

Left-handedness

George Gobel, TV comic, once did an amusing article on the problems of left-handed people. Localize this idea by interviewing a number of southpaws. What about a simple thing like writing a letter? Eating in a crowded place?

Legal Aid

Then there's the story of the man who wrote in his will: "Being of sound mind and body, I spent every darn cent I had!" How tough is it to convince people that they should make wills? Most folks admit they should make a will, but comparatively few do it. Why not? Talk with attorneys. Let them tell you some of the unusual provisions made in wills.

Letters

Did you hear about the firm which mailed one of its creditors this collection letter: "Dear Mr. Jones: Can you recommend a good lawyer in your town? We may have to sue you." To what extent do local firms use collection letters? What are some of the most effective types? Does one letter bring the desired response from most people?

Sign over the letter slot in a post office: "Have you mailed your wife's letter?" Jokes are told and many cartoons drawn to show that hubby always forgets to mail his wife's letters. Is this true? Do most women mail their own letters? What do post office employees think about this situation?

A letter addressed only to "Tony's Sister, Allegan, Michigan," was delivered to the right girl. It won a bet for her brother, Roger

(Tony) Nichols, a sailor aboard a Navy destroyer escort. What unusual addresses have been observed by your local postmaster? Do postal officials make every effort to locate the addressee of every letter, even though the address is not complete?

Every year two hundred million letters are written by Americans to family and friends in Europe alone. Many more millions go to other parts of the globe. The Common Council for American Unity urges that those who write letters abroad (1) write at least one friend or relative each week, (2) describe the American way of life, (3) express interest in conditions abroad, and (4) make your letter tell the story of America. How many persons are co-operating in your city? Is the number increasing?

Does anyone in your city have a collection of old letters? If so, what were some of the topics of discussion? Were any of the phrases given in an odd way? Is the handwriting clear and legible? What is the date of the oldest letter?

Libraries

A book borrowed from a Fitchburg, Massachusetts, library was returned after thirty years. Its title: *Half Hours with an Idiot!* What percentage of books in most libraries are never brought back? What excuses do persons give when they bring in a book they've kept for months or years?

Have you ever done a "night story" on your city library? Who uses the library at night? Adults who work during the day? Youngsters who need a quiet place to study? Club women looking for material for speeches?

Puzzled people often call your city librarian. "What are the dimensions of a bridge table?" or "How much sugar should I use when I deepfreeze strawberries?" are typical questions. What's the most amusing question? Do crossword puzzle fans call a lot? Is the librarian asked to provide an answer which will settle a bet?

Your state library association is worth a story. Some slants: early history, growth in membership, extension of library services, and prominent leaders through the years.

As one of the features of Book Week, children often portray characters from their favorite books. What are the favorites from year to year? Are some of the ageless characters just as popular as modern TV, comic strip, and movie personages?

Does your local library circulate phonograph records? Paintings? Tape recordings? More and more libraries are adding to their services by offering these and other materials.

Every library loses books. Do people just forget to bring them back? What types of books do people keep? Do books show up after being lost for years? How often do library books show up in used book stores? About how many volumes are lost from your city library each year?

One of the objectives of the American Library Association is to protect freedom of information. To what extent is your local librarian allowed freedom in the types of books which are ordered and placed on the shelves? What types of books cannot be ordered or placed in circulation? Have certain books been banned by members of the library board?

What do library patrons leave behind? Purses? Umbrellas? Notebooks? What are the most common objects left there? Does your library maintain a "Lost and Found" drawer?

Your local library keeps valuable papers and documents. Are they kept in a special place? Who is allowed to use them? List the most important items and show how they were acquired.

How does the owner of a rental library select books? What are some of the favorite authors of current readers? Do certain types of books—mysteries and novels, for instance—retain their popularity through the years? Who reads the most books—men or women?

Thousands of persons haven't stepped inside a library since their high school term paper assignments. But that is changing. Many libraries today have added extra services—providing tape recordings, film, and paintings. Some provide art, displays, current events discussions, college credit courses, and other services. What are some of the new services of your library? Are others being planned? How do the newer activities affect circulation?

Many large libraries now have a map room. In a university, for instance, cases which hold hundreds of maps and large tables for consulting and processing maps are maintained. Does your city library or nearby college have a special map room? Who are some of its regular users? Do people often consult a map to win an argument? How often are maps revised? Oldest map? Newest map?

License Plates

In many states, the battle for license tags with significant or low numbers is an important one. How does it work in your state? Are numbers handed out as rewards for safe driving? Are low numbers given to the same persons year after year? Do political leaders get the numbers or letters they want more easily than other citizens?

Lions Club

Date tie-in: The International Association of Lions Clubs was organized November 8, 1917. Use this date as a peg on which to do a story of your local club: its activities, its history, and its plans for the future.

Literary Criticism

It's been said the seven big drama critics in New York control the American theatre. That's a good peg for a piece on criticism. Does a man who can't, or hasn't, written a novel have the right to criticize a novel? Drama critics praise or condemn a play without being dramatists. What makes a critic? How well trained should he be? Is vitriolic criticism ever justified? Talk to local teachers, the man who reviews books for the newspaper, and the college professor who teaches literary criticism.

Literature

Family reading sessions in the home are being neglected, an expert on children's literature believes. Why should the family read together? What are some of the values of such an activity? Is there a substitute? Ask your librarian.

"Livability"

Your city's general appeal—the sum total of its churches, schools, parks, and other facilities—is often the big factor when new industries and new people come. An expert has defined this as "livability." What is your chamber of commerce doing to emphasize the "livability" of your community in its promotion efforts?

Lodges

What's the oldest fraternal group in your town? When was it organized? Who were first officers? Have any of its members been honored by state, regional, or national offices? How many members have been initiated since it was founded?

Luck

Heard this? "Luck is what happens when preparation meets opportunity." What part does luck play in life? Does the average person feel that he is lucky or unlucky? How many people still carry some type of good luck charms?

Machines

A huge machine called a ripper has just about made dynamiting a thing of the past in digging trenches for pipelines. Except for solid rock, the ripper can move along behind a tractor rooting up sandstone, shale, and rock layers at depths of up to four feet. The iron monster weighs from four and one-half to six and one-half tons. Railroads now have machines that can place long sections of rail with one operation. What other types of big machines are making difficult work easier? What has been done with the men they have replaced? Big equipment men can discuss their products and problems.

Magicians

Do you have a local magician? If so, do a feature on him showing how he became interested, his sources of new tricks, how much he must practice to perfect his techniques, and some of his experiences.

Magazines

How do nationally distributed magazines reach their destinations on the same day? Are magazines destined for the west coast simply mailed earlier, or do big magazines maintain printing plants far enough west to meet delivery deadlines? Another aspect of the magazine business: how are circulation lists maintained? Where does a new magazine get prospect lists?

Mail Service

A postman in Marblehead, Massachusetts, successfully delivered a letter addressed to "Cow's Corner." The man for whom the letter was intended lived at Jersey and Guernsey Streets. How far will the post office go in trying to decipher hard-to-read or unusual addresses? Are there any laws pertaining to the legibility of addresses? How many letters are not delivered because of illegible or improper addresses?

If you are doing a feature on stamps for publication in July, tie it in with July 14. It was on this date in 1845 that the first affixable postage stamp in the United States was issued by the New York postmaster. Show how many changes have been made in the speedy handling of postage through the years.

Early October is the time to do a feature urging that everyone mail overseas Christmas gifts early. Are perishables accepted? What are the limits on size and weight of packages? Should list of contents be placed inside the package?

Does your post office have many women employees or a postmistress? What do they consider the most interesting phases of their work? Show length of service and the capacities in which each has served.

What do postmen find in corner mail boxes besides mail? Usually it is something that kids stick in. Do many letter writers forget postage? Is mail in boxes heaviest during Christmas?

Management

An expert at Ohio State University declares that management is making strides in two ways: how to get employees and how to keep them. What does a large organization offer a prospective employee? Must they offer more to compete with other companies? Does modern management recognize the emotional needs of its employees? Directors of personnel can shed light on this topic.

Despite the best efforts of management to combat it, absenteeism is frequently a serious problem. What are some of its causes? What are some justified reasons—jury duty, military duty? Is it increasing or decreasing? Are women absent more than men?

Manners

A sixty-five-year-old man says, "It took me many years to realize that women don't appreciate a 'perfect gentleman.' " How do girls in your high school feel about such a statement? Have times changed? How do high school teachers and other youth leaders feel about manners of today's teen-agers?

Mansions

What's the oldest yet one of the finest homes in your city? What home has been the scene of several memorable occasions? What notables have been entertained there? When was it built and by whom?

Manufacturing

Technicians and radiologists in hospitals and clinics aren't the only persons using the X-ray in their work. Radiographs are now being widely used in industry, mainly to discover defects in metals. To what extent are X-rays used in industry? Are industrialists increasing their use of X-rays?

Maps

Officials of a large map company reveal that many persons collect maps. Do you have one or more in your city? If so, ask how many maps have changed. What are the oldest maps in the collection? Where can a collector locate maps?

Marines

Aim at a November 10 edition if you plan to write a story about the Marine Corps. It was on this day in 1775 that the Marine Corps was created by the Continental Congress. Show its growth, training program, and any unique features which make its work outstanding.

Marksmanship

How do members of your city police force keep in trim as marksmen? Must they keep up to certain shooting standards to remain on the force? Who serves as instructor? How do they feel about sometimes having to shoot at a criminal? Who is the best shot on the force?

Marriage

"Until the modern young woman can change the stigma of Miss to the magic of Mrs. she can't even think." So states an education professor. What about early marriage? Does it bring responsibilities too early for husband and wife? Do early marriages "trap" both husband and wife?

Headline: "70-Year-Old Man Weds Sweetheart of 50 Years Ago." Of the oldsters who marry for a second time, how many marry childhood friends? How many had courted in their younger days?

A chap in Tulsa bought a marriage license, had a quarrel with his fiancee, and then tore up the license. He was given another license when he brought the scraps of the old one to the clerk. How many people lose their licenses? Under what conditions can a duplicate be issued in your county?

Marvin Samples of Atlanta, Georgia, fell in love, but his 307 pounds was too much for the girl. So he trimmed his weight to 180 pounds in eight months by rigid diet and exercise, and won the bride. Examples of other pre-wedding agreements will make an unusual story. Suggested sources for comments: ministers, marriage counselors, and others.

Would delay between application and marriage prevent some unhappy marriages? Psychologist Margaret Brainard found that even the three day's delay required in Los Angeles prevented, in one year, seven hundred applications from being completed. Ask ministers, judges, family life experts, and even some couples their opinions of a waiting period?

Are elopements likely to end unhappily? A study of 736 elopements showed that 356 ended happily, 66 fairly happily, and the remainder unhappily. Are there fewer elopements today than a few years ago? Do ministers who suspect that a couple may be eloping try to get the ceremony postponed?

Mascots

Folks of Alresford, England, approved the spending of six pounds and three shillings ($18.60) to perpetuate the memory of Hambone, the dog mascot of an American regiment. The dog died, and the soldiers erected a wooden cross which rotted in several years. Then the English put up a new oak cross. Has your community ever had a mascot which was buried in a marked grave?

Maternity Homes

Does your state require the licensing and inspection of homes for unwed mothers? Under whose jurisdiction do they operate? What is the process required when a couple adopts a baby?

Mathematics

An Arizona man, arrested on a charge of catching more than his limit in fish, miscounted the number. He is a mathematics instructor. Does a CPA ever make a mistake in his income tax returns? Does a mental wizard at the office have trouble in helping his children with their arithmetic lessons at home?

Mayflower

There are approximately 8,600 persons in the United States who can rightly say, "My ancestors came over on the Mayflower." Organizations of descendants are found in more than forty states. Does your state have such a group? What are its objectives? Who are its officers?

Mayor

Your mayor is supposed to greet all "visiting firemen." Does he use about the same speech for each meeting? Has he ever gotten mixed up in his schedule by promising to be several places at the same time? Does he write his own speeches?

Meals

An expert reports that the average person spends about two and one-quarter hours eating daily. With most people on the run today, do you believe that the average family spends that much time at the table? Do some checking. Which meal is likely to be the most leisurely? The most hurried?

Medicine

Prodigious feats of strength are sometimes performed in times of great emotional stress. A Texas man was changing a tire when the car slipped off the jack and pinned his thumb to the ground. His wife, who weighed little more than one hundred pounds, lifted the rear of the car so he could free himself. Ask doctors how this can happen. How is strength tied to emotion?

Have any surgeons of your city performed operations with the aid of "controlled cross circulation"? In this procedure the heart and lungs of one person are "borrowed" so that surgeons may repair defects inside the heart of another.

You'll find an excellent feature in the work of pathologists and their assistants at your local hospital. Each patient who sets foot in the hospital may have at least four laboratory tests, and the average patient may have about fifteen. How has the volume of work increased? Have new tests been devised? Do the pathologists do autopsies?

A survey shows that more than half the chronically ill people in the United States are under forty-five years of age. What are the most common ailments? How much of that illness is psychological? How often does illness in persons under forty-five result in death?

Figures show that a typical medical student must study about thirty hours a week, attend a weekly total of thirty-seven hours of lectures and laboratories, and increase his two thousand word "working" vocabulary to six thousand in the space of two years. Visit the nearest medical school and show how students are taught, what they do in clinical assignments, how they work with specialists, and how they must have "living laboratories" in which to prepare for their profession.

Many persons have abnormal fears, or phobias. Some are victims of acrophobia (fear of high places). Others have mysophobia (fear or dislike of filth or dirt). Still others have agoraphobia (fear of being alone in an open space). Are there ways to combat or cure these unusual fears? Your doctor or psychologist can help. Can reasons for such phobias be found?

Pain is actually a life saver in disguise. It's your body's sixth sense. Interview several physicians and get their comments showing the usefulness of pain, and how they trace the presence or origin of trouble by the pain experienced by the patient.

Always good: interview the oldest doctor in your county. Ask him about the new wonder drugs and if he still favors some of the old-fashioned remedies. How many hours does he still practice? What about his hobbies?

Memories

Babe Ruth struck out 1,330 times. But that isn't what we remember about him. His 714 home runs completely obliterate the 1,330 strikeouts. Thomas A. Edison failed in many experiments. But we remember his successes. Does fear of failure keep many people from attempting new activities? Are we afraid of what people will think? Interview a psychologist and do a story on the theme, "Nobody Is Successful All the Time."

Dr. Bruno Furst, memory expert, says that everyone is born with a potentially good memory. It merely needs training to work properly. Interview several persons who have exceptionally good memories. What is the secret of their success? Did they just stumble on to their systems or did others teach them? How do they exercise their memories?

Everyone knows the Wright brothers were the first to fly, but how many can remember even approximate dates. When was Jack Dempsey heavyweight champion of the world? When was the Panama Canal completed? When was Taft president? Choose big events well within the lifetime of those you question. You can assure those you talk with that their names won't be used if their guesses are far from right.

Dr. George Gallup found in one of his national polls that less than one-third of all motorists can remember the numbers of their automobile license. Is this why so many seek to get short numbers or combinations which they can remember? Do police in search of stolen cars remember many numbers or only a few?

Men

Do gentlemen prefer blondes? One nationwide survey showed 60 per cent of the men preferred brunettes, 30 per cent blondes, and 10 per cent redheads. But, as someone pointed out, this doesn't prove much, since there are about three times as many brunettes as blondes —the natural variety.

Do your local haberdashers now make charges for alterations on new suits and other apparel? If so, does most of the work go to tailors, or do the husbands take the garments home and explain to their wives that "all it needs is a little taken out here and only a little taken in here."

What do women first notice about men? The way they walk? Voices? Expression of the eyes? Pace in speaking? Interview a number of well-known women in your community or state and the resulting feature will have high readership.

Men's Ties
Women buy 80 per cent of all men's ties, says *Changing Times*. And they buy louder colors, fancier patterns, and ties that resemble draperies, the article stated. What kinds of ties do men prefer? Do manufacturers make ties to please women rather than men?

Menswear
In summertime women put on fewer clothes; men simply suffer. Why don't men go in for shorts, sandals, and other summer wear as readily as women? What do women think of men in shorts? How do weights of men's summer clothes compare with those of women?

Oklahoma City Mayor Allen Street is a bow tie fan. He hasn't worn a "four-in-hand" in over fifty years! How many bow ties do men's stores sell to every four-in-hand? Is the ratio about the same in department stores? How do already tied bows compare in sales with the "tie-it-yourself" variety?

Mentally Retarded
Today, America has about two million mentally retarded children and approximately an equal number of adults. Does any agency of your community provide special services for the mentally retarded? Are children helped in special groups? Get the views of child psychologists, welfare officials, and ministers on what should or might be done.

Menus

A New York man made the headlines when he gave his collection of more than ten thousand menus to the New York Historical Society. Is there a menu collector in your city? (Restaurant and cafe owners will probably know.) If so, how have menus changed through the years? What items of food are still popular?

Merchandising

Is the customer always right? How do merchants handle complaints and adjustments? Ask clerks if they believe most customers are reasonable? Are there chronic complainers? How do stores handle their exchange business after Christmas, Mother's Day, and other special occasions?

Merchants

What are the pet peeves of local merchants? Find out how they are besieged by representatives working on all types of drives. Do they believe that too many drives are conducted?

Meter Readers

How does a meter reader look at life? How many customers "jump on him" because their water, gas, or electric bills are too high? Do housewives invite him to have a cup of coffee on a cold day? Or a cold drink in the summer? How many meters can an average reader check in one day?

Milk

Milking has come a long way from the old days of three-legged stools and a person with "pull." Visit a modern dairy and see how modern equipment—even "push button" milkers—has taken over some of the old jobs.

Mind-changing

Men change their minds two or three times as often as women, it is reported by Dr. Karl Robinson of Northwestern University. Would most women agree with that comment? What do the men think?

Ministers

You won't have to travel far to find an aged Negro minister in your region. Find out the amount of his training, if any. Get his views on Bible reading. Are any sons following in his footsteps? Does he think that churches of today are attracting more members?

An observer of the current scene believes that "faith has been reduced to a self-help . . . and the church becomes a kind of service station." What are local ministers stressing in their sermons? Do they believe that Christian faith has been altered by modern thought? Is Christianity merely a set of devices? Do church members have an obligation toward the social order of which they are a part? You can get some lively comments from church leaders on these and related questions.

Ministers' sons have included statesmen like Wilson, Hughes, Cleveland, Clay, Buchanan, and Arthur; financiers like Harriman and Cecil Rhodes; scientists like Agassiz, Jenner, and Morse; artists like Reynolds; and authors like Tennyson, Ben Jonson, Goldsmith, Coleridge, Matthew Arnold, and Emerson. Show some of the outstanding work now being done by ministers' sons who once lived in your city.

The typical American Protestant minister is between thirty-five and forty-four, is married, and has two children. And, says *Time*, his church has approximately four hundred members. Its budget is about $12,500 a year, some $3,000 of which is given away to good causes. How do these figures compare with the situation in your community?

Does your city have a pastor who is also an accomplished singer? Does he appear on many programs other than those of a religious nature? Does he often sing a solo and preach at the same service? What are his favorite hymns? Has he composed any hymns?

It's a standing joke to make fun of the large appetites of preachers. Do most of them really like to eat? What are some favorite dishes of several of the leading ministers? Are some of them fairly good cooks?

A New York minister recently made the headlines by living on the bowery for several days and nights and then delivering a sermon on his experiences. What is the background of some of your ministers? Social work? Business? Youth work? Do ministers feel that varied experience with many types of persons helps in performing their duties?

A minister asked a little girl who went to church for the first time how she enjoyed the service, and she replied, "I thought the music was very nice, but your commercial was too long." How long should a sermon be? Are modern sermons shorter than those given by ministers ten and twenty years ago? Do ministers feel that their listeners' span of attention is limited?

Mint

How are commemorative coins struck off by the U.S. mint? Who suggests them? Who authorizes them? Who designs them? Is there a special department for such work? The Treasury Department can give you material for an interesting feature.

Miscellaneous

People who want to disappear, for one reason or another, find it's a tough job! Americans are too well documented, what with birth certificates, social security cards, local, state, and federal tax rolls, and other records. What about a feature on the importance of these records to the average American?

When residents of Hutton Gate, England, protested to the officers of the nationalized railways that ancient gas lamps on the station platform were old fashioned, the lamps were taken down. Now they have oil lamps! Is there some aspect of life nearby that seems to have been by-passed by the mechanical age? Any gas lights, coal oil lamps, player pianos, indoor water pumps, or outdoor bathrooms? Now that most modern conveniences are comparatively low priced, what is the reason for the delay in installing them?

An Oklahoma City driver told a traffic judge he lost control of his car and wrecked it when he tried to keep water in a goldfish bowl in the front seat of the car from sloshing out. Police court judges have heard a variety of stories from drivers. Has your local judge got any good ones to build a story on?

Each year the Burlington (Wisconsin) Liars Club picks the World's Champion Liar. Why not find some of the whoppers being told in your community? Are some of the tall tales new, or have most of them been told before?

Do people like to visit? Are many people at home these days? Interview several meter readers and get their experiences. Do many people welcome a visit?

Watermarks were first put in paper by metal wires bent into a design and fastened to the mold in which the pulp was formed into paper. Has the process changed? How are color watermarks made? Foreign currency makes wide use of the watermark. Has this country ever used watermarked paper in currency?

Diogenes was the ancient Greek who spent his time with a lamp, looking for an honest man. How would he fare today? Most people think of themselves as honest. How do they rate the honesty of others? Is a little white lie all right? When does the lie begin to change color from white to a tinge of black? Make your own survey on honesty. Are most folks naturally honest, or are they afraid of getting caught at something dishonest?

Psychologist M. N. Chappell found that city people are overawed by what other people own; country folks are more interested in what the people are. What impresses most people? Does wealth still impress the majority of people?

"If you want something done, ask a busy person; any others you ask won't have time." What are some of the secrets of completing tasks? To what extent should a person budget his time? Interview several persons who are known for their numerous and varied activities and find out their secrets.

Clifton Fadiman believes that listening is a lost art in America. Seek comments of preachers, teachers, mothers, and others. How many people keep the radio turned on but never actually hear the programs?

Time picks a "man of the year." Do a feature by asking a number of people if they agree with the selection? If not, who would be their nominees? Why?

John Newton Baker once said, "It's easy to avoid criticism—just say nothing, do nothing, be nothing." Do people like criticism? In what form should it be given? Can you criticize without offending? Get your answers from supervisors, teachers, managers, and others who deal with people.

A Malayan proverb states that "one can pay back the loan of gold, but one dies forever in debt to those who are kind." Are most people kind? Ask some taxi drivers, elevator operators, store cashiers, and telephone operators. Are men kinder than women? Do children's manners show that they are kind?

When a Denver woman was asked by a census taker how much her husband earned, she replied, "Do you want to know how much he tells me he earns, or how much I suspect he earns?" Any person who does polling or similar work can tell you many humorous answers which people give to questions.

If hindsight is so much better than foresight, then try this feature: Get the comments of ten successful persons on the topic, "If I Were 21 Again."

A career expert says that a good letter of application should be (1) arresting, (2) compelling, and (3) convincing. Under what circumstances is a letter better than an interview? Should you enclose a photograph? Is the letter written from the YOU angle? Is it conversational in tone? Enumerate a list of general guideposts for letters of application by getting suggestions from employers, guidance experts, or instructors in business correspondence.

Does anyone like criticism? Or does it depend upon who is giving it and other circumstances? Interview several people who hold management positions or who supervise others and get their suggestions on tactful ways of criticizing others.

Louis Agassiz once wrote his brother, "Read much, but only good and useful books." What are the favorite types of reading preferred by businessmen and professional men? Do they read certain types of literature for escape? How many books does the average businessman read in a year? Sources for answers: librarians, booksellers, and newsstand proprietors.

John H. Patterson, founder and for many years president of the National Cash Register Company, filled many notebooks with facts and ideas during his busy lifetime. Do a story about people who are "jotter-downers." Does this collection of ideas make them more creative?

Roadside diners sell dozens of items from cards. Visit a diner or cafe and ask if this merchandising technique helps sales. Make a partial list of things now available on cards: lighter flints, cigarette holders, handkerchiefs, key rings, knives, puzzles, and the like.

A group of sociologists at Michigan State University have found that the "New American Woman" is a little uneasy in her role as an equal to the American man. They say that many women would be happier if they had fewer decisions to make. What do local women think about that? What about women over forty-five or fifty, who were born in a time when women didn't work alongside men at their jobs, yet who live in a time of more feminine equality than ever before? How do they accept their new role?

Missionaries

Thanks to Gospel Recordings, Inc., a California non-profit firm, a missionary can now deliver the gospel in scores of tongues. Missionaries send in more than one thousand tape recordings of native languages. From these have been made recorded messages and services in more than seven hundred languages. Local slant: find local pastors who use recordings of church services to take to those who are ill, elderly, or handicapped.

Mistaken Identity

Rev. George Bennard, author of the hymn, "The Old Rugged Cross," was often confused with other composers. Several thought he wrote "Rock of Ages." Is someone in your town often mistaken for someone else? Or do you know of a local person who is often mistaken for a celebrity whom he resembles?

Modeling

Sure, a fashion model's life is frequently a glamorous one. But it's a hard-working life too. What about a feature on the advantages and disadvantages of modeling? How many hours of work are necessary for a single fashion picture? How many women actually make a living as models? What "types" make the best models? Is beauty alone enough? What's the story on some of the big model agencies? What part do advertising agencies play?

Even a small town has a few women and girls who act as models at style shows sponsored by organizations, stores, or school groups. How are they chosen? Would some of the younger girls like to become professional models? Who coaches the local models?

Model Trains

Men enjoy running model trains because it gives them a power of dominance, a psychologist says. Visit the next meeting of the Model Train Club and chat with a few members. Have they always been interested in trains? Are some of them former railroaders? Who has the largest amount of equipment?

Money

With today's rising living costs, it is difficult for most persons to "get ahead of the game." So ask eight or ten persons, "Will you ever reach the point where you have enough money?"

Monuments

How about doing a story on the inscriptions on the monuments in your city and county? If you can, include a brief description of the dedication ceremonies for each.

There are few southern towns that don't have a memorial to the Confederate soldier in the square. When were most of them erected? Who provided the money? Who were the sculptors? How were Civil War cannons distributed for memorials after the conflict? Many towns have them—what's their story?

Does your region have any monuments erected on old battle-grounds? Tell highlights of the battle or battles, and heroes. What interested group marked the site? Are ceremonies still held at certain periods?

Morals

Who regrets more their departure from accepted moral standards —men or women? Men, according to the late psychologist Knight

Dunlap, who had years of experience in counseling. Would your ministers, psychologists, and other folks who do a lot of counseling agree?

Motels

One hotel manager cut down on pilferage after a convention by announcing to a lobby full of departing guests that a search would have to be made for a missing diamond necklace. Many guests had to hustle back to their rooms to get rid of towels, bath mats, ash trays, and stationery! What other techniques do hotel and tourist court men use to reduce such pilfering? Where do hotels draw the line between minor thefts and major ones? Do they keep records on guests who leave with more than they came with?

Mother's Day

You'll get the kids' angle by asking them to disclose "Why I Like My Mother" as a Mother's Day story. Interview about twenty children, and in the summary story give the name of each, the names of parents, and the address and age of each child.

What do teen-agers think of their mothers? What are some of the things which teen-agers wish their mothers wouldn't do? On the other hand, what are the things youngsters like about their mothers?

Movies

The proprietor of a movie house in a mining town filled his house to capacity every night he showed *Julius Caesar*. "It was easy," he said, "I just advertised it as a straightforward, wonderful gangster story." What other methods do owners and operators of movie houses use to attract customers? Can a bad or mediocre picture be publicized so well it draws as well as a good picture? Or is any movie that attracts patrons considered a good movie?

Sign outside movie theater: "Feature's Running Time: Three Candy Bars and Two Bags of Popcorn." Sales of confections and drinks have boosted income of movie theaters. Do kids consume a lot more food and drinks than adults? Is popcorn still the favorite with all ages?

Brief comments on current films are published in some magazines, both general publications and those issued by special groups.

Do many parents check the lists, or do they just "send their kids to the movies"? Should parents be more careful about the types of movies that their children see?

Every coach tries to use movies in increasing the strength of his team. Do movies show everything? Are there disadvantages? Are movies more important in some sports than others? Is it easy for a player to realize his mistakes when he sees them on film? What happens to old movies?

A veteran projectionist in one of your movie theaters is worth a story. How many pictures does he see each year? What does he consider to be the ten most outstanding pictures of the past five years? Who are his favorite actresses and actors?

Oldsters will remember the movies starring Douglas Fairbanks, Harold Lloyd, the Keystone Cops, Charlie Chaplin, Fatty Arbuckle, Rudolph Valentino, Joan Crawford, and others. How do some of the stars of yesterday compare with today's big names? Do they believe that some of the stars of the silent screen would have been successful in sound movies?

Treasury officials discovered that making a coin cost more in one mint than another. A movie crew filmed operations in each factory, and then the results were compared. Motion pictures revealed that in one mint the silver ingots had been topped too heavily and had to be trimmed. To what extent are movies being used in your city to study processes, developments, or manufacturing? What types of firms are the biggest users?

When announcement is made of the Oscar winners in motion pictures, you can always localize the story by asking folks if they agree with the results. If they disagree, what pictures or stars would they have given higher ratings?

Who are the animated cartoon favorites among the moviegoers of your city? How many of the old favorites, like Popeye, keep their audiences? Are animated cartoons enjoyed by movie fans of all ages? Any veteran theater manager can give you the answers.

More than two million American families make home movies. Look into your local situation and see if movie makers have a club. How many go beyond the usual routine of making pictures of children or vacation scenes? Who is the oldest movie maker? How has equipment changed in a few years?

A popular magazine comments that an actor "played the role of Sitting Bull in a manner wooden enough to qualify him as a Hollywood Indian." What do Indians think of movie portrayals of their race? Do they believe Hollywood has helped or hindered their acceptance in modern life?

Municipal Government

Just how much does crime or crime prevention cost your city each month? Show the total salaries of local police, jailers, desk sergeants, and others. What about the feeding and lodging of prisoners? Trace the history of your police force from the early days. And include a list of former police chiefs.

Interview your city attorney and get a number of specific instances to show his duties. What does he consider some of the most important cases in the city's history? Show the nature of his specific duties as city attorney—day-to-day situations which never make the headlines but which are more or less routine.

Newspaper editors and others are concerned with the increasing tendency of many committees, councils, and other groups to hold closed meetings. Is this a problem in your community? How many groups hold closed meetings? Why are reporters and others barred from the closed sessions? Does your local newspaper carry the names of those who attend closed sessions? And how they vote on certain issues?

Municipalities

In an average community less than 15 per cent of the street lighting is adequate, experts declare. How is the lighting in your city? Has it been improved in recent years? Has any study been made to reveal current needs? Does your city still have quite a few dark streets which should be lighted?

Museums

Did you know that a church in your region may have an interesting museum? If you find one, get the history of the museum—who started it? First objects displayed? What have been some recent additions?

Every museum has one exhibit which usually outpulls all others. What is the particular one in a museum in your city? What does the museum director consider the secret of its appeal? Does the exhibit interest people of all ages? Is the exhibit a fixed one or is it changed from time to time?

Music

Lots of fond parents start Junior or Sis on the piano or violin at an early age. So there are plenty of piano and violin players for orchestras. But where do oboe players come from? Who plays the bassoon, and how did he get started on the instrument? What about the piccolo? Or the tympanist who "plays" the triangle, the wood blocks, and cymbals?

A veteran music teacher is worth a story. How many pupils has he or she taught? Who are some who later became famous? Does TV encourage more youngsters to take up music?

Many have believed that Stradivarius used a secret varnish to give his violins their rare tone. If you have a violin maker or repairman in your city, ask him if this is true. What really gives a violin tone? Does the age of the violin necessarily mean that it is worth quite a bit? Are modern violins made partly by hand?

How do music boxes work? Your gift store manager probably has the facts, or can find out for you. Can music boxes be mass produced? Do the best ones still come from Switzerland? Some have three or four selections. Do any music boxes have more?

General U. S. Grant wasn't musical. He used to say he knew only two tunes. One was "Yankee Doodle" and the other was not. Do most people have musical memories? How many know all of the words to "The Star Spangled Banner" and "America"? Does the average person know all or most of the words of his favorite hymn?

National Music Week gives you an opportunity to summarize the musical activities and achievements of your community. When was the first band organized? What honors have come to local high school or college groups? What have been some of the outstanding programs of church groups? Bring your story up-to-date by telling of current musical activities.

Recent headlines told of an Illinois hatchery where twenty thousand birds enjoy piped music. Anything like this operating in your community? If so, does the music keep the birds contented? Make them healthier? Good sources to find if the music idea is used near you: feed stores selling to poultrymen, or your county agent.

Who composed the official song of your state? How was it chosen? Under what conditions was it written? How long has it been used? Was the composer a native of your state?

Juke boxes are found in many places. Is the juke box as popular as ever? How often are the records changed? Who are the principal patrons—teen-agers, couples, middle-aged folks, or others? How does the box owner know what records to buy?

Many celebrated musicians started their public careers as children or in their teens. Do they usually come from musical families? Did they enjoy practicing even as youngsters? Were their careers decided for them by their parents?

Sheet music is still with us. How does TV, radio, and movies affect sales? Who are the biggest buyers? Are requests often received for some old-time favorites? What have been some of the really big sellers through the years? Are sales increasing? Down? About as usual?

Highbrow music isn't as highbrow as it once was. What does your music store manager think of the increasing popularity of serious music? What effect does radio and television have on popularity? How much has the sale of operatic and classical records picked up with the advent of long-playing records, high-fidelity sets, and colorful packaging?

How many establishments in your community use piped-in music?

Is music used in any of the factories or industrial plants? Does this help morale or production?

Tunes of the Gay Nineties still appeal to many persons. Check music dealers and see how many still prefer sheet music or records of the old music.

Cartoonists often picture Johnnie in agony as he practices on the piano while the rest of the kids in the neighborhood are enjoying a baseball game. What incentives will cause a child to practice regularly? How can parents help? Do boys enjoy appearing at recitals as much as girls? Seek the comments of a veteran piano teacher.

A successful carillon player, like a boxer, must pack a punch in both hands and be quick on his feet. Is a carillon played like an organ? What does a carillon keyboard look like? How are tone and pitch adjustments made? How many schools in the nation offer instruction?

A symphony orchestra is big business in many American cities. What are the workaday aspects of an orchestra the public seldom hears about? Who takes care of the music and instruments when the orchestra is on tour? Who handles ticket sales, advertising, and publicity? Few symphony orchestras are self-supporting. Where does the rest of the money come from? Are the players full-time musicians, or do they earn part of their living at routine jobs?

To lots of folks the singing of the choir is an important part of the church service. But it takes a lot of work to present a fine choir. Ask the directors of several choirs how many hours of work go into a single hymn. Does competition for time make recruitment of choir members difficult? What effect has the employment of a minister of music had on church music? Many churches now have them. And lots of churches have several choirs—one for adults, another for intermediates, and another for children!

Is there such a thing as a popular new hymn? How long does it take for a hymn to become known and liked by a congregation? The ministers of music in local churches can give you the facts. What makes an enduring hymn?

March 24 is an excellent date on which to publish a feature on hymns, because Fanny Crosby was born on that day in 1820. Although blind nearly all of her life, she wrote at least six thousand religious poems and scores of hymns. Some angles for feature: What are the favorite hymns of people? Do many old hymns continue to hold their popularity?

Pleasant music is an aid to digestion. Where does recorded restaurant music come from? Why are there no vocals? How many firms supply this sort of "canned" music to dining places? Are requests possible?

You may not know it but the chances are that there are some hymn writers in your community. Music dealers or music store employees might be able to tip you off. How did the composer get the idea? Has the hymn been published? When was it introduced? Has it been played on any radio or TV programs?

Does your city have a symphony orchestra? Good! What happens when the organization goes on a tour? Do men wear nylon shirts because they can be washed and dried in a hurry? Who makes all of the arrangements? How much space is required for the instruments and music?

"Vaya Con Dios," a record featuring Les Paul and Mary Ford, sold more than two million copies. Many records by popular stars sell more than one million copies. What's behind a hit record? How many hours of rehearsal? How many "takes" are necessary before the music men think it's right to sell? Is a tune recorded straight through from start to finish, or are segments pieced together into a finished work?

Given reasonable care, any record will last indefinitely and lose little of its original clarity and purity of sound. Talk to a local record dealer and find out the best ways of caring for them. What about dull needles? Should a record be cleaned before it is played? Is vertical storage best? Should you ever touch the playing surface of a record?

If you've watched a high school band march by, you have probably wondered how the director finds enough uniforms in all of the sizes which are needed. Must some of the uniforms be altered each year? What is the largest size? The smallest? How long does the average uniform last?

Names

Old, but good at intervals: Run through your city directory or telephone directory and pick out a list of persons who have famous names. Often there's an angle when an explanation is given why the person was named. Does a child or an adult endure a certain amount of good-natured razzing when he or she bears a well-known name?

They did it in West Virginia in 1949. Residents of Mole Hill changed the name of their town to Mountain! Trace the history of some of the unusual town names in your state. Has pressure for a name change ever been exerted in any of them? What is the usual attitude toward such a change? How many towns have had three or four names?

One out of every one hundred persons in the United States today is a Smith, according to studies of the National Geographic Society. The Veterans Administration has had as many as 13,000 John Smiths enrolled at one time. How many John Smiths in your community? How many of them have no middle name? Are there mixups in letters, bills, and other material?

A Jasper, Alabama, woman was christened Luqincy Raine Martha Jane Eldorado Julie Dean Delma Ruthie Matilda Felma Jacka Cina Sophi Husky Charlotte Moss Stone. Her friends called her Lu-Ma. The need for nicknames isn't as extreme in most cases. What's the origin of nicknames? How does Richard become Dick, John become Jack? How does a parent feel about nicknames? Do some try to choose names for which nicknames aren't appropriate? How do children like nicknames?

H. F. Weed was named beautification expert by the city park and recreation department in Columbia, South Carolina. Do you have anyone in your city whose name has any tie-in with his title or duties? By checking various lists or asking friends, you will probably find one or several.

The Apple family of Winston-Salem, North Carolina, named a daughter Etta. How much of a help or a hindrance can names be?

Chances are you can find people with unusual names nearby who will help you. Do those with unusual names have a tendency to give their children similar names, or do they choose more common ones?

See the alias name file of local police and see what person has the most. How do police keep up with the various aliases? Show the origin of some of the names.

Do you like your name? Most of us, at one time or another, dislike our given names or hear others we like much more, says Eldon C. Smith, president of the American Name Society. Do this: Ask fifteen or twenty persons the question: "Do you like your name?"

National News

It's almost a cinch that your readers will be interested in the local end on any popular fad or national movement. Here's the main thing: get local opinions or the local picture.

Nature

How do autumn leaves get their colors? In the fall, maple leaves turn scarlet red, aspen and birch leaves turn yellow, and oak leaves turn dark red. Interview your local florist or high school botany teacher. Were the rich autumn hues in the leaves all summer?

What are the largest trees in your community? How old are they? Are some of them linked to the early history of your city? Have some of them required treatment from a tree surgeon? Sources: old-timers, nurserymen, and sometimes farmers.

News

You've heard persons ask, "Why do newspapers play up the news of crime, tragedies, and the unpleasant things of life?" Ask a number of persons if they think the press places too much emphasis on the wrong events? Do they admit reading those stories? What would they do if they were editors? Do they overlook the fact that newspapers devote a great deal of space to the bright side of the news?

Newsboys

A former newsboy and now a furniture store owner in Texas entertains more than three hundred newsboys at an annual Christmas party. Does any group or individual entertain the newsboys of your city? If so, does the party include a meal and entertainment? Presents for all?

Newspapers

Weekly newspapers and small town daily newspapers rely on country correspondents for much of their rural coverage. How are these local reporters chosen? What do they write about? What training do they get, if any? Ask small town editors about some of the unusual stories country correspondents have written.

Your veteran drama reporter is worth a feature. How many plays has he witnessed? Who are his favorite playwrights? What are the ten best plays he has seen through the years? Has he ever tried to write a play? Ask him: What are the ingredients of a successful play?

Find a local reporter who has covered the state capitol or the Washington scene. What were some of his problems? Typical experiences? Any scoops scored by him? Did he face any problems of censorship?

How many newspapers have been published in your city? What was the first one? Were some of them merged? Who have been some of the colorful editors? How have facilities for gathering news changed through the years?

Does your community or state have a women's press club? If so, describe some of the experiences of several of the prominent members. Any big scoops? What do women enjoy about journalistic activities? Do they advise young women to consider journalism as a career?

Newspaper Carriers

William R. Searcy gets up every morning at 4:00 A.M. to deliver the *Texarkana Gazette*—he's only eighty. Who is your oldest carrier or salesman? How long has he been carrying or selling newspapers?

An Ohio newspaper reader suggests that someone develop a repeating spring gun for carrier boys, so papers could be accurately fired at front doors. How important to reader satisfaction is prompt delivery? How important is dry delivery on rainy days? Local editors will probably be interested in the results of your personal survey, and so will readers.

News Services
Big news stories are flashed all over the country in a minute's time by the wire services. How do they work? Where does the news that comes in on a teletype actually originate? Is someone typing it out manually on the other end of the line? How do local stories get on the wire? How do wire service correspondents get their stories in? What are some notable examples of fast wire coverage?

New Year's Day
Check through a history of your county or city and show significant milestones in history. Paul Revere and Betsy Ross were born on this day, so perhaps you can create a tie-in by showing that some of your famous citizens observe their birthdays on this day.

The first of January has not always been New Year's Day. In fact, it became so in Protestant England, and therefore in the American colonies, as recently as 1752, when the British finally accepted the Gregorian calendar. What are some of the superstitions which apply to New Year's Day? Do Americans follow some of the old customs on this special day?

Nicknames
For a light treatment try this: Get the nicknames of quite a number of the best-known citizens. Show how each originated and when. Include men and women.

Numbers
Lewis Brent of Alton, Kansas, was born in 1877, and has seven children, seven grandchildren, and seven great-grandchildren, according to a "Believe-It-or-Not" drawing. Can you find anyone whose life involves a set of numbers?

Numismatists
Shoot at April 2 the next time you do a story on coin collectors. It was on this date in 1792 that the United States Mint was established at Philadelphia. Show how different kinds of money have been used

through the years. Describe some of the more interesting items in one of the better collections.

Nurses

The National Student Nurses' Association has active groups in all states, the District of Columbia, Hawaii, and Puerto Rico. What are the activities of your state association? How do professional nurses help the student groups?

Most people think of a nurse working in a hospital. But there are several types of nurses. What about a company nurse? What are the special qualifications needed? To what extent does she influence morale of employees? Does she work closely with the safety director and supervisors? What does she do in a typical day?

Most Visiting Nurse Associations (540 out of the nation's 684 such services) receive their operating funds from Community Chest or United Fund campaigns. The nurse and her patient offer a wide variety of interesting stories—educational as well as entertaining.

The menace of atomic warfare and the continuing shortage of nurses and doctors (which local hospitals, medical societies, and nurses' associations can verify) have made it imperative that homemakers learn how to care for illness in their own families and act as nurse assistants in time of major disasters. Talk to the Red Cross chairman of home nursing about its course in the home care of the sick, for feature angles.

Florence Nightingale, high-born Englishwoman who took a group of young women volunteers to the Crimean front in 1854, first dramatized woman's role in nursing the sick and wounded. Her work reduced the warfront death rate from 42 per cent to 2.2 per cent in six months. Give the modern story of nursing in your community—its needs, its many services, and its high standards.

Observances

Does your community or state observe National Shut-Ins Day? If so, start weeks ahead by talking to shut-ins who earn all or part of their livelihood. How many are successful in small business enterprises? What is their philosophy of life? Point out those who have succeeded in spite of terrific handicaps.

236

Occupations

"If all the baby pictures in America were laid end to end, most of them would still be out of focus." So says a well-known newspaper columnist. The baby trade is one of the most profitable for photographers. Your home town portrait photographer can tell you what troubles he has with most babies and their doting parents. How does he keep them quiet long enough to "pose"? What tricks does he use to get the "just right" expressions?

Any unusual occupations in your area? There may be tree surgeons, worm farmers, chicken sexers, hypnotists, bullfighters, steeplejacks, and glockenspiel soloists right in your home community. If you have a hard time finding full-time workers at unusual occupations, perhaps there are some interesting part-time jobs to write about.

Experienced trash men say a lot can be learned about a family by the things it throws away. What are some samples? How much tougher is the job during annual clean-up campaigns? Is anything of value ever mistakenly dumped in the trash? What is done with it? How is ordinary trash and garbage disposed of?

Cleaning skyscraper windows is a dramatic job. Who does the work on the biggest building near you? Are windows cleaned more often in winter than in summer, or vice versa? Do window washers strike up friendships with those on the inside? Does a man in this kind of work start from a ladder and gradually work up to higher windows?

Meter readers may doubt that the dog is man's best friend. The bad dog is one occupational hazard with which the men who check water, light, and gas meters have to contend. Any dog-bite victims in your city? What about other problems of meter men: weather, locked gates, broken meters, and the hostility of the overdue consumer? Do meter readers have foot trouble? Need special shoes? How many miles do they walk a day?

In city office buildings a clean-up crew takes over for night work almost as soon as the office personnel go home. Talk with a long-time janitor. Is the work different now than a few years ago? Do most folks realize and appreciate the service performed by custodians and janitors?

How many measurements are taken for a man's tailor-made suit? Let a tailor tell you the differences between a department store suit of clothes and a tailor-made one. How did the tailor get started at his trade? Does he assume the traditional tailor's position of sitting cross-legged? What percentage of tailor-made suits to ready-mades are sold? What styles are most popular? Fabrics?

How many parts are there in a wristwatch? How long does it take to train a watch repairman? Ask a jeweler about the best ways to care for a watch. What kind of lubricant is used? Are watch parts hand made or machine made? A good watch seldom wears out, so how is sales appeal made? What percentage of watches are bought at Christmastime? How many have messages or names engraved on back of the watch case?

Legal terminology is unintelligible to most laymen. Why is it that way? Why do attorneys keep phrases such as habeas corpus, party of the first part, president pro tempore, *modus operandi*, hereinafter, and sine die? Is the law more just with those terms than it would otherwise be?

Everyone wants to be an author. Perhaps someone in town has had a book published. (Chances are the librarian can tell you.) Almost certainly some local person has had an article published in a popular or limited-circulation magazine. What are his techniques? Where did he get the idea for the story or article? Is it true that writing is "10 per cent inspiration and 90 per cent perspiration"?

How are locks made? Ask your local locksmith if an expensive lock is harder to break open than a cheap one. Which is safer: a combination lock or a key lock? How many different kinds of locks are made? What is their history?

Got a taxidermist in town? Lots of your readers wonder about the steps involved in getting a moose head from moose to living room wall. How did the taxidermist learn his trade? Is business better during the hunting season? What's the most unusual animal or bird he has ever worked on?

How does one get to be a crane operator? How does a man learn how to drive a bulldozer? There are no training schools for learning the operation of heavy machinery. How does a man jump from a passenger car or truck to a road grader? Talk with men in the heavy equipment field.

Do you believe in signs? Then interview the owner of a local sign company. Is it just a joke that sign painters cannot spell? What are some facts about sign painting? Do more people want signs that are readable during the day and also after dark? Unusual requests? Largest sign ever made?

Many women are now employed as "traveling salesmen." Find a successful one and ask why she likes it, how many miles she travels each year, and what means of transportation she uses. As a girl, did she have a yearning to travel? Cite a few of her interesting experiences.

Your oldest businessman is good for a story. How did he get his start? Does he suggest both education and experience as prerequisites for success? Have buyers' habits changed? What advice would he give to anyone who plans to enter business for himself?

James Abbott McNeill Whistler, the famous artist, was dismissed from West Point in his third year because of low grades. Afterward he said that if silicon had been a gas, he would have been a major general. Are there businessmen or artists in your town who have been trained for other fields? Any engineers who became theatre managers, or teachers who became salesmen?

A Detroit garbageman wept upon his retirement, and said, "It's surprising what you can tell about people from their garbage." What do people throw away? Are many people wasteful? What is thrown in the garbage by mistake?

Nowadays many persons have two jobs: one full time, another part time. What are some of the "extra" jobs done by folks in your town? Do they work at them more now because of higher living costs, because they are a form of relaxation from their regular jobs, or because there is more time now for leisure and other employment?

Octogenarianism

William Hardner, a St. Louis cab driver, was pictured in newspapers because he could still do a day's work at the age of eighty-two. Who are some of the oldest persons still active and on the job in your community? More men or women?

Odors

Chemists say there are but four fundamental odors: fragrant, burnt, acid, and caprylic. How about a feature on smells, and how the modern world is making use of them. Paris authorities shoot perfumed odors into the subway; some perfume ads in newspapers are printed with perfumed inks; household deodorants sell by the millions. There's even talk of bolstering movies with perfumed air in the theaters. They'll call 'em "smellies."

Oil

The first transportation of oil was made by rafts or flatboats, onto which were loaded oak barrels of crude oil, in about 1862. Bring this fact up-to-date by checking with oil company officials on the role of the barges of domestic waterways and privately-owned tanker fleet vessels in transporting oil.

Samuel Kier constructed America's first oil refinery—a one-barrel still—in the early 1850's. During the past thirty years the quality of gasoline from U.S. refineries has improved so greatly that two gallons of present-day gasoline do the work of three gallons of the 1925 product. You may want to use these facts in writing a feature on a refinery in your locality.

It costs between two and three times as much to produce a barrel of oil from an offshore site as it does from a land rig. Yet more and more oil companies are drilling for oil through water! What are some of the difficulties in this new technique of oil discovery? Who drilled the first off-shore well?

Today five hundred thousand different compounds can be made from petroleum. Oil-based compounds are now used to make everything from cosmetics to tires, from plastics to clothing. Get in touch with research experts with an oil company and do a story showing the amazing number of products made from oil-based compounds.

Early oilmen used a crude man-powered sapling drill. But today giant derricks drill for oil below the ocean's floor—more than twenty miles at sea.

Old Clothes

Unwritten tragedy: a bag of discarded clothing donated to Goodwill Industries of Dallas contained one unused wedding dress. What types of clothes show up in the drives in your city? Are some of the clothes out-of-style? Are some of them new?

Oldsters

Mark Twain kept up his billiards until shortly before he died at the age of seventy-five. He often spent as much as nine hours a day at his table. Who are some of the old-timers in your community who still play certain games? If possible, find several men and several women.

Opera

No matter how small your village, it probably has several opera fans. Do they often meet and discuss current operas? Who has seen the most performances? Do some of them take part in local programs or those in nearby cities? Does the group meet to hear an opera on TV?

Date tie-in: Enrico Caruso sang his last role at the Metropolitan Opera House in New York on December 24, 1920. Was he the greatest of all tenors? Do his records still sell? What was his particular claim to fame?

Opportunity

"Opportunity knocks but once." True? Untrue? Do successful people make their opportunities? Must you expose yourself to opportunities, or wait for something to happen? Are opportunities as plentiful or more plentiful today than formerly? Sources for comments: employment heads, supervisors, managers, and others.

Optimist Club

Using the slogan, "Friend of the Boy," your local Optimist Club is good for a story on the ways in which it is helping youth. Once each year the club observes City Official Day, at which time it emphasizes its local program.

Orchestra

What are the duties of the librarian in a large orchestra? What

are some of his problems? How do the sizes of scores differ in pages?
Does the conductor have the largest score? How is the music filed?

Organizations

Many organizations have auxiliary units. What are their objectives? Do they tie in with the work of the main organization? What
are some of the oldest? The youngest? What are some of the most
active in community projects?

Outdoor Advertising

Huge, taste-tempting third dimensional pictorials of attractively
served foods are among the new ideas used by outdoor advertisers.
How has advertising to the outdoor public changed through the years?
Do faster automobiles mean shorter advertising messages? How is
lighting used at night?

Outdoor Life

The great outdoors will come under tremendous pressure from
expanding population within the next twenty-five years, says Dr.
Charles B. Loomis, a sociologist at Michigan State University. "The
poorest man is just as good as the millionaire when both get outdoors,"
he says. What are local and state agencies doing to expand recreation
facilities—hunting, fishing, and others—for coming generations?

What types of guns are preferred by the leading hunters of your
community? Ask each why he prefers a particular one. What are the
advantages and disadvantages of the different types?

Overseas Aid

Many of your citizens contribute to the overseas aid programs of
the three major religious faiths—the Catholic Relief Services, Church
World Service, and United Jewish Appeal. Who heads these groups
in your community? What are some of the appeals? For what specific
purposes is the fund used?

Pageants

Does your city or county present a pageant at an annual event?
If so, interview the director and get his side of the affair: the long-
time planning, writing, casting, properties, weather, costs, and other
details.

A human interest story about children is assured of high readership, particularly if accompanied by a lively picture. (See Children.*)*

Photograph by Martha Frederick

Unique hobbies always make a good feature story. (*See* Hobbies.)

Photograph by Jim Boatright; courtesy *The Tulsa World*

Painters

Have you ever had a friend who was ambitious enough to start painting his house by himself? Then what happened? He probably gave up and called in a crew of painters. How often does this happen? Show some of the dangers, such as working from high ladders, which the typical citizen may not be aware of.

Palmistry

Palmistry has been practiced for centuries. Does your city have any palm readers? What do they know about human nature? How did they learn their techniques?

Parks

One park director admitted that adults, not children, damaged more property. Is some of the damage intentional? Do some adults use equipment which is meant for children? What is the annual cost of vandalism and damage to park equipment?

Parking

Employees of merchants in many towns are being urged to use side streets rather than space in the shopping district. Why? Largely because their cars take up space needed by customers. Is your city doing anything about this? What do merchants think of parking meters? Have they helped business?

Parking Meters

Motorists often insert metal slugs and other objects in parking meters. What do city employees find when counting money from parking meters? What percentage of the "take" is slugs and other objects? Are meters often damaged by motorists who stick knives, nail files, and other objects in them?

Parties

Has anyone in your city played host at a "do-it-yourself" party—to which guests come dressed to indicate the thing they do best? Find one if you can, and do an amusing feature, both on the garbs worn to the party and also on the interests of the guests.

Two tombstones stolen from a dealer in Denver were located at a local fraternity which was observing its annual "Morticians Ball."

What are some of the unique parties held in your community? Are some of them annual affairs? Which ones feature unusual costumes?

Patents

There's feature stuff in this: All patents are dated on Tuesday of the week in which they are issued. Makes no difference even if Tuesday happens to be a holiday. Why is this practice observed? When did it start, and why? How many patents have been issued by the federal government since the founding of the U.S. Patent Office?

What are the steps in obtaining a patent from the U.S. Patent Office? For how long is a patent good? Is it necessary to use the services of a patent attorney? Is a model required? Perhaps someone in your town has secured one or more patents. Let him tell you the steps and costs involved.

Pawn Shops

To what extent do pawnbrokers assist police in tracing stolen items? How can a pawnbroker tell if some person is trying to dispose of stolen goods? What are some of the odd articles which have never been redeemed?

Peeves

According to George Gallup, our nation's three main peeves are: (1) honking horns in front of houses, (2) eating popcorn in the movies, and (3) coughing and sneezing in public. Interview a number of people and ask, "What are your pet peeves? What are some of the things that you wish people wouldn't do?"

Pencils

Experts reveal that the average pencil can draw a line thirty-five miles long. Have styles in pencils changed much through the years? Who are some of the users of colored pencils? Do many women carry purse pencils? Are many pencils purchased as gifts? Talk to the clerk in an office supply store or in a book store selling office or school supplies.

Pennies

Banks in a midwestern city reported a shortage of pennies. "More are going out than are coming in," officials said. Then a reporter started looking around and found this: children were saving them. One little tot had two quart fruit jars filled with pennies. Ask bankers about the situation in your town.

Personality

Mrs. Osa Johnson, wife of the famous explorer and traveler, kept busy after his death by filling lecture engagements and personal appearance dates. The couple made thirteen movies and twenty lecture films between 1912 and 1940. It's always news when you write a story about a well-known woman, particularly one who is carrying on the work of her husband after he dies.

Psychologist Henry Link, with the aid of eighty other psychologists, studied over two hundred physical and mental habits. Here's what they found: habits involving physical activities were far better for developing personality than mental exercises. Localize these findings by getting opinions from a psychologist or teacher of psychology.

"Human nature never changes." You've heard that repeated, but is it really true? Do the basic drives remain about the same, even though philosophies change? Get some quotes from ministers, sociologists, psychologists, or prominent leaders who have shown ability to lead people.

What is the final test of a person's character? Frustration, eight Yale scientists believe. They concluded that all frustrations cause aggressive conduct—constructive or destructive. Ask local psychologists or teachers of psychology if they agree with this view.

Petroleum

Drilling an oil well can be a very expensive operation. How does a big company reduce the uncertainty of drilling? What role does a geologist play? At what stage is a physicist needed? Finally, who gathers all of the information? Who decides if a well is to be drilled?

About 68 per cent of the oil wells in this country—approximately 332,000—are known as "stripper wells." This means that they produce so little oil that further development of wells in their area is unwarranted. How many of these wells are found in your area? What is the average daily output from the wells? What is the oldest well?

Pets

Pets in an animal hospital in Tampa, Florida, enjoy many luxuries. Music is piped into each kennel room. Pups enjoy a small swimming pool. Your local veterinarian may not have such a ritzy place, but his work is worth a feature. New facilities? New treatments for old ailments? Are modern pets kept indoors too much?

Baby chicks and ducks are sometimes offered as prizes by certain business firms during the Easter season. This practice is being criticized by officials of the SPCA because it gives the pets to children who may not have space to keep them and who may not know how to raise them. Do local stores follow this practice? If so, do SPCA officials approve?

The forty-six million families in the United States own some forty-nine million animal pets. What are the most common pets in your area? What's next? Is one breed of dog or cat more popular than others? What range of treatment is accorded pets by different families? What do parents think of pets? What do children think?

An Illinois man, after some difficulty, finally found a casket big enough for his pet lion (weight, 325 pounds). How many pet owners use boxes in which to bury their dead pets? Where do they bury them? Do they erect headstones at the graves? Good source of information: veterinarians.

Do an occasional story by interviewing the owner of a local pet shop. Where does he obtain the pets? Are many pets purchased at Christmas? What are some of the more popular ones? Any requests for unusual pets?

Humans aren't the only ones who sometimes need tonsillectomies. So do dogs. Are there other afflictions that both man and dog are heir to? Interview your veterinarian.

Many parents of small children wonder, "How old should Susie be before we get her a puppy?" Get the answer from the kennel owners in your community. What kinds of dogs make the best pets for kiddies? What health precautions should be observed before the dog joins the family? What about food for the puppy?

In Chicago a lady lost her dog and asked police to find it. Identifying marks: red nail polish on its toenails. Can most owners identify their lost pets? Can they describe characteristics? For interesting sidelights, talk to classified ad takers at the newspaper office.

New drugs are being used by human beings. Are they adaptable for animals? Are special drugs being used by veterinarians? If so, what are they and for what are they used? Your veterinarian has the answers.

The first world convention for parakeet fanciers was held in 1954 in Harrogate, England. It attracted some eight hundred parakeet owners from eleven nations. Are other international organizations of similar limited scope? Do bird fanciers near you meet regularly to exchange ideas and suggestions? Do they wait for the parakeet's first word with the same keen interest with which parents wait for junior's first word?

The manufacture of dog food is a big business, but one in which Fido has little chance to voice a preference. How do dog food companies know what foods animals will like? How can they make it taste good to animals? Is the sense of smell a factor in the manufacture of foods dogs will like?

Feeding dogs has become a two hundred million dollar yearly business in the United States. What should dogs be fed? How many times a day? Do dogs, like humans, get too fat from over-eating? Do different breeds require different foods?

It is much easier to prolong the lives of cats and dogs by taking care of them while kittens and puppies, a noted veterinarian points out. Interview a veterinarian and get his suggestion for the proper care of kittens and puppies. What diets are best? When do they need shots?

Nobody knows how many cats are in the United States. To many folks, cats are charming companions, good friends, and a lot of fun. Swinburne, Hugo, Rostand, and Mark Twain were among the literary cat lovers of other days. Why do many people prefer cats as pets? Do they catch as many birds as some people think? Do they jump on tables, steal food, and trip people?

Pharmacists

Do you know what the initials "U.S.P." mean on a bottle of medicine? They mean that the product has been made according to the standards listed in the *U.S. Pharmacopeia,* a book which provides standards for the most important medicines. Your druggist can give you the story behind the book, which was started in 1820.

Phonographs

Does anyone in your community still have an old phonograph? And some old records? Then write a feature for publication on November 21, because it was on that date in 1877 that Thomas A. Edison announced the invention of the phonograph.

Photographers

You've seen the photographs taken by lens daredevils. Is there such a photographer in your city? How much courage is required to take pictures of skyscraper workers, window washers, and others who earn their living way up in the air? Must a photographer overcome a fear of height?

Every much-photographed celebrity has a wisecrack or two he can use to break the ice when he is being photographed with "visiting firemen." Dwight Eisenhower would do this: if a baby were in the crowd he would tell the mother, "He parts his hair like I do." What does your mayor do to get a smile on the face of everyone in a group being photographed? Or your governor?

Every commercial photographer takes hundreds of pictures over a period of years. How does he file the negatives? Does a person often order a photo many years after the original was taken? Do relatives often order prints of someone after his or her death? Are photographs sometimes requested by newspapers or magazines?

What's the story behind a sidewalk photographer? What percentage of the people who stroll by want their pictures made? What are some of his techniques of getting people interested? Does he rely for the most part on tourists and visitors to buy prints? Does he need a city permit to take pictures?

Photographs

Look around and you'll find a studio which specializes in restoring old portraits and photographs. What methods are used? What are some of the oldest ones that have been restored? Have some of the paintings been of more than ordinary value?

Date tie-in: The first aerial photo was made from a balloon over Boston, November 13, 1860. How are aerial photos made today? What are some of their uses? Who are some of the biggest users?

Everybody likes pictures. But not too many persons enjoy having their photographs taken. Why do people dread to go to the photographer? Is it a matter of taking the time? Ask a veteran photographer about his experiences. Are men easier to please than women? Do relatives often come along and suggest poses? What are some of the best ways of getting pictures of babies and small children?

Many of your citizens possess collections of war photographs. Tie in their collections with the work of the famous war photographer Mathew B. Brady, who died on January 15, 1896. Who has the largest collection? The oldest? Newest?

There's one photographer in your city whose subjects don't always pose willingly. He's the police photographer. How does he go about getting the pictures he needs when the suspect is unco-operative? Does he have special tricks? Any unusual experiences?

Is the fashion photographer's job as pleasant as it would seem? How did top photographers in this specialized line get their start? Who designs the settings? Who creates them? How many shots does it take to get the one that's "just right"? What problems are peculiar to the profession?

Ever since George Eastman said, "You snap the shutter, we'll do the rest," Americans have been doing just that. Millions of snapshots are taken each year. Some are good, some are not so good. Any professional photographer can give the amateur hints on how to take better pictures of the family, the pets, the summer vacation trip. How about a summertime feature on ways to make a better snapshot record of a family vacation or outing?

Thousands of Americans are photography enthusiasts. Show how persons of all ages and from all economic brackets enjoy this hobby. Who has the oldest camera? Who has been a "shutter-bug" the longest? Cite local persons whose photos have won awards.

A five-year-old Detroit boy jumped into the headlines when it was announced that he was to become a press photographer for the *Detroit Times*. His assignment: to make a photo feature of pictures taken by himself. Who is the youngest photographer in your community? Has he won any awards? Have any of his photos been published?

Physicians

Twenty years ago a physician spent only about 30 per cent of his working hours actually doctoring. Today, thanks to modernized equipment, transportation, and communication, and more and better assistants, he spends approximately 90 per cent of his time treating patients. Why not follow a busy doctor through a typical day and tell what he does?

If you're doing a story showing the progress of medical training, then remember this date: May 3, 1765. It was on that day that Dr. John Morgan and Dr. William Shippen, Jr., established a medical department in the College of Philadelphia, now the University of Pennsylvania. This was the first medical school in the nation. Point out the high standards of medical schools, how teaching methods have changed, how full and part-time staff members are named, what is involved in internships, and the number of graduates each year.

You've heard a lot of jokes about the old magazines in doctors' offices. Are they true? What magazines are found in doctors' offices? Do patients carry off some of the publications? Does a doctor try to provide a variety of reading material for his patients?

Different types of operations demand different types of sutures. One used in an eye operation, for instance, is different from one used for a brain operation. Interview a surgeon and ask him how sutures have changed through the years, the advantages of the newer types, and how he learned to stitch skin and human organs.

Doctor's Day is observed once each year by the women's auxiliaries of medical associations. Purpose of the day is to honor members of the medical profession, both living and dead. The red carnation, official flower for the day, is given to each member. What will be done in your county or state? Special programs? How many retired physicians live in your community? Does your community have more or fewer doctors than ten years ago?

The dictionary defines sneezes, coughs, and itches, but doesn't say what causes them. Lots of readers would like to know what causes these normal functions. Can your doctor tell you what prompts a sneeze, a cough, or an itch. What are the bodily processes involved?

Two Iowa doctors cleaned out their old offices before moving to a new clinic and found magazines dating as far back as 1921. What magazines are found in local doctors' offices? Which magazines are read the most? Do patients ever make suggestions for their favorite magazines?

In a great many localities county medical societies have organized an emergency medical service. If there's one in your community, describe how it operates. Can any person get in touch with a doctor at any time? Have telephone operators been trained to help the caller in finding a doctor?

Who has the oldest medical library in your county? What is the oldest book? How has the practice of medicine changed since some of the old books were published? Did some of the old-time doctors practice psychosomatic medicine under another name?

Picnics

It's spring! And too many people become sun lovers, picnic fanatics, and hiking enthusiasts as caution is thrown to the wind. What precautions should be taken? Like swimming too soon after eating a big meal? Staying in the sun too long? Getting in a patch of poison ivy? Overexertion in games and sports? Any health authority can give you enough pointers to make an informative story.

Pipelines

Burrowing through mountains, bridging rivers, tunneling under lakes, heading all across America, are gushing streams of natural gas and petroleum, channeled through a five-hundred-thousand mile network of pipelines. The first successful pipeline was laid in Pennsylvania in 1862. What are some of the oldest lines? Their load? How is the flow of oil regulated? Do lines require many repairs? What about inspections?

Plants

About 350 different plant diseases damage crops heavily each year. Your county agent will know which ones affect your area most. How many plant diseases are common to your county? Is research in ways to cure these plant diseases as constant as is research in human diseases? What important steps have been taken in recent years?

Remember this tie-in date when you write a feature on flowers, vegetables, or plants: March 7, 1849. That is the birthdate of Luther Burbank, who produced many new and valuable varieties of fruits, flowers, and forage plants. Is the anniversary of his birth observed by any local groups?

Plays

A leading playwright explains that he tries to give all of his works happy endings. Do most drama lovers want happy endings? Do they want to know exactly how the hero got out of the predicament? What do theatergoers and TV fans consider happy endings?

Plumbers

Every veteran plumber can tell many interesting stories. Some angles: how plumbing fixtures have changed, shortage of supplies in war time, his advice to water users during extremely cold weather, and some unusual emergency calls he has answered.

Poetry

Interview eight or ten of your leading citizens on this question, "What is your favorite poem?" What are their reasons for their choices? Did some of them learn the poems while in school? Do any of them have framed copies of the poems in their offices or homes?

Charles Darwin, in his late years, said if he could live his life over again, he would read some poetry and listen to some good music at least once a week. How many read poetry today? What are some of the most popular types of poetry? Check your bookseller, your librarian, or a local poet.

Police

A child called the police in Morgantown, West Virginia, and asked that they "come right away." They investigated and found that someone had taken the child's modeling clay. How do police in your city handle calls from children? Should they be taught by their parents not to call the police unless something is really wrong? Get the comments of the chief of police.

Strange murder weapons possess a peculiar interest. Let a veteran officer tell about unusual objects used by slayers in their crimes. Were some of them homemade? How did officers recover some of the weapons? What happens to confiscated weapons?

Small children get lost from time to time. How do your local police find them and get them home? How does a policeman win the confidence of a youngster? What have been some of the puzzling cases? Do most small children know their address, telephone number, or the names of their parents?

Every day the police in a city will hear complaints of crimes which have never happened. How do your police handle fibbers? How do police sense a false complaint? What constitutes the largest number of false reports—petty larceny? Stolen automobiles?

A burglar broke into a factory warehouse in Los Angeles and stole seven hundred pogo sticks. Has your local police chief or sheriff had to work any thefts as unusual? What percentage of robberies or thefts are eventually solved in your town or county? How does it compare with the national average?

Recruits on the Los Angeles police force, like those of many other cities, are prepared for their jobs by a thirteen-week course that has all the rigors of basic training in the Marines. How are your local and state police trained? What subjects are stressed? Who sets up the course of study? How are instructors chosen?

How do your local police keep in good physical trim? Are they required to practice wind sprints, walk regularly, or pass a physical examination at regular intervals?

Make the rounds with a night watchman some night. Or if that isn't convenient, then ask him about his unusual experiences. Why does he prefer night duties? What are some of his typical experiences?

There's a story waiting to be written about the police vehicles—cars, motorcycles, and patrol wagons—of your city. What kinds of officers get in the most mileage each month? How often are cars checked? Are police vehicles involved in many accidents? How are routes of scout cars determined?

Police work in shifts. And often their shifts are rotated. Which shift do most policemen prefer? At night when the "criminal element" is usually more in evidence? Or during the day when more people are moving about in their everyday tasks?

The first aerial policewoman in the United States was Cora Sterling, commissioned in Seattle, Washington, in 1934. Does your city have a policewoman with special assignments? What is her philosophy toward offenders?

What goes on in your city in the wee hours of the night? Interview a night watchman about his experiences. Ask him how many businessmen often leave their front doors unlocked, how he watches for prowlers, and how he has detected fires.

Policemen are always doing something to disprove the belief held by many that they are unfriendly to children. Who are some of the cops who rank as favorites with children? Show how a typical policeman is a friend to boys and girls.

Are any of your local policemen known for their memory feats? How do they try to remember faces? Are they always concentrating on certain faces in running down criminals? How do they strengthen their memory?

You can't beat the foot patrolman, New York Police Commissioner Francis Adams points out. "He is what the infantryman is to the army." Does your city still use the old-fashioned beat pounder? What are his duties? Does your chief of police agree with Adams?

Politics
Almost no parents want their sons to go into politics; they are certain that a political career leads to graft and crookedness, a Gallup Poll revealed. How would holders of political offices react to this attitude? How did they become interested in politics? Would they encourage young people to consider careers in politics?

More women are attending political gatherings, heads of both the Democratic and Republican national groups report. What's happening in your community? Are more meetings being held in homes? Are the meetings attracting many young women? What is being done to interest women in political affairs?

Population
The restless migrations of a restless age are creating many problems. Rural folks are moving to the city, city folks are moving to the suburbs—boundary lines are being pushed back. What is happening in your city? Are new churches springing up in new sections? How does a population shift affect the schools of your city?

Shoot at the publication of a census story on August 1, because the first national census got under way on that date in 1790. Who were the first settlers in your county or city? How fast has the community grown? What have been some interesting facts in the population figures from time to time?

Postmen
On his last day of carrying mail a veteran postman was kissed by 386 women on his route! Check with your postmaster and find out when a postman will carry mail for the last time. Will the patrons do anything for him? Will he be honored by any of his associates? Approximately how far has he walked on his route through the years?

Post Office
What are the most violated postal regulations? Leaving off stamps? Marking the envelope "air mail" or using an air mail envelope and then forgetting to use enough postage? Leaving off part of the

address—like the city and state? Failure to pack "fragile" articles? Check with post office officials for other angles.

The days of the olive drab corner mailbox may be numbered, as the U.S. Post Office Department hustles for more business. Experiments in red, white and blue mailboxes are being carried on in several parts of the country, to remind passersby of unanswered correspondence. What other methods does the Post Office Department use to attract business? How are techniques changing? Are the brightly colored corner mailboxes doing the job?

What has happened to the rural mail routes of your county? Talk to a veteran carrier and find out the requests which people make of him, how many miles he travels each day, how he sorts his mail early each day, and about how many people on his route receive newspapers or magazines or both.

Check with your postmaster now and then and find out any gains or losses in outgoing or incoming mail—first class, parcel post, second and third class. Do people write more letters in the winter or summer? Do the vacation months mean more mail?

Few persons know exactly what happens to a letter from the time it is dropped into the mail until it is delivered to the addressee. Visit the postoffice and watch the steps followed by employees in their duties. How is mail sorted? How fast do machines cancel letters? What are the rush periods for this step? Describe the duties of the employees who work at the sorting table.

Congress established the United States Post Office March 12, 1789. With this date as a peg, write a feature on the local postal service, how many persons use air mail and special delivery, how the system has grown, whether people write more letters today than they used to, and how many postmasters have served in the local office.

Censorship of mail isn't new. According to the *Connecticut Gazette* of November 29, 1755, a letter written in New York was adjudged "false and scurrilous and tending to beget ill will" and was "accordingly, at four of the clock this morning, after proper notice by beat of drum, publicly whipt, according to Moses Law, forty stripes save one, by the common whipper, and then burnt." What types of mail are forbidden by federal regulations?

Power

Hundreds of old-fashioned water mills are still at work grinding meal, flour, and a variety of cereals. If there's one in your region, find out who built it and when, its owner, what it is used for, where its water comes from, and if it attracts many tourists.

Predictions

On her 101st birthday in Chicago, Mrs. Demitra Gekas recalled that fifty-six years before doctors had given her only twenty-four hours to live. Who are some people in your community who have lived far beyond the prediction of medical experts who had given them a limited number of days, weeks, or months to live? Does a person facing a limited stay on earth change his philosophy?

Premiums

Lee Priestly spoke of a friend by stating that "he was as impatient as a kid who had mailed in a boxtop." Does the use of premiums speed up the sale of many products? What are some of the unusual ones? Do most premiums appeal to both boys and girls? Look over the cereal shelves at your nearest supermarket, then talk to the manager and you'll have a story.

Premonitions

Can you count on premonitions? When are they likely to be experienced? Do some persons receive warnings before disasters or tragedies? Can you find persons who "felt" that something was about to happen?

Prescriptions

More than 90 per cent of the medical prescriptions today could not have been filled twenty-five years ago because the medicines did not exist. Talk to a veteran druggist and see what some of the standard remedies were when he entered the profession? Have most of them given way to newer drugs? Does he ever get a call by a person who wants an old-fashioned remedy?

Presidents

A reporter wrote a feature after he had discovered that one man served as president of five organizations. Can you find a person who heads that many groups in your city? If so, how does he find time to perform all his duties? What does he enjoy most about serving as president?

At 42, Theodore Roosevelt was the youngest United States president? What do most people consider the desirable age for the president of the nation? At about what age do most people believe a man should not attempt to get the nomination?

Printing

Observance of National Printing Week, tied in with the anniversary of the birth of Benjamin Franklin, will make you a good story. New printing processes, the role of printing in communications, and how Americans depend on the printed word are just a few possible angles.

The ratio of apprentices in the printing industry is one to ten but it should be one to five, according to a report of the Printing Industry of America. Are newspapers training apprentices? Is instruction in printing and other graphic arts offered in any schools in your community or state?

Prisons

Does your state operate a prison farm? If so, does it show a profit? How much of the farm output is used by the inmates? Do state officials believe that a farm keeps a lot of inmates busy and thus keeps them from brooding? Does the farm ever have a surplus which is sold to other state institutions or to the public?

Did you read about the Alabama prisoner who did not want to accept his parole because he sang bass on the penitentiary quartet and "didn't want them to have to go to the trouble of breaking in a new man"? Do many prisoners regret leaving jails and penitentiaries? What are some of the reasons? Does a long sentence cause some prisoners to want to remain even longer? Wardens and jailers should be able to elaborate with interesting comments.

*Animals, from Pliny's day to ours, have absorbed
human interest.* (See Animals.)

Photograph by Jean Mattox

Excellent feature articles distinguish The Saturday Evening Post.
*Here Senior Editor Richard Thruelsen gets enthusiastic
about a new idea with Pat Schneider.*

When Virginia State Penitentiary inmates were offered the opportunity of taking courses in practical subjects, many of them asked for a course in keymaking! What courses are offered in your state and federal penitentiaries? How are the instructors chosen? Are most of the inmates really interested in their assignments? Are they given certificates when the courses are completed?

How should convicts be treated? You can get an interesting feature by interviewing the warden of your state penitentiary. What is the philosophy of his administration? To what extent does he believe an inmate can be trusted? Does a penitentiary sentence change the lives of many inmates? Under what conditions are privileges taken away from inmates?

If you live near a federal or state prison, find out about the rehabilitation program for prisoners. Are all prisoners required to learn new habits and skills? Do some continue the work which they followed in civilian life? What are some of the products made by prisoners?

Progress

"Discontent is the steam in the boiler of progress," Gerald Horton Bath says. Is this true? Are the leaders of your city dissatisfied with things as they are? Is this the secret of American progress? Get the opinions of several well-known people who have succeeded in different fields.

Which brings about more improvements, conservatism or radicalism? E. D. Marshall, in his *Farewell to Revolution*, shows that nearly all improvements have come from intelligent, progressive conservatives. Is man torn between a desire to remain the same and yet do something different? Is the radical too aggressive in seeking changes overnight? Has most progress been rather slow?

Proofreading

"If readers think a lot of mistakes get in the daily newspaper, they should see some of the ones we catch," a veteran proofreader stated. What are some of the boners which slip by the proofreader? Does he read the proof once or several times? What special abilities are helpful to a proofreader?

Proverbs

Turkish propaganda experts believe that through its proverbs its people can best be understood. Proverbs, they say, are the wisdom of centuries distilled into everyday use. Are proverbs used by teachers today? Ministers? How many proverbs can an average person remember? Have they helped him?

Psychiatry

A prominent psychiatrist says it is possible that psychiatric illnesses have been "oversold." He believes that "psychosomatic illnesses have become fashionable." Can people read so much about certain types of illness that they gradually believe that they have them? Are too many articles about mental illness being published?

P.T.A.

On February 17, 1824, in New Ipswich, Connecticut, a "Maternal Association" was organized which was a forerunner of present-day "Mothers Clubs" and possibly of the P.T.A. One of its objectives was "the bringing up of our children in the nurture and admonition of the Lord." To what extent are religious values stressed in P.T.A. groups today? Is there a committee on character and spiritual education?

Cartoonists often aim their gags at P.T.A. activities. Actually, these groups perform a great variety of tasks, many of them virtually unknown. So why not check with past and present P.T.A. officials and get a list of the scores of activities sponsored by the groups through the years.

Public Apathy

Too many Americans show a "low level of public interest in many of the country's major issues," Dr. George Gallup of the American Institute of Public Opinion declares. Why aren't more Americans interested in great issues? Does education increase interest in major problems? Do people really know what's going on in the world?

Public Speaking

Where does a toastmaster find his jokes? Does he keep a file? If so, are the jokes filed under certain topics? What kind of joke gets the biggest response? What kinds of jokes does he avoid? What about telling a joke on a stranger?

One speaker, addressing inmates of a state penitentiary, opened his speech by saying, "I'm glad to see so many of you here tonight." Query several prominent speakers about their slips of the tongue.

Americans have always found plenty to talk about. And the time has passed when programs can be dominated by a few persons who know it all. So there are new ways of holding meetings—ways in which all members of a group can participate. Some of the best sources for such a story: speech teachers, adult education leaders, and anyone who is active in community groups.

Do commencement addresses which give advice do any good? Ask ten adults if they can remember any advice given them at either high school or college commencements. Then ask the college president or superintendent of schools what they think about advice offered by commencement speakers.

Quarrels

Most of the quarrels between Mr. and Mrs. America are prompted by money, jealousy, and children—in that order—a Gallup poll discloses. Would money be the chief quarrel producer today? Are most persons jealous to a certain extent? To what extent do children cause quarrels between adults?

Questions

"Only a fool asks questions." True? Thomas A. Edison once said, "I learned mainly by reading and asking questions." Ask teachers if the student who is curious is usually any brighter than the rest of the group. And ask supervisors if employees who are "on the way up" possess more curiosity than their fellow workers. Is curiosity a sign of mental alertness?

Always good: Put this question to eight or ten of your leading citizens: "What was your most embarrassing moment?"

Quilts

Quilting isn't a lost art. A Ponca City, Oklahoma, woman had made more than one thousand before her seventy-ninth birthday.

Who makes quilts in your community? How are the designs chosen? How many pieces are in an average size quilt?

Old quilts still have a peculiar fascination. Do women still make them as they did years ago? Does any group in your community ever hold a quilting party? Do young wives of today know how to make quilts? Who owns some of the oldest?

Radio

Where do radio stations get those sound effects? Do they create any of them in the studio, or are they all recorded? Is there a difference in sound effects and their use in radio and television? How important is a sound effect in the creation of illusion? Talk to a sound effects man at a big radio or TV station.

About one-third of all the radios built in the United States were designed for automotive use. What are the peak hours in listening for owners of car radios? What programs are preferred? Music? News? Sports? Quiz shows? What percentage of the new cars come equipped with radios?

Surveys show that radio listening suffers temporarily in new television areas, but increases after the TV newness has worn off. Is this a typical reaction in your community? Let radio men tell you the advantages of their medium. Then get the television side of the story. Follow up with a survey of your own on listening and viewing habits.

Do listeners like their radio news with the accent on facts or on interpretation? Do they know and appreciate the difference between a newscaster and a commentator? At what time of the day do most people listen to radio news?

What types of letters are received by local radio and television stars? Do some of the admirers write regularly? Which sex receives more letters? What are the most common types of letters?

Are radio and TV announcers trained in the pronunciation of musical numbers, composers, authors, and other proper names? One boner on the air probably brings a deluge of letters. And what about the pronunciation of towns with strange names in your area?

About 35 percent of homes have at least two radios and about 21 per cent have three, according to a survey. Have radio listening habits in the home been changed by the coming of TV? Do listeners prefer music and news on radio? Do many housewives continue their housework with the radio operating? At what periods do most people listen to radio programs?

Who is the best-known radio minister in your city? What kinds of letters does he receive? Does he make a special effort to reach the elderly, the handicapped, and other shut-ins? What kind of sermon is likely to get the best reaction?

A columnist in the *Detroit News* wrote, "We're always grateful when the moderator of a radio panel discussion repeats at the end of the program what the subject was, as there is no way of telling just by listening to the arguments." Does your local station present panel shows? Who chooses the topics? What topics are likely to interest listeners? Are some topics too controversial to be discussed?

Quiz shows are eagerly followed by many radio and TV fans. What makes a good quiz show? How difficult should the questions be? Have amusing answers been given to some questions? Do many contestants "freeze up" and seem to forget everything before a mike? Which seem to possess more poise before the mike—men or women? Any experienced quizmaster can give you some interesting answers to these questions.

Since the middle thirties, the Federal Communications Commission has had a rule for assigning the initial call letter for radio and television stations: those east of the Mississippi River start with W, those west of the Mississippi start with K. But who chooses the letters that go with the W or K? Do they have any meaning? Can any combination be used?

When technical difficulties force a radio or television station off the air, the station usually gets a flood of calls. The receptionist or telephone operator at your hometown station can tell you about unusual calls she has received. Are most people sympathetic to the problems of the station? What unusual information do people want from radio and TV stations?

Railroads

The duties and experiences of railroad police are unknown to many people. If there's one in your region, get an insight into his duties in protecting railroad property. What are the most common types of law violation? Do many young men try to get free rides on freight trains? Is the old-time hobo still around?

Not too far from you you will find a hospital maintained by a railroad for its employees. Interview the surgeon and ask him what are the principal illnesses and injuries of railroad workers and what rare operations have been successful. And ask him to tell you what his company does to watch the health of its employees.

Who is the oldest depot agent in your county? Ask him how times have changed, how he started his career, and what he thinks of the competition offered by airlines, trucks, busses, and other means of travel. Be sure and ask him to explain the safety measures observed by his railroad.

Do any railroad engineers live in your city? If so, ask them about some of their experiences, about the children who regularly greet them along their runs, how the speed of trains has been increased, and be sure and get some of the experiences of yesterday.

Locate a Pullman porter with years of experience, and you'll get a live story. Is the most asked question, "Where are we?" Does the porter have to be a travel guide, amateur psychologist, shoe shine boy, nursemaid, and finder-of-lost-articles? Does a porter ever forget to awaken a passenger at the right time? How many traveling salesmen still use trains? Have a porter's duties been changed by the air conditioning of trains?

Monthly auctions are conducted in many cities by various railroads to dispose of refused and unclaimed freight. Is a preview held the day before? How fast does the merchandise move? Is most of the merchandise repaired or offered "as is"? Will anyone buy a broken mirror? Your source: the auctioneer.

What is the fastest train which stops or goes through your town? What is its average speed? What is the length of the run? If your local agent does not know all of the answers, get in touch with the nearest public relations office of the railroad.

You'll never lack for a story if you'll visit a railroad station in a city. You see people of all classes, all ages, all races, in all kinds of clothes. Interview a few to get a "Welcome Traveler" angle and then round out the story with some bits of conversations you hear and a few observations.

The average freight car today wanders far and wide—moving on as many as thirty-nine different railroads in the course of a year. Talk to a freight official and see how they keep track of cars, how far a car may travel in a year, the different types of cars, and the speed with which freight moves in comparison with the old days.

Railroaders have traditionally been identified with uniforms or with jewelry such as watches with steam locomotives on the back. A conductor with his gold buttons is just as proud of his buttons as the policeman is proud of his shiny badge. Do a story on railroad buttons, jewelry, and fraternal emblems.

About fifty cents out of every dollar of operating revenue taken in by American railroads is paid out in wages to employees and taxes on payrolls for the support of railroad retirement and unemployment compensation systems. Check with railroad officials and see how the other fifty cents is spent? Increased facilities? New equipment?

Good tip: Interview a railway mail clerk. Find out how the treatment and handling of mail has changed. How is mail sorted? Does he dread the Christmas rush? What does he enjoy about his work?

Rats
Rats are the deadliest, most destructive of all animal enemies of humanity. Government biologists estimate that there are as many rats as people in the United States. But new poisons are being developed and used. What are they? Are they safe for domestic animals, pets, and children?

Readership
Does your town have the annual rodeo fever? If it does, run up the thermometer of support for your newspaper with stories on the

history and origin of rodeos, tied in with a local riders' club or a scheduled rodeo. These riders' clubs are active almost all year.

Combine both news and circulation promotion by running a series of feature stories on some of your oldest subscribers. Play up the person's hobbies, beliefs, and his or her role in the early days of the community. Use plenty of direct quotes—let the person talk.

It's an old idea but it always clicks. Do a humorous feature on or just before January 1 on New Year's resolutions. Use a lot of names rather than quoting just one person.

Reading

Officials of the Chicago Public Library have discovered that TV has increased the use of books. They believe that TV boosts reading by (1) stimulating interest in new subjects, and (2) boring the viewer and encouraging book reading as a substitute! Get the opinions of your local librarian.

A man in Wilmington, California, can read 6,200 words a minute—about twenty-five times the average reading speed. He's a teacher in "how to increase reading speed." Many colleges now have such courses. How do they work? Does increased speed in reading increase comprehension? How is faster reading taught? Can everyone learn to read faster?

"To acquire the habit of reading is to construct for yourself a refuge from almost all the miseries of life," W. Somerset Maugham said. Select four or five community leaders and find out what they read regularly, what publications have priority, why they choose what they do, and about how many hours each reads per week.

The average book contains a mile of reading matter. And because people who do little or no book reading make up for that by working with records, inventories, and other written material, the average American adult now is estimated to read the equivalent of eighteen books—or eighteen miles of written matter—each year. Talk to your local librarian about this estimate. Who reads the most books—men or women? How many books does the average library patron check out each year? Do children read more than adults?

How can you interest small children in reading? At an early age give children picture books of all kinds, advises Morton Schroeder. What's next? Get the views of teachers of little boys and girls—either those who teach in public schools or in Sunday schools. Ask them, "How can you teach a child to love books?"

Real Estate

Can you find a bargain in an old house? What are some of the advantages (many have abundant space) which an older house may have over the modern ones? How do you find symptoms of aging? How much would be required to repair the old house? Should you trust an enthusiastic salesman, or should you seek the advice of an expert appraiser? Get your story from the latter.

What do most families look for in a house? What are some of their reasons for wanting to sell their own? Are houses sometimes bought because of their sentimental value? What affects the real estate market?

Records

Record dealers have a hard time keeping up with the demand for hit tunes. Ask your local music store operator how long it takes for a hit parade record to reach the top in local sales. Or do local sales precede hit parade popularity? Which record has sold the most copies in the shortest time? Does he have stocks of records he thought would sell but didn't?

Mitch Miller, authority on records and hit tunes, says that the tune people remember is the one they associate with their courtship. What do record dealers think of this theory? Do they have any way of predicting whether a tune may hit the top list?

Recreation

What do the high public officials of your state—governor, members of the supreme court, attorney general, state treasurer, and others —do for recreation? What are their favorite sports and amusements? Good slant: how recreation activities refresh their spirits and strength.

Five cents out of every consumer dollar is spent for recreation, a national survey shows. Do most families set aside a certain amount for recreation? How many have a year-round program rather than seasonal ones? What are some of the biggest "bargains" in recreation for families?

"Kids of today depend too much on toys and gadgets for their fun," a child psychologist declares. Did your grandparents have more fun with simple things? Do kids of today build as many of their playthings—wagons, scooters, and the like—as those of yesterday? Do modern youngsters need more playthings because so many live in crowded apartments and do not have the yard space which was available to yesterday's kids? Talk to youth leaders and get their comments.

Most persons spend about 11 per cent of their income for fun and recreation—travel, boating, fishing, TV, reading, plays, gardening, golf, football, and other diversions. Would this percentage apply to most citizens of your community? Do most persons enjoy some type of recreational activity?

Red Cross

Members of the Junior Red Cross, with programs in elementary and secondary schools, make millions of articles from paper favors to furniture for use in hospitals and other institutions. Check with your Junior Red Cross chairman for ideas.

Your Red Cross chapter is a local terminus of a worldwide network of telegraphic and radio communication. Each year this network carries thousands of messages relating to the well-being of U.S. military personnel and their families. Obtain from the chapter's home service chairman or director data for a story on local messages sent and received. Bear in mind that actual names cannot be used except in very rare instances.

The hospital at the military installation near your city is worth a story. How is your community serving patients? What are the services of the Red Cross staff and volunteers in recreational and other areas? How are families of patients cared for when they come from a distance to visit their kin?

What are some of the problems of men in service? What are the most common? Check with the Red Cross field director at the military installation near your city. And you can give your story more human interest by getting case histories from chaplains.

What is the disaster potential of your community and county? Do you have a substandard residential section which is a fire hazard? A dangerous curve on a highway? A river without dams controlling its flow in times of high water? Are you in a tornado or hurricane area? Check with municipal authorities and the Red Cross on what measures have been taken to lessen this disaster potential?

Does your local Junior Red Cross participate in the high school chest program—providing chests of school supplies for foreign classrooms? Or perhaps the younger students are sending gift boxes to school children in other countries.

Religion

Here's a feature idea which is particularly effective just before Easter: seek the comments of ten or twelve leaders on the topic, "What My Religion Means to Me." Choose a variety of persons so that all major denominations are represented in the story or the series.

Does your state hospital for the mentally ill have a full-time chaplain on its staff? If so, what are his duties? Show his special training, the unique problems which he faces, and the ways in which he helps patients.

Of an estimated global population of nearly two and one-half billion, over a billion persons believe in Christ. How fast is that figure being increased? Is church membership making gains proportionate to the increase in population? Ministers will be glad to give you the facts you need.

Restaurants

What are the most popular foods of people who dine out? What are some of the old stand-by items which will always be popular? Do families eat out as much as they once did? Interview a local restaurant man for answers.

Does your town have a restaurant owned and operated by women? Do the cooks and waitresses believe in "calorie counting"? What are some of the most popular items on the menu? What are some of the "headaches" in operating a restaurant? Can waitresses judge people by the type of food they order?

Eating is a great national—and local—pastime. Then it's a natural for you to write about the most popular foods locally, judged by surveys of cafes.

Rodeos

Rodeo, once a Western sport only, is now popular through most of the nation, with about six hundred being held annually. Chances are you'll find one near you, so find out who sponsors it, who supplies the rodeo stock, how it is advertised, and the events which give the spectators the greatest thrills, together with something about the performers.

Safety

Say what you will about teen-age drivers, statistics prove the largest number of accidents for any age group and any one violation comes from drivers from twenty-five to thirty-four years of age. Safety experts can give you other facts about accident-prone age groups. Why is one age group more likely to have a greater number of accidents than another? Is it simply because there are more drivers in that group? How does your safety expert suggest correcting the situation?

More policemen are hurt in routine accidents such as slipping off a curb than are shot in gun battles, a study shows. Do your policemen take a safety course? Do they have many accidents? Get the views of the chief of police.

New traffic lights are fifty per cent larger and almost four times brighter than the usual city systems. Does your city have any of the new ones? Do your city traffic experts believe that larger lights will reduce accidents? How many offenders say that they did not see the lights? How do city planners determine where to place lights and what kinds?

What's the best method of punishing motorists who violate laws? Get tough with traffic offenders like Los Angeles? Send drunk drivers to jail like they do in Detroit? Educate drivers? Seek the comments of safety officials, policemen, and judges.

Insurance men say the courteous driver rarely causes—or gets caught in—an accident. Get comments from traffic judges and police on this view.

Is safety being commercialized? With more and more advertisers using safety signs and standards, some people think so. What legality is there in, say, a stop sign with a tag, "Furnished Courtesy of Joe Blow Soft Drinks." Does your city allow advertising on any of its safety signs or standards? If so, are there limitations? Who determines the size and nature of the advertising message?

Unmarked patrol cars are being used to nab traffic violators. Some folks think that this practice is "unsportsmanlike." Others ask, "What's wrong with slipping up on law violators?" If your state police are using unmarked patrol cars in their work, get the opinions of motorists, judges, traffic experts, and others.

Has the Jaybird visited your city? It works like this: Citizens are asked to keep a sharp lookout for anyone violating any pedestrian safety rule. To the person who spots the Jaybird, a cash award is given. What other method has been used in your city to call attention to violations of safety rules?

Even the tiny tots are taught rules of safety. Talk to a safety expert and find out some of the ways—films, demonstrations, stories—in which small children are taught some of the main safety rules. What is the best age to start the instruction? How can parents teach safety in the home?

Training in driving automobiles is provided in more than ten thousand American high schools. How is driver training handled in your public schools? Is it required? How many take the course each year? Do boys or girls learn to drive quicker? What are some of the hardest things to teach?

Scarcely a day passes without headlines telling how a small child has taken some kind of medicine by mistake and died. What are some of the safety precautions which should be observed in keeping harmful drugs away from small children? What do doctors and druggists advise?

In many states the department of public safety makes regular inspections of brakes, lights, horn, and other safety devices on cars. What are the most common defects? What reasons do motorists give for driving without safety features in proper working order? What percentage of accidents is caused by mechanical defects?

Skid marks left by synthetic tires do not provide accurate clues for determining the speed of a car at the scene of an accident, officials of Motor Vehicle Research have announced. Furthermore, they pointed out that a tire's stopping ability varied from make to make. Do your local traffic police and state police still measure skid marks at scenes of accidents? What is their opinion of the value of these marks?

Motorists in a Washington community see this sign: "Our Speed Limit is 25 Miles Per Hour With a Fine of $3 Per Mile for Faster Driving. Pick Out A Speed You Can Afford." Do these signs reduce accidents? Do motorists pay much attention to them?

You are 266 times safer while in an airplane than you are at home. And deaths in the home account for 30 per cent of all accidental deaths. Do a feature story on "There's No Place Like Home—For Accidents."

Sales

You are three times as apt to remember a can with a red label as a can with a white label, an advertising expert declares. Find a commercial artist—preferably one with some sales "know-how"—and get his opinion on color as a factor in buying. Are certain colors avoided in packages? What are the most attractive colors?

Billions of dollars are spent each year in advertising. Are such expenditures justified? Talk to the advertising manager of the biggest store in your community. What success stories can he give you? Are advertising claims extravagant? Do newspaper readers, radio listeners, and TV viewers want advertising? Do they buy widely advertised products?

Salesmen

The United States needs more salesmen now than ever before. But fewer competent young men are turning to careers in selling. Is a good salesman born or made? How can a salesman be trained to increase his sales? How do salesmen get leads? Talk to some of the best sales persons for tips for a good feature.

What's happened to the old-fashioned drummer? How have the duties and assignments of salesmen changed? How much of the buying is still done through salesmen who call on merchants? How much territory does today's salesman cover?

One top business executive predicts that twenty-five years from now half the nation's working force will be selling or making products unknown today. Get local salesmen's comments. List some of the newer products which have been placed on the market within the last year.

Chances are that your community has one or more Bible salesmen. Talk to one or more and get their experiences. When are most Bibles bought? By what age group? How many are bought as gifts? If you can't locate any salesmen, then get some comments from local booksellers.

The modern manufacturers' salesman is likely to be a far cry from the "drummer" of fiction. He is likely to be experienced in jobs other than his own, middle-aged, and the possessor of at least a year, and sometimes more, of college. Here's an angle: contrast yesterday's salesman—duties, territory, travel, approach—with the modern salesman.

Who takes longer to buy a suit—an introvert or an extrovert? Can a salesman tell in the first few minutes which type he is waiting on? If so, does he vary his techniques? Is the extrovert likely to change his mind after reaching home and then want to exchange his purchase?

Have you heard of a gentleman who serves as a "bird dog" for salesmen? In a word, he makes contacts in barber shops, drug stores, and other places and thus uncovers prospects for the salesmen of his organization. Pick out a successful sales force in some business of your city and show how its members operate.

273

Salvation Army

Activities of the Salvation Army are many and varied. The organization was founded in London in 1865 and came to this country in 1880. Point up the many worthwhile services and help correct the popular idea that the organization is concerned chiefly with street-corner services.

William Booth, the founder of the Salvation Army, was born April 10, 1829, and died on August 20, 1912. Show the many varied and far-reaching activities of the Salvation Army today by writing a feature timed for publication on April 10. Have the activities of the group changed much from the early days? How are workers chosen? In what ways does it perform services which are unique and beneficial?

Date tie-in: The Salvation Army was founded July 23, 1865. Describe the program and activities of your local citadel, what it means to the community, and its many unique objectives.

Cartoonists often poke fun at the music furnished by Salvation Army bands. So talk to the local leader and find out how music is used, not alone in street services but in other ways. How many of the workers are trained musicians? Is every person in the local group required to help in the services at some time or other?

Ringing bells greet many shoppers when the Salvation Army conducts its kettle drive to make Christmas a little brighter for scores of persons. Members of civic clubs often man the kettles. Is this done in your city? Find out which group did the best job the year before. Are members of a women's group better "bell ringers" than members of a men's organization? How is money used?

Schools

Schools are using more audio-visual aids. Educators are using peg-boards, slides, films, felt-boards, flip charts, and other devices to get across ideas quickly and effectively. Interview a few successful teachers and find out how they are using more visual aids in keeping kids interested.

Used to be that high schools and colleges were the only schools that bothered with graduation exercises. But no more. Nowadays it's not uncommon for kindergartens to stage commencement ceremonies! So do elementary and junior high schools. Get the opinions of several educators on the wisdom of such exercises.

Since 1890 the number of high school graduates in the United States has increased about thirteen times as fast as the total population. Find out the figures for your city or state. How does the number of boys compare with the number of girls? What is the average age of the graduate today? Do school authorities predict even more graduates in the future?

Behind truancy lies anxiety, says John G. Milner of the University of Southern California. Avoidance of school is the child's own way of trying to handle his anxiety, he believes. Talk to several local educators —principals, teachers, attendance officers, and others—and get their reasons for the truancy of many children.

Parents often criticize school methods without really understanding them. They look forward with eagerness to new models in automobiles, dresses, and hats but are reluctant to accept new methods in teaching, says H. J. Otto of the University of Texas. What are schools doing to acquaint parents with modern teaching methods?

When schools forbid debates on controversial issues, they do not live up to their obligations in a democratic society, says Dr. J. Jeffrey Auer of the University of Virginia. What topics or issues are banned from discussion in your schools? Who makes this policy—superintendent, board members, teachers?

Should students be required to take world history or world geography? Many people think so. Get the opinions not only of teachers and parents but also of persons engaged in a variety of occupations.

Communities and school systems are working together to orient new teachers. Social events (mixer, breakfast for new staff members, or luncheon), handbooks, welcome meetings, and other ideas are being used. What is the most popular idea? Who plans the affairs?

What is the driving force behind the good teacher? Leonard B. Irwin says that the good teacher "is always trying to do better what most people would not care to do at all; help children in general to grow." Select eight or ten outstanding teachers and find out what makes them tick.

Are comic magazines influencing today's youth? Do kids bring them to school? How can teachers dramatize their presentations enough to compete with the highly emotional stories of the comics? Ask teachers if they consider many of the comics salacious or loaded with stories of horror and violence.

Because of world conditions, changes are made from time to time in certain textbooks. Check with teachers of history, government, geography, and other subjects and see what changes, if any, have been made in recent books.

Hundreds of school districts are holding citizens' advisory conferences on education. Citizens and educators study the major problems facing schools. What's happening in your city and state? Are citizens participating more in school affairs?

Johnny isn't sent home for dry clothes when he shows up on rainy days at Monteith school in Detroit. The P.T.A. installed an automatic clothes drier. What are some of the facilities which have been installed in your schools for the convenience of the students?

What types of excuses are given by students who are tardy or absent from school? What are some of the more common ones? What are some of the most ridiculous? Do boys fib more or less than girls in giving "their side"?

School officials often use unusual methods to stress regulations. A school in a Southern town keeps its cafeteria clean by placing this sign over each wire wastebasket: "Can You Hit This"? Kids love it. Has your school done something unusual by stressing obedience in a positive sort of way?

A high school jumped into the headlines when its seniors decided to convert a used storage room into a chapel for student use. What have been some of the senior high school class gifts in your city? Who decides what will be given? How is money raised to finance the gifts?

What does it cost to educate a child in your state or city? What factors are considered in the total cost? Has the total increased in the last five or ten years? Is the cost more in a city than in a rural school? Two sources: your county or state superintendent.

Many parents are often shocked when they visit their younger children in school. Often they find them acting strangely—at least much more shy and quieter than at home. Ask teachers what parents should do when they visit schools? What are the best times? How long should they visit?

In the latter half of the nineteenth century, one man was responsible for most of what was taught and studied in grammar schools all over the country. He was William Holmes McGuffey, a young professor at Miami University, Oxford, Ohio, who wrote a series of books to teach children to read. Nearly 130,000,000 copies of his books were printed. Does your community have a McGuffey Society? How many of his books are owned by individuals or libraries in your community? Best angle: Get comments from oldsters who used the books, or talk to folks whose parents used them.

A press dispatch states that California psychology students were asked to write down "their most valuable asset." Several wrote "intelligence" and misspelled it. What makes a good speller? Is a student who is excellent in spelling also likely to be above average in other subjects? Teachers of English will have the answers for you.

What kind of schedules are followed by college students majoring in education? How do they learn the techniques of teaching? Do they have opportunities to observe, learn, and practice teaching before setting out with a diploma to take charge of a class of youngsters? Do they grow in self-confidence and assurance?

Tours to places of interest in the community are now a regular part of many school courses. What are the objectives of tours? How are they tied in with classroom topics? In what courses are they especially valuable?

Is geography being taught as it was when you were a kid? How much instruction in this subject do youngsters receive today? How do instructors keep up with all of the changes? Are movies used to show world conditions? Does the typical student know quite a bit about world geography?

Hundreds of teachers take summer tours, both in this country and abroad, and thus expand their knowledge of other countries and other people. Are the teachers of your state or community encouraged to travel? Do they receive similar credit to that granted students at summer sessions? Who is the most traveled of all the teachers?

Here's an old question which can form the basis for a live interview: Can teachers be rated? If so, by whom? Should teachers rate each other? Could each one rate herself? Could the students rate their teachers? Could the principal do it? Would it be best to ask a supervisor to perform this task? Get the comments of teachers, principals, superintendents, supervisors, and even a few parents and students.

More students are learning foreign languages, both in public elementary schools and in college demonstration schools. Hundreds of grade school children are receiving language lessons in special radio programs. To what extent does a knowledge of foreign languages foster intercultural understanding? International understanding? Should every student be required to take at least one foreign language? Teachers of languages can supply you with facts and comments.

Teacher-scouting has become the big league way. Each spring in California, for instance, more than one hundred scouts—many of them school administrators—fan out in search of classroom reinforcements. And it pays off. Between twenty-five thousand and thirty thousand of the sixty thousand new teachers hired by California schools during a five-year period came from out of state. How does your superintendent find new teachers? Where do new teachers come from? What are some inducements offered to teachers who are considering your community?

Should we have specialized teachers in elementary schools as we have in high schools? Is it more important for a teacher to spend practically the whole day with young children and thus know them intimately? When is it advisable for experts in various subjects—art, music, physical education—to assist the classroom teacher?

278

"U. S. College Students 'Flunk' Geography" reads a headline. And the story revealed that less than half of the students reached in a nationwide survey knew even the approximate population of the United States. Locally, find out if geography is required of all students and how much. Is a knowledge of geography more necessary today than ever before? How is the subject being taught—lectures, films, slides, field trips?

Should school children look down on their teachers? They should, not socially or mentally but literally, says London optical expert W. C. Weston in *Science Digest*. He believes that classrooms should be built so that children look down at their teachers instead of up, because continually looking up causes more eye fatigue. Ask school superintendents, teachers, and school architects what they think of this suggestion.

How does a good teacher maintain discipline in the classroom? Is the problem more acute in certain grades or in certain age levels? Do teachers feel that students should learn some discipline in the home? What approaches and techniques produce the best discipline?

Schools are often named for scholars, generals, poets, and presidents. And often a local or state citizen with a distinguished career is honored by having a school named after him. What system is used in your city? Are patrons or children allowed to suggest names? Vote on the names?

George Santayana, the famous philosopher, said: "A child educated in school is an uneducated child." How do the schools of your city provide students with a variety of learning experiences? Do they provide field trips, excursions, and other planned activities?

It isn't too unusual now to find an elementary school child who has lived in several parts of the world. Who is the "most traveled" youngster in the schools of your city? Where was he born? Is his father connected with some branch of the armed forces?

To what extent are magazines used in the schools of your city? Are more teachers using them in their classes? Which has been used the longest? How are magazines used to bridge the gap between school and the world?

Only 140 of one city's high school enrollment of 1,800 students did not sign up for some kind of activity. How would this percentage apply to a high school in your community? Do students have a wide choice in extra-curricular affairs? What is done for the few who may not find anything of interest?

Business and professional men who serve as members of school boards devote an average of thirteen hours per month to board affairs, according to a survey made by *Business Week*. Thirty-four per cent devoted from six to ten hours per month, while 24 per cent devoted from eleven to fifteen hours per month. Localize these figures and see how much time is used in an average month by school board members. Is more time demanded of school board members now than a few years ago? Have new problems brought added responsibilities?

Lack of interest is the chief cause of low grades, according to a survey made among advisers of high school students. Do high school kids listen to too many TV programs? Spend too much time tuning in on disk jockey programs? Overdo club activities? Try this slant: Ask several advisers of high school students in your city, "In what specific ways can students raise their grades?"

Many high school senior classes write a "class prophecy" near the end of their final year. A home town class prophecy after ten years makes interesting reading. Compare the prophecy with real life.

Study is an important aspect of life, both in school life and out of it. Young folks learn to study while in school, then use the techniques in later life. Ask about their study habits. Do they have one spot at home set aside for study? Do they have the radio or the TV set turned on? Compare high school study habits with those of college students.

There's a rising flood of instructional materials, and it is causing a major headache for administrators and school teachers, according to a study made by the American Association of School Administrators. Some of the material is biased and some is obvious advertising, school men say. Does your school system have any policy on the use of free instructional materials? Should it all be screened? What materials are of value?

Do a story on the school days of the Governor and First Lady of your state. What were their favorite subjects? Did either ever teach school? Get their comments on current education.

What is the largest rural school in your section? Discuss some of its unique programs and show some areas in which its students have won high honors. What is the educational philosophy of the superintendent? List some of its outstanding graduates.

Queens have always been a part of school life—from grade schools through the university. Current queens are news. But what about some of the queens of yesterday? Is the 4-H Club queen of ten years ago, for instance, a farm wife today?

More and more students are participating in science fairs sponsored by colleges and universities. Why? Mainly because one of the problems facing the nation is the shortage of technical manpower. Contact college or high school science teachers about regional or state science exhibits. Do both boys and girls take part? What branches of science attract the most entrants?

Teachers must know more than subject matter. They should combine instruction with career guidance to halt "drop outs" in high school, according to a study made by the National Education Association. To what extent should interests, needs, and capacities be examined before a student is advised to follow a certain type of work? Are standardized tests really effective? Should career counseling be given a more active role in instruction?

Schools of tomorrow will have more outdoor work and play areas, and students will take part in various activities in different buildings, an expert predicts. Ask your superintendent, the business manager in charge of buildings, or an architect, "What will the school of tomorrow look like?"

Jesse Stuart believes that modern children who do not walk to school miss so much—walking and breathing fresh air, seeing birds, eating nuts. What percentage of the students in your city always ride to school? Do some of their parents bring them every day even though they live near the school? What students walk the farthest?

Who's the youngest school board member in your county? Why is he interested in educational matters? How does he think parents could help in school affairs?

Dr. Lee A. Dubridge, president of the California Institute of Technology, says that we must "make thinking popular" with students today. Get comments from local teachers, the president of the P.T.A., a college president, or others.

Who writes better poetry—boys or girls? Ask several elementary, junior high, and high school teachers. Quite a few students, mostly boys, dislike the study of poetry. Why? Ask teachers the real values of poetry.

What's in a name? Maybe plenty of confusion if several students have the same names. Check with local school officials and see how many students have the same names and whether a boy and girl have the same name, and then find out what names head the list in the various schools.

Science
This is an age of research. Charles "Boss" Kettering once said, "Once you get the research bug, life will always be exciting." Find some of the important areas of research being emphasized by some of the larger companies in your area. Show how staffs have been increased, the expansion of equipment and facilities, and what has been discovered through research.

Marco Polo reported the use of eyeglasses in China in about 1275. They have changed a lot since then. How are glasses "fitted" to the individual's eyes? What kind of glass is used? What materials are used in frames? How do frame styles change? Do dime store glasses help the wearer?

Some folks are doubtful of the new science of rainmaking. But several firms now specialize in increasing rainfall by seeding clouds with chemicals. Got a rainmaker near you? How does he do it? What results has he obtained? How does he deal with public doubt about man's ability to "make it rain"?

Scientists can divide and weigh out one ounce of sugar so that every human being would get an equal share—less than a millionth of a house fly's weight each! So states an article in *Scientific American*. Tie this fact in with any research equipment which weighs a small amount. Or you might contrast the huge scales which weigh large objects with scientific instruments which weigh electrons or something as light.

Oil researchers are now using a microscope that enables them to look at objects ten thousand times smaller than a human hair. Visit a research laboratory of a company near you or check with local high schools or colleges and do a story on some of the modern equipment and research facilities.

Scouts

There's a bright side to the experiences of college coaches in luring high school stars to institutions of higher education. Talk to several coaches, explaining that no names will be used, about some of the amusing situations which they have experienced or heard about.

Sculpture

Bet lots of people have wondered how a sculptor goes about his work. Does he start by drawing outlines of his subject on a block of stone? How does he know when to stop chiseling? After the work is completed, how is it smoothed and polished? Is it possible for sculptors who aren't teachers to earn a living with their work? You get information from nearby art schools.

Sea

Although few people know it, the radio signal sent out by lighthouses is more important than the beam of light. When were radio transmitters first installed in lighthouses? Who operates the lighthouse system in the United States? Where do men train for work as lighthouse keepers? What are their schedules?

Seals

Official seals are interesting. Take your state seal, for instance. Who is its official keeper? What are some of the ways in which it cannot be used? Trace its history. Has it had any unique uses?

Secrets

Who can keep secrets better—men or women? Psychologists explain that we like to tell secrets because it inflates the ego. Query five men and five women with the question which opens this paragraph.

Service

Roy W. Harp of Richmond, California, heard that the local hospital needed radios so he began to collect and repair old sets. He has given more than 150 sets, and he services all of them. What have certain individuals done for your hospital? Or does your hospital have a certain need which some interested person might solve?

Service Uniforms

Do a contrast feature on the new and old styles of service uniforms. Give your feature more reader interest by running a photo of the old-time uniform. You can also show how certain uniforms—U.S. sailors, for instance—have remained about the same for many years.

Sewing Machines

Who has the oldest sewing machine in your county? Is it still in use? Interview the owner and see if she still uses it.

Tie-in date: Elias Howe patented the first sewing machine on January 10, 1846. Local slant: newest types of machines, interest of today's women in sewing, and instruction being offered in high schools or colleges of your community.

Sex Guidance

A Church of England publication says that "the church is bypassing one of its most imperative tasks" if it fails to give Christian guidance on problems involving sex. How do church leaders who deal with youth feel toward this proposal? Is anything special being done by the churches of your city?

Shakespeare

Date tie-in: William Shakespeare was born April 23, 1564. Give the story a local angle by showing how his plays are still studied, his influence on drama, and his uniqueness. Best source: teacher of subject.

Sheriff

Does the county sheriff hold auction sales from time to time? If so, how often are they held? Are there ever any bargains? Do antique collectors attend? Any amusing incidents?

Your sheriff probably receives some of his tips and clues by mail. Does he receive letters from cranks? Or from relatives of criminals? What was the strangest request to come by mail?

Shoes

You've probably suspected it—the average child now wears out a pair of shoes in about forty-five days, with the average boy wearing out his shoes about 25 per cent faster than the average girl. What affects styles and fads in children's shoes? Do some kids prefer the same kind of shoes year around? What should parents look for in seeing that their children are fitted correctly?

Show Business

The famous dancing group, the Rockettes of Radio City Music Hall in New York City, enjoy movies, television, or games between shows. Localize this by writing a story showing what members of the theater orchestra do between shows at your local theater. Do they write letters? Play games? Take a nap?

Show people who do imitations seem to vary little in their choice of characterizations. Why is it easier to do James Cagney, Lionel Barrymore, Cary Grant, and Jimmy Stewart? How does a mimic go about learning a new routine? What part do mannerisms play in imitating a voice?

The next time a group of performers—musicians, dancers, or circus performers—are in your city for Thanksgiving or Christmas find out how they observe holidays on the road? Do they have a Christmas tree and exchange presents at Yuletide? Do they have a big dinner on Thanksgiving?

Shrubbery

Homemakers should beware of the many self-styled tree experts, some of whom are nothing more than "wood butchers" who can ruin the looks of any tree they trim. Get the views of nurserymen or the county agent on what should be done if the person plans to do his own pruning.

Signs

Sign in a Boston bakery: "Cakes, 66 cents. Upside down cakes, 99 cents." Sign on a rendering company truck in Temple, Texas: "Your friendly used cow dealer." Find a merchant who has an unusual sign or other advertising device. How successful has it been? What comment has he had? Does his other advertising use a similar theme?

How can you say "No" in a positive way? Here's the way one park superintendent solved the problem: he used signs with the words, "Keep Off—Your Feet Are Killing Me—The Grass." Be on the lookout for clever signs, and then make a story about them. You may find a local sign painter who can give you more than enough to make a feature.

Some organizations are now using signs on dividing lines between counties. What are some of these? Are most of them in the nature of a welcome? Are they torn down or defaced by pranksters?

Sleep

One in three Americans has a terrible time getting up in the morning, but only one in five has any trouble in dropping off to sleep, a national poll shows. How many people actually enjoy getting up? How many would like to sleep longer? What would most people consider a reasonable time to get up?

Seventy-six per cent of all Americans are asleep by 11:00 P.M. each night. Does that apply in your city? What percentage go to bed before then? What do the night owls do? Read? Watch TV? Play games? See late movies? Interview eight or ten people and ask them about their evening schedules.

Slogans

The slogan used by the Mystery Writers of America is: "Crime Doesn't Pay—Enough!" Do any of your city, state, or regional groups have unusual slogans? Who coined them? Or were they chosen in a contest? How many groups have used the same slogans for years?

Smiles

"If you want to be not only successful but personally, happily and permanently successful, then do your job in a way that puts a light in people's faces," a sales expert advises. How important is a smile in one's personality? Does it help you to feel better to wear a pleasant expression? How do employment officials, directors of personnel, and others rate a pleasant personality?

Smoking

One contestant at the International Association of Pipe Smokers set a new world record by keeping his pipeful of tobacco going for one hour, forty-two minutes, and twenty-six seconds. How long does a pipeful last local smokers? Do many of them prefer pipes which hold more tobacco?

Are pipes as pleasant as cigarettes? Cheaper? More cumbersome? Can you stoke a briar at a formal dinner? If you are switching to a pipe, what should you look for in a good pipe? Visit your neighborhood tobacconist for the answers to these and other questions.

Sound

Literally thousands of insects are capable of making sounds. Scientists at Ohio State University say they can recognize certain courtship songs from records they have made. How do insects make sounds? Do they use their wings, legs, head, or antenna? What is the relationship of sounds to insect behavior? Best source for observations: zoologists and entomologists.

Souvenirs

It's been said that in wartime other nations fight for freedom, for God, and for country, while Americans fight for souvenirs. True or not, it is a fact that G.I.'s were sometimes loaded down with more souvenirs than combat equipment. What has become of those relics now? Ask some ex-servicemen what they brought home, where they keep their souvenirs now, and how often they look at them or think of them.

Speeches

Are your thoughts clear when you cannot put them into words? Psychologists believe you can't think clearly without words. Interview a few good speakers and writers and get their views on this topic.

Abraham Lincoln delivered the Gettysburg Address on November 19, 1863. Use this tie-in date to publish a feature on modern public speeches. How do they differ from the old-fashioned oratorical type? Do many hearers still prefer an oration? Have radio and TV altered public speaking? Quote a speech teacher or a well-known speaker in your community.

Spending

Can Uncle Sam act as Santa Claus to all demands of citizens? Some people evidently believe that Uncle Sam should take care of citizens from birth to death—homes, health, education, employment at high wages and short hours, food production underwriting, pensions, and many other things. Shall we go on piling up higher federal debts? Does anyone hope that the federal budget will ever be balanced? Obtain the views of a cross section of your citizenship, including comments from some people who have a knowledge of government finance.

Spiders

Children should be taught to beware of the deadly black widow spider because its bite can cause death. How can it be identified? Where is it likely to be found? What emergency treatment can be used? Should you call a doctor or go immediately to a hospital?

Sports

One of your schools or colleges probably features a gymnastic team. How are the members trained? Are many beginners discouraged when they start their training? What precautions (like testing physical facilities) before an exhibition or practice? Youngest and oldest members? Experience of coach?

The better the golfer, the less distance he walks. He gets from hole to hole the shortest way. But most men (and women) get plenty of walking on a golf course. How far does a man walk in playing eighteen holes of golf? Attach a pedometer to an average player. Is there a correlation between score and yards walked? Is there a difference in miles on the golf course and miles of shopping with the wife downtown?

The ball used in polo is made of specially selected willow root. What about balls used in other sports. What is a bowling ball made of? A billiard ball? How are they made perfectly round? What's in a baseball? A medicine ball? Golf ball?

Next time you catch four or five coaches in a meeting, ask each one to tell you the funniest thing he has ever experienced as an athlete or as a coach.

Success in wrestling is often a matter of using the right holds. What are the most effective ones? Which ones are particularly dangerous? Are some of them barred in amateur contests?

An estimated 60 per cent of all U.S. civilians cannot swim. What is being done in your city or state to teach swimming? Get the comments of physical education teachers and others about the value of knowing how to swim. Do many kids still learn in the old swimming hole?

More than fifty thousand young gladiators, aged nine to twelve, are now playing spectacular half-pint football in towns and cities of the nation. Who sponsors the teams? Are there regional and national contests? What precautions are taken against injuries? What percentage of the young athletes continue as high school and college players?

Good football players become famous in their teens if they make a few of the many All-American teams picked each year. But that fame may be short-lived. What are the All-Americans of the 1920's and 1930's doing today? Do they keep scrapbooks? Has their football success helped in the business world, or has it sometimes hindered?

Teddy Roosevelt, among others, was sickly as a child and later developed a marvelous physique. Do you know of a coach or an athlete who overcame physical frailties? Is he an inspiration to other youths?

For years shot-putters delivered the sixteen-pound iron ball from an upright, forward-facing stance. Then some athletes began to use the "wrong-way" pitching style; they started with a back-to-the-target crouch, then they hopped, spun, uncoiled, and pitched. What method is used by local athletes? Do coaches believe the new method more effective?

End of the year story with chuckles: Relate some of the amusing incidents which have taken place during the year in various sports. Coaches and players will be happy to relate them to you.

Do referees, umpires, and other officials mind the boos and Bronx cheers which come from partisan fans? What are some of the tense situations in which they have found themselves? Do they believe that most crowds have a sense of sportsmanship?

What's the most important characteristic of a successful athlete—speed, spirit, level-headedness, enthusiasm, love of the sport? You'll get interesting answers by interviewing coaches.

Pre-tourney story: Get predictions of coaches, sports writers, team captains, and radio and television sports editors on probable winners.

Some sports officials have had more than their share of hard knocks from fans. Is there an umpire, referee, or other official in your town who has had an unusually trying experience? What about humorous incidents? Are most fans good sports?

If your child is injured playing ball in a recreation program, would he be covered by insurance? One type of policy, for groups affiliated with the National Recreation Association, pays up to one thousand dollars in medical expenses. Premiums run higher when the sponsoring group is not connected with a national organization like the N.R.A. Does your community make a provision for accidents on playgrounds? When kids are members of teams?

Many fish and game clubs are active in conservation work. Perhaps your local club restocks fishing streams regularly, helps raise quail, collects funds, and aids in reforestation. Show how hunters and fishermen are not only concerned with taking game but also with putting it back for future trips into the outdoors.

Tall Tales

Who tells the biggest whoppers, men or women? A psychologist points out that women are more adept at "small fibs, deception, hoodwinking, evasion and exaggeration." Ask a number of men and women: Who are the glib fibbers, men or women?

Taxes

An official of the Internal Revenue Office in Minnesota was startled to find that a man had claimed a twenty dollar deduction for "mice." Investigation proved that was the taxpayer's abbreviation for "miscellaneous"! Tax collectors have lots of similar cases where poor figures and abbreviations make checking difficult. How does the Internal Revenue Bureau decipher the illegible writing of some folks?

The U. S. Treasury has a "conscience fund"—a place where folks conscience-stricken because of non-payment of taxes can send their money. It was started in 1811 when some citizen sent six dollars. In 1950 the fund hit an all-time high: $370,285! Does your nearby internal revenue office receive much "conscience money"?

An Ohio woman emptied her attic of old clothes for Korean war relief and listed this charity contribution at $2,400 on her federal income tax return! What are some of the strange things which tax officials see on the returns they examine? In their frenzied search for refunds and tax savings, what do some people claim as deductions? Without using names, tax officials will tell you some of the queer statements they read on tax returns.

Taxes are high, but so are collection costs. How many thousands of forms are mailed out by your nearest internal revenue office? How much did they weigh? How many revenue officials assist taxpayers in filling out their returns? How much do the government workers travel?

Taxpayers can usually save money by keeping more careful records, a federal expert says. Use of a desk calendar or pocket diary is recommended rather than relying solely on check stubs. Follow this angle by interviewing a federal tax expert and asking him about the best ways of keeping records.

Teachers

Your school system has a group of shock troops—the substitute teachers who take over the duties of regular teachers, often on short notice. How many substitute teachers are on call? Are some of them versatile enough to teach in a variety of situations? Are most of them former teachers? Under what circumstances are they asked to teach?

Experts tell us that the nation will need 1,365,000 teachers by 1960. Total enrollment at that time is expected to be about 34,000,000. Where will your city find additional teachers? Seeking out former teachers? Employment of more part-time teachers? Check with your city superintendent or director of personnel.

S. M. Brownell, U.S. Commissioner of Education, says that teachers in many places are nothing more than baby sitters. What do parents expect of teachers in addition to their teaching? How much extra curricular work do some schools require of their teachers?

It's the first year that is hardest in teaching. That's what a group of teachers revealed in a survey. Is this true in your schools? Does your system help new teachers to get off to a good start? What is the major problem of most new teachers? Discipline? Lack of confidence?

More than five hundred young would-be teachers attend college on P.T.A. scholarships each year. Anyone chosen from your community? Does your local P.T.A. participate in this program? If so, how is the winner chosen?

A survey of 785 young elementary school teachers in Minnesota disclosed that 524 of them had gone into the profession for just one reason: "Love of children." Interview a number of teachers of various ages in different situations and ask, "What is your biggest thrill in teaching?"

Quite a few mechanics teachers attend classes in service training centers maintained by automobile manufacturers during the summer. What are some of your local teachers doing to step up their skills in special summer programs? Do physical education teachers work in summer camps?

Teaching methods change from one generation to another. How do such modern practices as finger painting compare with drawing on slates? What about teaching with motion pictures, television, and other recent techniques? Get the opinions of the newest teacher in the school system. Then ask a veteran teacher his views.

With more responsibilities assigned to schools, will the teacher have more influence on the moral habits of children? How can a teacher "get across" certain moral teachings? How do the best teachers do it? Is the best teaching always a combination of attitudes and skills?

Teen-agers
Teen-agers, especially girls, are taking over telephones with their timeless, tireless conversations. Many families are installing a telephone for their children. Is this happening in your city? Will it solve the problem? What do teen-agers think of the idea?

Telegrams
What is the longest telegram ever sent by your local office? Are emergency messages given priority? Are the messenger boys of yesterday disappearing?

The first telegram was sent January 6, 1838. With this as a tie-in, do a story on local facilities. Point out modern facilities and how they differ from those of the old days. And best of all, try to interview an old operator.

Telephones
Pay telephones are worth a story. How often are they robbed? How many users try to use slugs? Do users argue with the operators about the amount of money required for calls? How are the locations of pay telephones determined?

Pioneers are telephone employees with twenty-one years of service. Their organization carries on many activities of local interest. One of their older members could reminisce about early telephone service, contrasting it with today's.

The spirit of service is a time-honored tradition in the telephone company. Your local operators probably have many stories to tell about help summoned in emergencies and service rendered beyond the call of duty.

Telephone women in many towns have a "Design for Living" program under way. This is a personality development program that covers many fields. Design for Living members can pass along their tips for self-help to your readers.

A telephone company open house takes customers behind the scenes, shows them the operating room, the equipment, and the business office. A telephone employee hostess can give you the customers' reactions to their visits.

Is there a child in your town who's attending school via the telephone company's school-to-home service? With this set-up, a home-bound child can listen and recite by telephone, and thus keep up with his classmates.

Information operators get many unusual and entertaining requests from telephone customers. These anecdotes will brighten a feature about the scope of the information service in your town. How many calls are handled every day? How many operators are on the job?

The publication and distribution of telephone directories is a newsworthy event in many communities. Who handles the job in your town? How far in advance must preparation begin? How many new phones are installed between directories? How many numbers are changed? Do new directories decrease the number of calls to "information"? How are new directories distributed? What efforts are made to get old directories out of use?

A telephone directory in an Oklahoma town carried "Zyss, Whois" as the final name for several years! Telephone office managers can tell you of other attempts to be last, or first in the directory. Another telephone angle: how valuable are easily remembered business phone numbers? How are easy-to-remember numbers given out? Is there ever an extra charge for a number that can earn extra money for a businessman?

A Poughkeepsie, New York, housewife was hauled into court when she refused to yield a country party line to a volunteer fireman trying to report a fire. How do telephone officials discourage lengthy conversations on party lines? Do they believe party line listening is as popular an indoor sport now as it once was?

A Dallas man boasted that he memorized the telephone numbers of 817 persons and firms which he called regularly. Who knows the most numbers in your city? What is the secret of his unusual memory? Do most persons keep a sheet of frequently called numbers near their desk?

Long distance lines are always busy on Christmas. How many calls were handled by your office? What was the approximate distance covered by some of the longest? How did the total compare with the total of a year ago?

The information girl at the telephone office is paid to answer questions. But those questions are supposed to pertain to telephone services. Ask an experienced operator the kinds of questions she gets. How many calls a day does she average? Any unusual requests?

Advertisements of telephone companies often glorify the lineman —how he performs his duties in all kinds of weather. Interview a local lineman and ask him about his experiences. What safety precautions does he keep in mind? Is he alerted before a storm or other sudden change in the weather to be ready to go into action?

A date to remember if you do a "backward look" feature on the telephone industry: Alexander Graham Bell, inventor of the telephone, was born March 3, 1842. Insert this fact into your story showing the history of the local office. Tell of early-day operators and some of their experiences. Localize your story by telling the peak hours, how operators are taught to handle emergencies, and other interesting facts.

A night telephone operator asked police to go to a certain address when the signal appeared on the switchboard but no one answered. Cause? A kitten had knocked the receiver off the hook. How are operators trained to watch the board and thus be alert to unusual situations? Have your local operators, particularly those who work at night, sensed danger by the lights on their switchboard?

Five physicians answer to the name of "McKinley" in Brookville, Pennsylvania. Are there mixups in telephone numbers in your city? People who have the same names or initials? A residence and a business which have similar numbers?

Chicago police finally caught a man whom they accused of telephoning them at least two thousand times in a year to curse them. Do pranksters operate by telephone in your community? Do funeral homes, the police station, and other offices receive strange calls? You might show the danger of sending in false fire alarms.

Television

How much makeup does a television performer need? Is it the same as women's everyday makeup? Does a suntan help? Why is makeup necessary? Do TV stations employ someone to help actors and others who appear before the camera with their makeup?

Members of the Houston, Texas, school board televised some of their meetings over KUHT-TV. And informal surveys indicated that many persons saw the program. Are any local meetings televised over any of your stations? What seems to attract the most viewers?

With the growth of television, new words have popped into use. Visit a studio and learn the meanings of a few terms, including bite-off, barn doors, eighty-eight, dupe, dish pan, dubbing, gaffer, lock jaw, fish bowl, Madame Cadenze, and others.

Your local television station probably has at least one program of primary interest to women. How does the person in charge choose the topics? Do suggestions come from TV viewers? What types of programs have been the most popular? Does a TV program aimed at women differ greatly from the typical run of shows on the air?

Does a television antenna afford any kind of protection against lightning? Experts point out that a TV antenna is not a substitute for the lightning rod. An improperly grounded antenna could actually increase the danger of lightning's striking. Ask TV dealers and repairmen how antennas should be installed to decrease the danger of being struck by lightning.

Servicing of TV sets has become a big business. Show how it has grown. Do most shops provide day and night service? Does the average person want his set fixed in a hurry so he won't miss a special program? Show some of the odd ways in which sets have gone on the blink.

The fearful eye of a television camera has frozen many a non-professional into stony silence. How do TV stations help participants get over such "stage fright"? Talk with TV personalities and ask them how long it took to learn to be at ease before the camera. Do they have advice for persons who appear on TV only occasionally?

Laughter and applause on some radio and television shows sound suspiciously "canned." What big shows can you find where the audience "participation" is dubbed in this way? Is a live audience reaction so important to the listener or viewer at home? How do networks and stations decide which shows will be opened to the public and which will not?

The average American doesn't exactly know the best posture. And it is getting worse as more people spend more time watching television, health experts say. Ask doctors: Can too much TV viewing cause eye strain? Overeating? Incorrect breathing?

Too many TV commercials do not sound like the average woman's conversation, one woman editor complained after listening to a lot of messages aimed at women. Do women think they are being talked down to? Do they think that many of the commercials lack a ring of sincerity? Are some of the phrases and words commonly used likely to irritate women viewers?

Testimonials

Testimonials have been used as a technique in sales and advertising for years. Are they still as effective as ever? Are testimonials of local folks better in some ways than testimonials of celebrities? What are the special advantages of testimonials? Your answers can come from almost anyone in any area of advertising.

Thanksgiving

Nearly three hundred men from the skid row district in Chicago were freed of drunk and disorderly conduct charges on Thanksgiving morning and given tickets to a free Salvation Army dinner. Are your courts more lenient on Thanksgiving, Christmas, and other holidays?

According to old reports, the first Thanksgiving at Plymouth featured wild turkeys. Indians and whites joined in hunting the birds. If wild turkeys are found in your region, find out what kinds and if hunters are allowed to shoot them.

A Detroit man wanted a turkey dinner for Thanksgiving, and he got one—in a jail cell. He was arrested for trying to steal a turkey in a supermarket. Do many folks steal food for Thanksgiving or Christmas? Check with store managers and police.

Do the turkey growers of your state present a turkey to the governor on Thanksgiving? Does the governor and his family receive more birds than they can use? On what other occasions does the chief executive receive gifts of food?

Theater

Ever see the name George Spelvin on a theater playbill? It's traditional that an actor with more than one part use that name on the program, to keep his real name from appearing more than once. What other traditions in the theater: the show must go on, good luck pieces and omens, and so on? Why is New York headquarters for the legitimate theater? Why do shows open out of town, then move to Broadway?

Most theaters offer some kind of training instructions for ushers. What are they taught to do? How do some theater patrons make nuisances of themselves? Do small children ever get lost in the theater? What provisions are made for persons who suddenly become ill?

William Shakespeare went to London at the age of twenty, and it is said that his first job was holding the horses of patrons of the theater. Later he became an actor. How do "stage-struck" kids of today get experience in drama? With local little theater? Summer stock companies? Working around a theater? Organizing others of the same age into drama groups?

What abilities are needed by a makeup artist in the theater? How does he make lightning changes? What are some techniques which indicate old age, for instance? Contact a makeup man in your city or the drama teacher at your high school or college.

Thefts

An Oklahoma City firm reported the theft of a five-ton earthmover. What is the biggest item ever stolen in your city? Was it recovered? Do police believe that big trucks make it easier for thieves to haul heavier objects?

Then and Now

At least one World War II winner of the Congressional Medal of Honor went on to become a movie star. What about some of the others? How long does a man stay a hero? How has the nation's highest combat award changed their lives? Are most Medal of Honor men active in veterans' affairs? There's a national organization open only to those men who have won the Medal of Honor.

Americans have more labor-saving gadgets than ever before. But demands for time have increased. Interview prominent local citizens about public service activities. Do they feel time saved through modern inventions is paying off in community service? Is the modern pace really as fast as it seems?

It's been said that one of the strong points of the English language is its flexibility. What about slang in your community? Ask high school students what words are most used today. Are they different from those of five, ten, or fifteen years ago? Do popular words ever make comebacks?

Tickets

A court ruled that if a bus passenger loses his ticket it is his problem and not the bus line's. How many people lose their tickets in or around a bus station? Does the ticket clerk ever issue a second ticket (without cost) to a person who has lost his?

Time

On November 18, 1883, nearly one hundred "local times" observed by the railroads were abolished, and all the trains used Standard time—Eastern, Central, Mountain, or Pacific—each one hour apart. Why are time zones bounded by such uneven lines?

Most of us say, "If I just had more time I could do more work—I could get more done." Actually, Father Time is perfectly fair. He gives potentate and plumber the same amount of time each day. What are the secrets of using time effectively? What special patterns are followed by people who "get the job done"? Does a busy person learn to economize on his time?

Where does the "correct time" come from? Where is the Naval Observatory sometimes referred to in matters of precise timing? How is time taken from astronomical readings?

No person can tell time, because it is a "vague little thing" that has escaped absolute measurement, Dr. Dirk Brouwer, director of the Yale Observatory, believes. Do residents of your city rely on whistles, bells, master clocks, or other means to tell time? Do jewelers receive telephone calls from persons wanting to know the correct time? Here's another angle: How do railroad men keep their watches right on time?

Time is not our enemy, it is our friend, Dorothy Dix once pointed out in one of her columns. Ask people to enumerate some of the positive advantages and values of time: how it solves problems, how it helps us to forget, and so on.

Time Keeping

Now we have an "electronic supervisor." The IBM apparatus each morning will extinguish a rooftop neon sign, turn on ceiling, showcase, and display-window lights, switch on air conditioning, heat restaurant ovens, and sound a buzzer alerting employees for the start of business. How have time-keeping systems changed? How many places still use time clocks? Are there still quite a few clock watchers?

Timepieces

G.I.'s vacationing in Switzerland after World War II bought wrist watches by the hundreds. And they wanted them accurate. Many a watch that lost or gained thirty seconds a week was taken back to the jeweler for "adjustment." How accurate can watches be made? Does a pocket watch keep better time than a wrist watch? Does the size of a timepiece have anything to do with its accuracy? Ask a jeweler for hints for the care of a fine watch, to keep it "on time."

Timetables

If timetables confuse you, don't go to India. Timetables there are published in eleven languages. Contrast new timetables with older ones. Aren't the newer ones easier to understand? How have they been made more readable? Do many people miss planes, trains, or buses because "they thought" the departure time was different?

Tips

What about tipping? Americans pay to the tune of about one billion dollars a year. Tips are often a part of wages (bellhops, waiters, doormen, cab drivers, and others). How much should you tip? Seek the opinions of both seasoned travelers and officials of hotels, railroads, or other businesses in which some employees rely quite a bit on tips.

Is tipping on the decline? Do men tip more than women? Do many people resent tipping? What is the average tip? Highest? Lowest? Good source of comments: waitresses in cafes, coffee shops, and restaurants.

Tombstones

Lots of stories have been written about unusual epitaphs. But we've not heard much about the man who carves the inscriptions into the stone. Where does he learn his trade? Is he paid by the letter, line, or complete job? Is it a full-time job? Is any part of the job creative, or does he merely cut out letters and designs that have been traced on the stone?

Tourists

Interview a veteran service station attendant and get his slants on human nature as revealed in the customers—the friendly fellow, the suspicious guy, the taciturn person, and the others. Has he ever talked to any celebrities? What are some of the unusual requests? What advice would he give to those who plan trips?

Tours

Today we have tours for golfers, opera lovers, flower growers, farmers, and others. How many special groups visit your city or region each year? Are some tours for men only? Women only? Is touring becoming a big business in your region? What special attractions are offered by those promoting tours?

Towns

California historians have found accounts of well over five hundred gold rush towns, most of which have vanished. Among the more picturesque names are Whiskey Flat, You Bet, Muletown, Gouge-Eye, and Slumgullion. What were the names of some of the by-gone towns and communities in your state? Have some of them continued under other names?

Has your city ever changed its name? Who chose the original name? Why was it changed? Does it present name tie-in with the principal industry? Do other towns have similar names?

Toys

Now we have the station announcer who reels off the train stops— one of the latest additions for miniature railroad fans. Do you have a model train club in your community? Ages of its members? Have some of the members actually worked for railroads? How many build some of their own equipment? Do small trains provide fun for both fathers and sons?

Marketwise, the major toy demand is for children in the two to six age group. That bracket represents 36 per cent of the child population, experts say. What are some of the changes in toy requests as children grow older? Which toys (dolls, for instance) are often enjoyed by both small boys and girls?

When home permanents became popular, little girls thought it would be fine to give their dolls the same kind of treatment. Result: bald dolls. Then American ingenuity came along and perfected a machine that stitched hair directly on the doll's head. With this as an example, talk to a toy designer or manufacturer and find out how other toys have had to be changed to meet a new need.

Traffic

Traffic police have found that safety can be promoted not only through the apprehension of bad drivers but through the rewarding of good ones. Many cities give certificates to careful drivers. Is your city doing this kind of work? A feature might start such a plan.

Rewarding careful drivers for good deeds, while penalizing the reckless, is now practiced by the Salt Lake County (Utah) sheriff's office. How do police in your community handle careless drivers? Do they bawl out offenders? Or do they handle most of them with tact and courtesy? What are some of the alibis offered by offenders?

One authority says traffic accidents are caused primarily by one thing: emotional immaturity. What do others think? Why do we preach safety, admit the necessity of courtesy on the road, and then kill ourselves in ever increasing numbers? Everyone will have an opinion.

Travelers have discovered a road in Mexico, built about 1600 A.D., which has a line of white stones down the center. And there are markings on Brooklyn Bridge, presumably dating back to the late 1890's, to separate the different traffic lanes. Bring this traffic idea up-to-date by talking to your local traffic head on the various types of painted lines, their purposes, and their values.

Talk to the police who check parking meters and find out some of the usual alibis people use when overparking. How many people really tell the truth? What are some of the most unusual alibis? Who uses more alibis—men or women?

Telling motorists when to go and when to stop is probably an expensive business in your city. How much is spent for signals each year? How much does it cost to operate them? Are pedestrian "walk-wait" signals being installed? How do city traffic officials select crossings where signals are to be installed?

Routing traffic in a modern city is a science of one-way streets, no left turns, and "no parking from 4:00 P.M. to 6:00 P.M. this side of street." It's also a science of educating the driving public. How do city officials go about spreading information about a new one-way street or a new traffic plan? How is release of the information timed? How far in advance are new street signs installed?

When is traffic heaviest in your city? How does the weather affect the number of vehicles? How much has traffic increased through the years? What are the busiest intersections?

You'll perform a real service to drivers of emergency vehicles if you'll do a feature on their right-of-way privileges. Many a driver of a fire truck, police car, or ambulance has had to fight his way through traffic when private citizens refused to give way, despite a siren and a flashing red light. Get drivers' comments, then give motorists a few tips on what to do when they see or hear an emergency car or truck. Most cities have ordinances to govern such right-of-way.

About one of every twenty homes being sold is a trailer, according to officials of the Mobilehome Dealers National association. How many trailers are in your community? What are their special advantages? Has the number increased? Who has lived in a trailer longest? Who has lived in a trailer in the most states?

Transportation

School buses carry 30 per cent of the public school students. Describe the school transportation program in your county—the number of buses, miles traveled per month or year, longest routes, safety inspections of buses, and number of students who ride. Human interest angle: Interview a veteran driver about amusing experiences.

Have you done a story recently on the rent-a-car business in your city? Who are the biggest users? What is the limit, in terms of miles or days, on a trip? Is anything besides a driver's license and proper identification needed to rent a car?

A woman in Abingdon, Vermont, was hailed into court after she had blasted the radiator of a school bus and wounded a passenger. She told the judge the driver came too close to her front gate. Other school bus drivers have had other experiences, most of them probably less dangerous but some of them just as interesting.

How big is the automobile business? If all the registered motor vehicles in the United States were lined up bumper to bumper they would stretch from New York to San Francisco about seventy times! But that's only one aspect of this tremendous industry. Think of all the gas and oil these vehicles require, all the insurance, the tires, the fabrics for upholstery, the license tags. What about a feature on the far-reaching effects of America's automotive industry?

In the last ten years the United States railroad industry has changed over almost completely from coal to Diesel oil. Interview some railroaders—agents, conductors, engineers, and others—and see how they like the change. Do some believe that the old steam engine had certain advantages?

About one out of every three public school children in the United States rides to and from school aboard a school bus. How are bus routes planned? What is the longest route? How many hundreds of miles would a child ride if he rode a school bus every day during his entire school career? How are bus drivers chosen?

Catch some of the drama which is often enacted at the Travelers' Aid desk in the railroad station in your city. What are some of the major problems facing travelers? How many persons are helped each year? Do young folks who have run away from home ask for help?

Trucks provide much of the revenue on the new turnpikes. Some of the newer ones will spot special parking areas, restaurants, and sleeping quarters for truckers. Are these factors considered when new highways are being built in your state?

Many truck drivers lend a helping hand to motorists in trouble. Often they tow cars out of mud, help fix flat tires, provide gasoline, or make minor motor adjustments. Interview the owner of a line of trucks and find out some of the many services rendered by truck drivers.

An obelisk hitching post, dating back to 1890, was pressed into service as a bench mark for elevation control during the erection of a six-story building. How many hitching posts are left in your community? Are some of them lying around in barns and other farm structures?

Municipal transit is faced with headaches. In only ten years the transit companies have lost almost half the twenty-three billion fares they carried yearly. At the same time, operating costs have soared. Many major companies have gone broke. What is happening? Is the private automobile the biggest competition? Can old passengers be won back? Should buses be allowed to go faster? Find out what is happening to the bus systems in your state or region.

Buggy making, though not exactly booming, still is a business in the United States. Two groups, the Amish and the French-speaking Acadians of Louisiana, still use quite a few buggies. Any buggies in your neighborhood? Are some buggies in your neighborhood stored in barns?

You'd be surprised how many miles the buses of your city travel each week or each month. Get these figures into a story and then show how far a bus driver travels each year or in five or ten years. And back of it all, show the work of the mechanics and other maintenance men in keeping the big vehicles rolling.

Ask a taxi driver: Do you prefer young folks or old folks? How do your learn the names of new streets? When are your busiest periods? What are some of the articles which are left by people in cabs? How many miles do you drive each week?

Any ambulance driver who has been on the job for several years can recount many experiences. What special training does he have? How fast does he drive in emergencies? Is he accustomed to being awakened during the night? What special equipment does he always carry for use in emergencies?

Does your community have a trailer village? What are the ordinances set up by the city for its maintenance? Interview several of the wives and see how they feel about trailer life? How many of their husbands are engaged in work which requires that they move about?

Truck drivers have a jargon of their own. To them, gasoline is "push water" and a sleeper bus is a "pajama wagon." A poultry truck is a "cackle crate." Slant: show some of their colorful language and try to show the origin of as many terms as possible.

306

Yesterday's travelers, whether going by train or stagecoach, carried most of their belongings in large trunks. Do modern train and bus passengers use trunks to any great extent? Or do they use several smaller bags? Baggagemen at your depot, whether large or small, will have the answers.

Five former World War II pilots who needed jobs started an airline that handles any kind of livestock. Do any of the airlines serving your city handle livestock? If so, what are some of the special regulations? What was the longest flight? Most unusual?

Travel

Consumption of gasoline usually reaches its peak in July. As an index this means but one thing: more motorists are taking vacation trips that month than any other. What do most people consider the ideal month to take a vacation? Does a slowdown in certain business activities during July affect the number of employees who are assigned their vacation periods?

Does the American motorist prefer one long trip or several short ones? About sixty million Americans climb into about twenty million cars for jaunts each year. What is the mileage of the average trip? What is the average number of passengers in each car? Do motorists prefer the faraway place but often settle for some spot closer home?

Whether you live in a city or a village, you can get a story from the ticket seller at the bus station. How many questions does he answer daily? Odd questions? Do police officers often ask employees of bus stations to help in detecting criminals?

Remember when motorists built food cabinets on the running boards of their cars? And they carried cots and camping equipment because there weren't many auto camps or motels. How many still prefer the out-of-doors at night? Do many motorists carry food? If so, what kind?

Ask a much-traveled person: What is the favorite meat dish all over the nation? Steak? Beef? Ham? Furthermore, where is the best type found? Is the favorite meat cooked differently in different parts of the country?

Travelers Aid societies and USO Travelers Aid units and lounges help about two million persons a year. Heartbreak and happiness, laughter and tears, are to be found in the stories behind these figures. Talk to a Travelers Aid representative in your community.

How many local motorists bring home mementos of their trips? What do most of them seek—Indian curios? Leather goods? Unusual foods? Antiques? Books? Find someone who has collected articles of interest from many states.

World travel is increasing. Never before have so many Americans from all walks of life planned so many trips to other continents. What lures them? Are most of them older people? Have planes made it easier for more people to go farther in less time? Your local travel agent is worth seeing for a story.

Americans are on the go more these days. They move more, get to know more people. Are folks as neighborly as they once were? Interview several housewives in different parts of town. Are they as interested in their friends now as their mothers were a generation ago? Do they exchange cakes, recipes, lawnmowers, snow shovels, and other things?

What is the favorite honeymooning place in your state? Is June the big month for honeymooners? Does the place make any special "play" for the newly married?

Giving away road maps to travelers is a ten billion dollar annual business in the United States. Oil companies provide approximately half of the estimated annual total of three hundred million maps. How are maps kept up-to-date? How quickly does a map become outdated? Does today's highway boom add to the problem?

Trees

Florida's Treaty Oak in Jacksonville is about eight hundred years of age. Are any trees in your region known because of some historical event? If so, what was the event? Is it still observed? What is the condition of the trees?

Trees surpass all other organic things in height, magnitude, and longevity. Their life may range from forty to over four thousand years. Oaks, for instance, live fifteen hundred years, and the sugar maple lives to five hundred years. What are the oldest types in your community? Is there one tree which is especially old? Your nurseryman can give you interesting comments on the age of trees.

Trucks

Figures released by the Automobile Manufacturers Association reveal that 52 per cent of fruits and vegetables are received by truck at twenty-one of the major wholesale markets. Where do most of the fruits and vegetables in your city come from? What products come from the farthest points? How does the weather affect certain fruits and vegetables? Are special provisions made for perishable products? Get your answers from the head of a large wholesale firm.

Truck Drivers

Thousands of truck drivers are volunteer operators of Red Cross mobile first aid units. Find one among your city's trucking companies and interview him on his experiences. How many are prepared to respond to an emergency call in time of disaster?

Uniforms

If your city has a store which specializes in uniforms, interview the manager about the many different kinds. Have most of them been streamlined? Are some about as they were many years ago? Is more color being used? Any unusual requests?

Unions

In Detroit and other cities in which it has large membership, the United Automobile Workers Union has been alert to render constructive service to the aged. They have provided library facilities, hobby clubs, craft shops, and other services. What have the unions of your city done in special services?

Universities

Some colleges and universities attract graduates back to class reunions with gimmicks. A recent example: a prize was offered to the member of each class who had the "worst" job while in school. Can you find other techniques? How successful are they?

Class memorials are familiar sights on practically every college campus. Describe some of the oldest or most interesting memorials. How are they financed? Who chooses them?

Both government agencies and industry sponsor research grants and other forms of assistance at many universities. Security regulations may forbid news of some. But you can find some research projects on which you can build interesting features.

A modern university may need everything from live frogs to Grecian urns in its instructional and research programs. Interview the purchasing agent at a large university and get a list of the many items required in the various phases of higher education. Show the purpose of each.

Does your nearby college sponsor a Vocational Guidance Conference, or a special day for high school seniors to give them assistance in the choice of careers? If so, find out how many attend, in how many areas guidance is given, and what some of the trends in the choice of professions by high school seniors are.

Few college men wear hats. And just why, nobody knows. Some believe that young men who have been in the service are tired of wearing something on their heads. Others point out that some young men believe that hats make them look older. What do men think on a campus near you? Do they wear any kind of headgear? Anything special in summer or winter?

University presses publish approximately twelve hundred new books each year. Of these, about half are in the humanities and one-third in the social sciences. If there's a university press near you, find out how many books are published each year, what types it emphasizes, and which volumes have been especially outstanding.

Student Unions are now a vital part of higher education. With their many and varied services, they fulfill an important role in student life. What are some of their special services? To what extent are their policies determined by students? How are they financed?

Alumni funds have been established in scores of colleges and universities. In addition, a large sum of money comes to institutions from alumni in the form of gifts and bequests that are not credited to annual alumni funds. What percentage of alumni give? What are some of the appeals used to raise money? How are the alumni funds administered?

Nearly every university has dedicated some type of memorial honoring the war dead of various wars. By releasing this story around November 11, it might have more reader interest. Describe the type of memorial, when it was dedicated, by whom it was sponsored (the university or a special group), and other details.

An old college catalogue reveals the fact that coeds at early seminaries were often punished if caught dipping snuff. What are some of the regulations for coeds of today? How are the regulations explained and enforced? By college authorities? Other students? Both? Show how regulations have changed through the years and how the title of "dean of women" has been changed to "counselor" in many colleges.

What's the biggest problem of the college student? Here's what a counselor at the State University of Iowa believes: it is achieving an independence that will let him develop satisfactory new relationships. How can this be done? What part should his parents play in guidance? Do they interfere too much? It's easy to get a story on this from the dean of men, dean of women, or the dean of students.

Colleges today are full of young married undergraduates. How has this changed the pattern of campus life? Fewer dances and social affairs? Larger audiences at concerts and lectures? Do parents help support young couples? Do campus marriages face a hazard—like immaturity, for example?

Each student is certain that everyone but him was kept in mind by those who prepared the class schedule. Who prepares the schedule of classes? What are some of the problems? What are some of the facts which must be kept in mind? How can the planners anticipate how many sections of a class may be needed?

The Hollywood version always shows the old grad marching back to homecoming with a pennant. True? Untrue? Are pennant sales up or down? Who buys them? Alumni? High school students? University students?

Does a nearby university offer courses in geology? If so, ask the instructors about persons who send in samples of rocks or ore. Do some of them think they have discovered gold, uranium, or some other valuable metal? How are these requests handled?

What about an establishment which cashes student checks? What is the rush day? What season brings the most business? Who spends the most, men or women? Who writes the biggest checks? What is the largest cashed? The smallest?

What are the pet peeves of some of the better-known professors? What do they like and dislike in a student? Try to locate the oldest and one of the youngest to compare their answers.

Student religious activities are booming. Interview full-time directors of religious education for various denominations. How do they account for the new emphasis on religion? Who are some well-known athletes who take an active role in religious life? How are churches meeting the need? Enlarging student centers? Expanding programs?

Income of university professors dropped by 5 per cent during the unusually prosperous years between 1940 and 1950. Income of the average industrial worker during this period increased by almost one-half. You'll get an interesting story from the business manager of a nearby university by asking him what has happened to professors' salaries during recent years.

Scores of students, both from the United States and abroad, take part each year in the international exchange program. How are the students chosen? How long are they allowed to remain in another country? What are some advantages of the program? You can obtain answers to these and similar questions from a person or a committee at a university.

Class reunions are now held at many universities during commencement. Here's an opportunity for you to ask old grads about their undergraduate days, how college life of yesterday differed from that of today, and how the campus has changed.

Homecoming has a new note. Bandsmen of yesterday may return, rehearse once, and then play a number or two at the football game. Who is the oldest member of the alumni band? Have most of the musicians gained weight? How many still play their instruments, either as a hobby or as a member of a musical organization? What were some of the amusing things which happened on band trips when they were undergraduates?

All types of workers from ministers to merchandisers participate in short courses held at colleges and universities. What specialized groups often hold meetings? Which meeting attracts the largest attendance? Who plans the programs? Do some delegates want college credit for their attendance?

Students in the departments of home economics and agriculture at Ohio State University elect "professors of the year." Upon what basis do students choose the professors for special recognition? Is a popular professor usually brilliant as well? What qualities do students admire in their professors?

With the possible exception of Methuselah, nobody could live long enough to take all of the courses offered by Yale University. With 1,450 courses available, a student would need more than 350 years to go through them all. Apply this total courses-academic years possibility to your nearby college.

Hundreds of foreign students are away from home on Thanksgiving, Christmas, and other holidays. In some colleges, faculty members and townspeople open their homes to students from faraway lands during the holiday seasons. Is this done at the college in your city? Who sponsors the program?

It's not unusual now for a college graduate to have a wife and child looking on at commencement exercises. The story of a student earning a degree while he supports a family is frequently an interesting one. And the bigger the family, the bigger the story.

A fraction of every big university's graduating class usually comes from foreign countries. These students will be glad to tell you what influenced them most in choosing the school they attended. Was it the recommendation of other graduates? Professors with international reputations? Special fields of study? How many foreign students stay in this country after graduation? How will their new skills be used back home?

Many universities commission their R.O.T.C. graduates the same day commencement exercises are held. What percentage of the college men who start R.O.T.C. finish the course? How do R.O.T.C. commissions differ from those awarded graduates of West Point and Annapolis? How are honor R.O.T.C. students rewarded?

A college president recently stated that the emphasis in education should be on "analyzing, not on memorizing." Seek comments on this statement from deans and perhaps the college president. Where do professors of education believe that the emphasis should lie?

Each yearbook is usually built around a central theme. How is it chosen? When does planning begin? Where do ideas come from? What have been some of the most successful themes? Your source: the adviser.

Do a feature on the best-known college songs of your state. What is the oldest? The newest? Were some of the songs composed under unusual or special circumstances? Upon what occasions are the songs used?

One college raises money for its Campus Chest by sponsoring the "Ugliest Guy on the Campus" contest with professors as candidates. Another auctions off a dean who must wait on table at one meal for the group bidding the highest. Check your college for unusual ways in which the faculty aids student funds.

Your college or university may have a package information service for speakers, students, and others. It may have information on everything from atoms to zinnia culture. Who are the largest users? Is there any expense for borrowers? What are some of the most popular topics? How many requests are handled each year?

314

A coed at Brigham Young University keeps snakes in her room. She keeps the nonpoisonous snakes for pets. Do many college students have pets? Or is it against regulations to have any kind of pet? Does a group—fraternity, sorority, or a dormitory gang—have a pet? If the school has an animal as a mascot, is it cared for by students?

Here's a different angle on a health story: Interview the physician in charge of the health service at a college. What is the most common illness? What are some of the services of the program? Are X-rays required of all students? Are entering freshmen given checkups?

Over a lifetime the average college graduate can expect to receive about one hundred thousand dollars more income than the average high school graduate, officials of the Bureau of Census report. What are the approximate costs, direct and indirect, of a college education? How much have the costs risen in ten years?

What is the philosophy of the director of public relations at the college? What is the basis for the services which he directs? Does he interpret the public to the college and the college to the public? Show the variety of duties which he must handle.

Still good: any student who is working his way through college in an unusual way. What percentage of students earn all or part of their expenses? What are the advantages and disadvantages of working one's way? Do many working students keep up better-than-average scholastic averages? Best source for answers: the student employment director.

Do college women prefer marriage to a business career? One survey showed that 77 per cent of the graduates preferred marriage, 18 per cent preferred a career. Check with employment officials at your nearby college and find out how many senior girls want jobs? How many work full-time after graduation while their husbands finish requirements for degrees?

Unusual Occupations

Never throw anything away. That's the slogan of Stanley Slotkin, president of the world's largest rental company. His firm will rent you virtually anything. What do some of the rental agencies in your city handle? Tuxedos? Furniture? Appliances? Do many people find it cheaper to rent than to buy? How many people rent things temporarily to impress their friends?

Ushers

What qualifications are necessary for those who work as ushers in theaters? Are they taught to handle emergency situations? How do they handle patrons who may be critical or upset? Strengthen your story by interviewing ushers about their most unusual experiences.

Vacations

Vacations are an old American custom. What about the vacation policies of firms and institutions near you? Many companies, for instance, give five days vacation after one year's service. Some give ten days after five years. How is vacation pay computed for hourly-paid workers? If an employee is entitled to three weeks, can he take the three weeks in succession? Officials in charge of personnel and payrolls can give you enough facts and comments to make a timely feature.

About 83 per cent of all vacation trips in the United States are made by automobile, according to figures released by the Automobile Manufacturers Association. What percentage of travelers go by air? By bus? Train? To what extent does the amount of time allowed for vacation affect the type of transportation used?

Summer vacationists get an ideal picture of the cowboy's outdoor life. But what happens in the winter? Who takes care of the stock when winter comes? How many persons stay on duty at some of the dude ranches and regular ranches? How is stock protected in the cold winter months, particularly when the snow is quite deep? Must fences be mended?

With better cars and better highways, faster planes and lower fares, do folks go farther on vacations? Do they take advantage of better facilities nowadays to make longer trips? What are the vacation habits of the many folks in your community? Why is summer the traditional vacation season?

Good manners make good vacations. What advice should be given to folks before they start on vacation trips? What about those who

316

trespass on private property? Those who leave smoldering camp fires? Litterbugs? The sign and marker stealers? Those who travel with an unleashed dog? Answers to these questions give you a good story for late May or early June.

About seventy-two million Americans make vacation trips each year. The average stay away from home is eleven days. How does the average family choose its vacation spot? Because "we always go there"? "The Joneses liked it?" Is the decision usually unanimous? Is the average trip planned months in advance or just a few days before? How many families seek a cool spot in which to spend a few days?

Valentines

St. Valentine's Day, which is observed February 14, has had an interesting history. Not too many years ago the Chicago postoffice rejected thousands of comic valentines on the ground that their art and subject matter violated postal regulations. How have comic valentines changed? Do most people still prefer the sentimental types? What age group buys the most?

Vending Machines

Nowadays candy, cigarettes, gum, peanuts, soft drinks, fruit, insurance, and lots of other consumer items are sold through vending machines. Ask local distributors about machine sales as compared with earlier forms of merchandising. Does cost of machines increase cost of product? Do machines jam easily and prevent sales? What about rough treatment given vending machines by customers?

Ventriloquism

Is there another Edgar Bergen in your community? How did he learn to become a ventriloquist? How much practice is required to learn to "throw the voice"? Can you learn from reading a book? Or must you take lessons?

Veterans

Remember when Veterans Day was called Armistice Day? It carried the latter name for thirty-six years. Why the change? Do veterans like the new name better? The original name started November 11, 1918.

One manufacturer made the headlines and his story was told in a national magazine when he announced that he would employ no man except a disabled veteran. What are some of the problems in the rehabilitation of physically handicapped veterans into industry and business? Officials of a veterans' hospital should be able to give you the needed information and also tell about specific cases.

Have some of your war veterans or other folks brought back strange animals from overseas? If so, did it mean a change of climate for the pet? Is it easy to provide food, or does the animal require something special in its diet?

A popular song of World War I wondered "how you gonna keep 'em down on the farm after they've seen Paree?" That was a couple of wars ago. By now, millions of American men and women have seen Paris and dozens of other world capitals and faraway places. What does the ex-serviceman think about his wartime travels? Did he enjoy them then? Have intervening years mellowed his outlook? Has he returned to any of the places of his wartime experiences, or would he like to return?

On December 25, 1776, George Washington crossed the Delaware River to attack Trenton. Localize this fact by getting comments from former veterans on the ways in which they observed Christmas when they were in service.

Veterinarians

People and not their pets are the veterinarian's biggest problem, declares an officer of the American Animal Hospital association. Veterinarians are glad to help in emergencies, he said, but so often people become worried about their pets late in the evening or even in the middle of the night. How many calls does your vet receive at mealtime, late at night, and other inconvenient times?

Vision

One out of three American children have vision which is inadequate for school work if uncorrected, says the American Optometric Association. Are children starting to school in your city required to have eye examinations? Are regular examinations given to students in the higher grades? What percentage of the students wear glasses?

"Visual abilities cannot be determined by a test that ranks man with a chimpanzee," a leading optometrist declares. How are vision tests being conducted? What are some of the newer methods? Is there one "best" way?

Vocabularies

Stuart Chase points out that very few words carry only one meaning. Some English words, in fact, have more than a hundred meanings, depending on the context. How do teachers in the elementary grades show children how to distinguish between the differences in the same word? Do they ask the child to listen to the accent? Tone of voice? Or figure out the situation?

Voters

Often the members of a family may vote for the candidates of the same political party for generations. It has been estimated that about 75 per cent of the voters are "heredity" voters. Is the number of independent voters increasing in your county or state? Do government professors and political leaders believe that more people are voting for "the man" and not "the party"?

W. C. T. U.

With more than a million dues-paying members in over sixty countries, the W. C. T. U. is still pushing toward its historic goal: a bone-dry America. Today the Carrie Nation tactics are gone. Instead, the group relies on social pressure and a highly vocal public relations program to win its battles. Do a feature about the activities of your local group for publication November 18. It was founded on that date in 1874.

Waitresses

Do tips increase during the Christmas holidays? When are most diners likely to give larger tips? Do most tips total about 15 per cent of the check? Ask several waitresses. And ask each, "What is the largest tip you have ever received?"

War

When Caesar was defeating the Gauls, killing one enemy soldier cost the Roman taxpayer seventy-five cents. In World War II each enemy casualty cost the United States two hundred thousand dollars.

Do an article showing how modern warfare depends so much upon industrial production, scientific research, electronics, global movement of people, and supplies of all kinds.

Water

Few persons know about the evidences, movement, and work of ground water. Interview a geologist who has a special knowledge of water and ask him about wells, seepages, springs, and geysers. And he might be able to tell you about caverns, fossils, and deposits.

Wearing Apparel

What's happened to the umbrella? Women used to carry them; men too. Your department store manager can tell you how much sales have decreased, and why. Does he ever have calls for them any more? Does he ever sell an umbrella stand?

Weather

"Tomorrow's high will be 77 degrees." That's a familiar phrase in weather forecasts. How do weathermen arrive at such figures? Where does their information come from? How do they use it to predict temperatures and weather conditions? How has science aided accurate weather forecasting?

Funny thing, but the weather directly influences how we feel and act. Moderate cold, scientists explain, is mentally stimulating. Heat is usually troublesome. You can make an interesting feature by talking to teachers, supervisors, and others who work with people.

Many improvements have been made in forecasting tornadoes. Advances in meteorology have made it possible generally to alert an area two to three hours in advance concerning possibility of tornadoes. Are volunteer tornado spotters being used? To what extent have radar stations increased? About how far out can each station probe for severe storms? Do weather experts think that the advance alert can be extended several hours?

Your readers will appreciate your listing safe winter driving tips any time the driving gets hazardous. A local officer, preferably one who knows quite a bit about safety, will be glad to give them to you.

One of the heaviest cloudbursts ever thoroughly studied occurred on July 8, 1951, over North Central Illinois. Within six hours, as much as thirteen inches of rain fell. What particular conditions cause such extremely heavy rainfalls? At what time or times of year are they most likely to occur?

U. S. weather reports are accurate 88 per cent of the time, according to the U. S. Department of Commerce. Why do so many folks poke fun at forecasters? Are most people likely to forget the many times when forecasts are accurate?

Have television weather programs created a new interest in wind, rain, snow, temperatures, and other aspects of Mother Nature? Do a round-up interview.

Tell your readers what to do when a tornado—or similar form of disaster common to your area—is apparently headed in your direction. With the assistance of local authoritative agencies, you can be specific in explaining the ways to minimize danger.

Is your weather changing? Interview the weatherman and also a few old-timers. What has been the coldest day, wettest season, and so on?

Many cities and states, in seeking new industries and new people, point out the advantages of their climatic conditions. Aviation firms, for instance, usually locate where there is good flying weather most of the year and where much maintenance work can be done out of doors. Is the climate a "drawing card" for business or tourists to your community? How is the appeal used in promotion literature, advertisements, direct mail, and in other media?

After one forecaster had missed on several days, he received a note: "Seems like you should ask for a transfer to some other place. The weather here doesn't agree with you." Do many people write or call when he misses the forecast? Does your local weatherman get a lot of razzing? What percentage of the time is he correct in his predictions?

It's quite likely that your community has several amateur meteorologists. What's more, it is quite likely that some of them have home-made weather vanes, barometers, and other instruments. Can they predict the weather with some certainty? Have TV weather programs caused amateurs to become interested in studying the weather?

What's the difference between a hurricane and a tornado? In what months and regions are they likely to occur? How have meteor-ologists learned to predict the direction and strength of the various types of outbreaks?

"Everybody talks about the weather, but no one does anything about it." If folks like to talk about it, they'll like to read about it. A feature on what makes hail, snow, fog, and clouds would be interesting. A readable explanation of the cause of lightning would go well with the weather facts.

Has your community ever had an earthquake? If so, tell of the loss of life and property damage? If it happened quite a few years ago, you might find someone who can recall his experiences. If your com-munity has never experienced one, ask weathermen why? Show con-ditions necessary for an earthquake to occur.

An astronomer says that the sun will be cold in fifteen million years. How about getting some comments from some amateur astrono-mers in your community? Or your local college or university may have an expert on its staff.

Weddings

Weddings are big business! Just ask the jewelers in your town. Most wedding gifts come from jewelry stores. What system do jew-elers have of keeping wedding gifts from being duplicated? How lib-eral are stores in allowing brides to return duplicate gifts?

A western hardware dealer is becoming popular in launching marriages. Twice he's turned his store into a wedding chapel, with an altar and potted plants. Have any ceremonies been performed in the stores of your city? Under what conditions? By whom?

In Pennsylvania Miss Van Dyke was married to Mr. Foster Beard. And in Washington Mr. James Toogood and Miss Doris Goodenough took out a marriage license. Dig through your local records and you'll probably find some amusing combinations.

From time to time newspapers tell of a bridegroom being late for his wedding. How often does this happen? Interview a veteran minister and get his comments on this situation and other unexpected delays and mixups at weddings.

Do most bridegrooms pay in cash to ministers for officiating at marriage ceremonies? Do some forget to pay? Do some of them give checks? Has anyone ever given a "hot" check? What is the highest fee? Lowest? Average?

Weeks

Now we have a Pass the Laugh Week. Does everyone have a sense of humor? Select about four or five persons who are known for their sense of humor. Then ask them: "Have you always had a sense of humor? Has this helped you? Do you believe that anyone can develop this trait? What kind of jokes are the funniest?"

Sponsored by a large number of national, regional, and local groups, Farm-City Week is observed in many communities. Does your community observe this week? In what way? What are some of the misunderstandings between city dwellers and rural folks? In what ways do they co-operate in certain activities?

Weight

Julie Harris, Hollywood, told of how she reduced to one hundred pounds so that she could play the part of a twelve-year-old in a movie. What are some jobs in which applicants are overweight? Employment office officials can help you to fashion a feature around this idea.

Window Shopping

Your window shopping results in actual buying more than you realize. When a druggist kept his windows empty for three weeks, candy sales dropped 32 per cent, soda 14 per cent, and toilet goods 18 per cent. Where do window dressers get their ideas? Are some original? Do they often tie-in with local affairs? What are some of the newer trends in creating attractive window displays?

Women

A businessman who preferred to remain anonymous recently made the headlines by stating that housewives are inefficient—that they waste a lot of time. He mentioned telephone conversations, one- or two-hour naps, radio and television serials, shopping trips, coffee sessions with neighbors, and other things as time-wasters. What do women think of these charges? Exaggerated? Partly true?

Every woman wants a few extra dollars—outside dollars she can make while caring for a family. Many women make extra money doing something at home. One woman, for instance, makes pies for a local coffee shop. Another one runs a nursery for a few children each morning. How do housewives in your community make extra money? Any unusual part-time jobs? How many are doing something they created— new and different?

Each year the National Grandmothers Club names a leading grandmother. A recent winner had sixty grandchildren. She had thirteen children. Who has the most grandchildren in your community? Does Christmas mean a lot of headaches to a grandmother who has many grandchildren? Do grandmothers think that their sons and daughters are too strict or too lax in the treatment of their children?

Are women more practical than men? Ashley Montague so argues in his book, *The Natural Superiority of Women*. Are they greater idealists than men? Can they see further ahead? Whip up a feature by getting the views of four men and four women.

Thousands of wives are working outside the home today. Do many of their husbands object? Would most husbands prefer a well-run home, wonderful meals, and occasional parties for their friends? Seek comments on both sides of the question.

How much does hubby help around the house? Not that they should learn to make afghans, but husbands are usually roped in on a few duties. What are the comments of a few wives? A few husbands?

Here's something every woman knows: domestic help is vanishing. A recent national survey showed that only one out of fifty housewives can have help. The survey also revealed that only 15 per cent of all the workers live in the house where they work. What's happening? Will younger girls become part-time helpers?

Statistics show that every forty or fifty years Americans grow a full inch taller. Surveys have proven that boys now attending college are at least two inches taller than their dads were, that the American soldier of today stands a full four inches above his counterpart in the American Revolution, and that whereas the girl five feet four inches tall was a rarity at the beginning of the century, there are in America today some three million women over five feet eight inches tall—and proud of it! How have clothes designs helped the tall girl? Do most tall girls wear flat shoes?

Women's headpieces are always news. Try this angle: see how many women still wear sunbonnets. Check with local stores to see if patterns for sunbonnets are sold.

A survey of fifty banks shows that more women than men, particularly in young families, write family checks. Is this true in your community? Are women the financial heads of most households? Check with local banks.

Every hostess wants her party to be a success. So do an article showing new angles and new stunts which will guarantee "The Life of the Party."

Newspapers recently carried the story of Mrs. Margaret Ross, age eighty-eight, who holds down the job of Dominion government telegraph operator in Nova Scotia. Your angle: Find some elderly woman who holds a responsible job. Be sure to ask, "What is your formula for a long life?"

The United States government, through its Commerce Department, has tried to standardize clothes sizes for all American women. Can this be done? Who can define the female form divine? Do women come in so many assorted sizes that such a task is impossible?

Home sewing is staging a comeback. In 1954 it is estimated that fifty-seven million women and girls were buzzing away on more than thirty million sewing machines. Home sewing is interesting more teen-agers. More than four and one-half million girls are enrolled in sewing courses. Are more women and girls making their own clothes? Do many sew just as a hobby? Does today's woman have a wide knowledge of fabrics? How many hours does the average housewife spend in sewing each week?

In 1920 only 29 women served as state legislators. By 1954 that number had climbed to 303. Approximately 5,000 women hold important state appointive positions in the United States. Why do women enter politics? What are the backgrounds of those who enter government service? Are women better fitted for certain types of political positions?

Many men rely on their wives to help them choose suits, hats, shirts, ties, and other apparel. Get some comments from clerks on this situation. Do some men like to shop alone? Are most men anxious that their wives approve of their apparel? Must the clerk plan to sell two people when a man and his wife shop?

Some surveys indicate that in practically all types of TV programs women viewers outnumber the men. Have women's interests been increased by TV? Have many women been attracted to wrestling and other sports which they may have believed "unladylike" a few years ago?

Do women still visit over the back fence? Or do they still visit about as much but use the telephone? What hours do most women use in visiting with neighbors? Do some women still prefer to drop in on their neighbors for visits?

Grandmother used to spend most of the day in the kitchen. What does her granddaughter do today? How have time-saving appliances cut down on the number of hours spent in the kitchen? Do most families have sandwiches and soup for the noon meal? What are some typical breakfast menus?

Your state federation of women's clubs has an interesting story. Show how women have become more civic and welfare minded. Find out about the founding, early leaders, and the presidents with longest records of service. Trace some of the major projects and show what the clubs have done for the state.

The secret wedding is a poor start for matrimony, Dr. Ada Hart states in her book, *Successful Marriage*. Talk to a marriage counselor, to ministers, and to other qualified persons and show all of the disadvantages of secret weddings.

Barbara Stanwyck once said, "Women over thirty should not dye their hair—only the young dye good." What percentage of women use some sort of dye? How often must the solution be applied? Why do most women dread the thought of gray hair?

"When a woman tells you her age," Wilson Mizner once commented, "it's all right to look surprised but don't scowl." How many women try to keep their age a secret? How many sign "legal age" on various forms and blanks? Do some brides and brides-to-be ask the newspaper to omit mention of age in the column listing the marriage licenses?

Joint bank accounts prove that wives are quicker on the draw. How many husbands and wives have joint accounts? Has the number increased as more wives have started working? Who writes the checks for most of the bills?

Are women more conservative than men? It depends. Surveys indicate that on public questions without emotional content—tariffs, roads, and such—more men than women are conservative. Check the results of voting in your community, particularly in situations where you can determine the number of men and women who voted.

Optometrists report that 8 per cent of all men suffer from red-green color blindness, and only 1 per cent of women have this vision defect. Does this account for the fact that women can distinguish traffic lights better and therefore have better safety records? Get the views of police and optometrists. Best source: safety experts.

Talk to local florists and get a feature on wedding decorations. Any unusual requests? What are the greatest rush months? Amusing experiences?

Ask women to give a penny for every year of their age and you will make a lot of money, officers of the American Pen Women in San

Diego, California, discovered. Why? Largely because most of them will pitch in a dollar rather than reveal their age. Check with local groups and find out some of the unique methods used to collect money and play up the new and different.

A woman in Columbus, Ohio, started a one-woman rebellion against women's clubs. She is convinced "that club women don't have any fun. All they do is pass resolutions. They do not think for themselves, but do whatever their national headquarters tell them." Ask four or five prominent club women in your city for their reactions to the Ohio woman's views.

Women Cops
Female traffic officers in a large city expressed a desire to wear slacks on duty—and the police commissioner approved. If your city has "meter maids" or other women policemen, do they wear special uniforms? Is it permissible to wear slacks?

Wonder Drugs
A single one-hundred-thousand-unit dose of penicillin in 1942 cost twenty-two dollars. Today your doctor can give you a single injection of penicillin for from three to five dollars. What's the story about the decreasing cost of wonder drugs? What are some drugs which are still costly but which will probably decrease in price? Your pharmacist can provide interesting comments.

Words
The expression, "Mind your P's and Q's" probably originated in an English tavern, where they record the ale customers drink—by pints and quarts—on account sheets. Every business has words and phrases which are unique to that activity. You can write a feature on peculiar phrases of any of these: railroading, newspaper work, college life, or show business.

Work
"Work is the easiest way man has ever invented to escape boredom," declared Le Recueil. Do most people enjoy their workaday jobs? Talk to successful people and see if they get a kick out of their daily tasks and problems. Are the more successful always happier in their duties?

Arthur Rubinstein once said, "I play each concert as if it were my first one. If a law were passed making it illegal to accept money for playing the piano, I still would play." Can love of one's work actually make it fun? How many persons actually enjoy their day-to-day work?

"Hard workers are usually inefficient," Thomas Dreier says. Why? "Champions get their results in the easiest way—the relaxed way." How many persons approach their jobs with some kind of organized plan? How much motion is lost in everyday tasks? Is the efficient worker flexible and relaxed? Best source for answers: personnel directors.

Sir William Osler advised, "Throw away all ambition beyond that of doing the day's work well." How many people plan their work very far ahead? How many actually lay out a long-range plan and then follow it? Are many of them too impatient to stick to any task for any great amount of time? Among the good sources for comments: personnel managers, managers of employment offices, and executives of large companies.

Workers

Does the intelligence of workers increase in hard jobs? Psychologists gave intelligence tests to workers in five different levels of difficulty and the same tests to them two years later. Average intelligence on the lower jobs had decreased because the brighter workers had dropped out. In the harder jobs, the average intelligence had increased because the duller workers had dropped out. Get the opinions of management experts and supervisors on this survey.

In 1929 the average work week for the American worker was just under fifty hours; today the average man works about forty-two. How has the work week changed in several key industries in your community? Does a shorter work week mean increased production and higher morale?

Worry

William Bower Teal of St. Louis told newsmen on his one hundredth birthday, "People would get along a lot better if they would quit their darn fool worrying." Interview four or five oldsters and see if they give the same advice. Did they worry more when they were young?

Wrecking Business

How are large buildings torn down? What are some of the odd things found by workers? Are there certain precautions to be taken by all workers? What is the largest building ever torn down in your city? Source: the owner of such a concern.

Writers

Few people know much about ghost writers. Who gives them most of their assignments? Is it a widespread practice for busy people to have their speeches, articles, reports, and other forms of writing done by professionals? And don't forget this angle: How many college students use ghost writers to prepare their themes, term reports, and other assignments?

Every county usually has at least one person who is considered an authority on his or her particular region. So much the better if the person has written newspaper or magazine articles about the locality. How much research is done? How long was required to gather enough material for a particular article? Whom does the writer consider to be the most colorful people of the past?

W. Somerset Maugham's notebooks occupy fifteen thick volumes and cover a period of fifty-seven years. He used them as a storehouse of materials. Interview a fiction writer and ask: "Where do you get ideas for your plots and characters? Do you keep a file of incidents? What are other sources for your material?"

Chances are that some of the writers in your state use pen names. What are some of the best known? Why do they use pen names? How did they choose the ones which they have? Do they always use their pen names?

Do you have a writers' club in your community? If so, find out if most members write to sell or just for the fun of it. How many members have sold material? And ask about the market possibilities for various kinds of material.

Character changes may cause changes in handwriting. When an obscure young journalist, Benito Mussolini had a small, inconspicuous handwriting. After he came into power, he signed papers with a big, black, pretentious "Mussolini." Find a psychologist and ask him what he thinks of handwriting diagnosis? Does handwriting express personality or lack of it? Is the human ego projected in handwriting?

Most pen companies make points for lefthanded writers. They range from "fine firm" to "bold backhand" to "slanted" and "stub oblique" points. What percentage of the pens sold are sold to lefthanded writers? More men than women?

X-rays

William Konrad Roentgen, a German physicist who invented the X-ray machine, revealed his discovery to the Physico-Medical Society of Würzburg in November, 1895. Little did he dream of the many uses for the machine, not only in medicine and dentistry, but in industry and other areas as well. Is too much radiation from X-rays harmful to human tissue? Is the overuse of X-rays, for instance in the fitting of shoes, harmful to children? For interesting comments, interview a radiologist.

Y. M. C. A.

Adults aren't the only persons enjoying hobby classes. Courses in radio, photography, Indian lore, magic, and other subjects are offered by one Y. M. C. A. for kids. If your city has a Y. M. C. A., see if it offers classes for youngsters.

Date tie-in: The Y. M. C. A. was organized June 6, 1844. Do a progress story on your local "Y," showing its varied activities, newer programs, the number benefiting from its program through the years, and sketches of its leaders.

Youth

Would movies showing solutions of adolescent problems help young people? Psychologist Ira Iscoe found results with such movies in Texas. Are your local schools using movies of this nature? Do discussions follow the showings?

Should boys expect to pay all expenses on dates? Evelynn Duvall says smart girls find that Grandma has two theater tickets she can't use, or Dad has a pass to the baseball game but is out of town. When is it correct for a girl to foot the bill?

J. Edgar Hoover, FBI chief, praises the Junior Deputy Sheriffs League and similar groups. Why? He explains, "When you make a youngster an ally of law enforcement there is no need to worry about his becoming a delinquent." Has the sheriff in your county organized a league? If so, what are some of its activities? What ages of kids are members? Has it shown itself to be effective in reducing juvenile delinquency?

Are modern young people willing to pay the price for good jobs? Will most of them accept jobs with a lot of drudgery but which have promise of giving them a lift up the ladder? Or do many young people want to start at the top? Sources of comments: personnel directors, officials of firms or businesses, and employment office managers.

A young TV actress says that "young people are pushed into maturity long before they are equipped for it." And then she asks: at what age should bobbysoxers wear high heels and lipstick, smoke, and date regularly? For answers, seek the opinions of parents, youth workers, and youngsters who are recognized as leaders.

Judge Samuel S. Leibowitz of Brooklyn says that "the charge is now made that the courts are guilty of coddling the young criminal and thereby encouraging him to become worse, rather than better." Are courts too lenient? Are too many "repeaters" turned loose on probation? Is there a shortage of trained probation officers? Are police trained in handling youngsters?

The New York City youth board is making a study that may make it possible to identify potential juvenile delinquents before they are six years old. Is this possible? Can you determine a child's future behavior at an early age? Get the comments of teachers, youth directors, and ministers.

Why do boys and girls leave home? What can parents do to make their homes more attractive to their sons and daughters? What is wrong with the homes of today? Interview a judge or officials who are competent to discuss this situation.

To oldsters, it seems that youth possesses a strange sense of humor. What kinds of jokes amuse the teen-agers of your community?

Who are their favorite comedians? Tell some of the current jokes making the rounds.

The tongue of man is responsible for many broken romances. Phrases like, "I was out with a girl last night and she said . . ." or "I'll give you a call sometime" may be offensive. Ask ten popular high school girls what they consider awkward, inept, inconsiderate phrases.

When to write a letter? That is a question which puzzles many young people. Does your school system offer any help to youth in writing letters? Are they taught how to write congratulatory notes, holiday greetings, letters of application, and others?

Juvenile delinquency is overplayed in newspaper and magazine stories. Give this development a different twist by showing how the majority of youngsters—working in Boy Scouts, Girl Scouts, Camp Fire Girls, 4-H clubs, and other groups—are doing many fine things for their communities.

Once there was a frail, freckle-faced boy who refused to study. It took him three full terms to get out of the lowest prep school grade. He tried a military college's entrance exam three times before he was admitted. He had a speech defect. Now we know him as Sir Winston Churchill. Can teachers predict the future of unpromising children? Do they see possibilities in so-called "problem children"?

Is National Boys' Club Week observed in your city? If so, this is an excellent time to summarize the activities of all boys' clubs. Is any group doing something which is new and different? Which organization reaches the most boys? Who are some of the adult leaders in the various groups?

American youth is getting bigger. The average fourteen-year-old boy today is two and one-half inches taller and eighteen pounds heavier than his counterpart of thirty years ago, experts report. Your school physician should provide some interesting figures on average weight and height of students in various grades. Are most kids underweight? Overweight? What is the condition of their general health?

Are popular boys better in grades and behavior than unpopular boys? Psychologist M. R. Reinberg found that popular boys were in the top quarter in marks. These boys have many friends and like their teachers. A local feature awaits you when you ask your high school principal or dean of boys about this situation.

Time was when nothing pleased the high school girl more than a spin in her one-and-only's ancient flivver. Not so now. The girls think the old car's all right for short hops after classes, but for the most part they like the family car, with its comfort and accessories. Why the change? It's a good start for a feature on high school students' cars.

The Tom Pappas Chefs Club, a division of Boys Club of Boston, gives boys from six to sixteen the thrill of taking juvenile energy out of the fire and into the frying pan. From eighty to one hundred boys take the cooking classes. What is your community doing that is unique in youth activities? What ideas are being considered for the future?

Do children from ten to sixteen go through fairly definite emotional stages? Yes, Dr. Arnold Gesell reports in *Science Digest*. He believes that a youngster is farthest away from his parents at fifteen. If this is true, get suggestions from a dean of girls, dean of boys, youth director, or minister for parents who wish to strengthen their ties with their children during this particular period.

Sockhops are enjoyed by today's youngsters. Do these differ from the old dances? Do kids dress more informally for dances today? How has the music changed through the years? What type of music is the most popular with the youth of your city?

Oldsters aren't the only ones who make New Year's resolutions. Interview eight or ten junior high or high school students and get their resolutions for the New Year.

Today's teen-agers are often criticized. Have you ever given them a chance to answer? If not, invite about three outstanding high school students to give their views on modern youth—its problems, its dreams, its hopes.

Does your rural Boy Scout program differ from that of the boys who live in town? How many boys are engaged in this activity? Are more scoutmasters and other adult leaders needed?

Always good: the story of any youth who succeeds in spite of handicaps. Find one in your schools, and in the story show his philosophy of life, together with his special interests and activities.

Shyness is one of youth's handicaps. So do a feature interview with a well-known and popular youth leader on the subject, "How to Cure Shyness."

Zoos

A zookeeper revealed that his most finicky eater was the hippopotamus. Is this true at your zoo? What special diets are followed by certain animals? Are the peanuts tossed by spectators good for monkeys? What is the monthly food bill at your zoo?

"Most animals are better off in a zoo than in the wild. They are healthier, and most of them are happier." This is the belief of Dr. William M. Mann, director of the National Zoological Park at Washington, D. C. Find your local zoo director and ask him what he thinks. Do zoo animals live longer? Does a lot of pacing mean that animals are trying to break out, or are they merely working off excess energy? Are zoo animals kept more free from diseases and parasites than those who live in the wild?

Index

337

The Feature Writer's Handbook

was set into type on the Linotype machine in ten- and eleven-point Electra with two points of spacing between lines. Electra was designed by W. A. Dwiggins and has a crisp, modern feeling ideally suited to a book for today's writers. The hand-lettering on the title page, taken from the typewriter keyboard, helps carry out the theme.

UNIVERSITY OF OKLAHOMA PRESS: NORMAN